The World of GEORGE WASHINGTON

By

RICHARD M. KETCHUM

PUBLISHED BY AMERICAN HERITAGE PUBLISHING COMPANY, INC., NEW YORK

BOOK TRADE DISTRIBUTION BY McGRAW-HILL BOOK COMPANY

STAFF FOR THIS BOOK

EDITOR
Richard M. Ketchum

ART DIRECTOR
Murray Belsky

MANAGING EDITOR
Brenda Bennerup

PICTURE EDITOR
Maureen Dwyer

———

AMERICAN HERITAGE
PUBLISHING CO., INC.

PRESIDENT AND PUBLISHER
Paul Gottlieb

GENERAL MANAGER, BOOK DIVISION
Kenneth W. Leish

EDITORIAL ART DIRECTOR
Murray Belsky

Library of Congress Cataloging in
 Publication Data

Ketchum, Richard M   1922-
  The world of George Washington

  1. Washington, George, Pres. U. S.,
    1732-1799.
I. Title.
E312.K47 1974 973.4′1′0924 [B] 74-8020
ISBN 0-07-034409-4
ISBN 0-07-034410-8 (deluxe)

HALF-TITLE PAGE: Washington's presidential seal.

TITLE PAGE: Detail of a 1787 painting of Washington by Charles Willson Peale.

MASTHEAD PAGE: Bookplate used by George Washington, displaying the family coat of arms.

INTRODUCTION PAGE: 1796 watercolor by Benjamin
Latrobe, showing the Washingtons on the piazza at
Mount Vernon.

FRONT JACKET/SLIPCASE: (Clockwise, from top left)
Portrait by Charles Willson Peale; detail from
Capture of the Hessians at Trenton by John
Trumbull; daguerreotype of a portrait by James
Sharples; detail of a portrait by Gilbert Stuart.

CONTENTS

6

FOREWORD

To a majority of his contemporaries, George Washington must have seemed the towering figure of his time. He was, to begin, an authentic frontier hero to a people for whom the wilderness and the menace it held were very real and present facts of life. As the military commander who led the new nation to victory, Washington — more than any other individual — personified the rebellion against British imperial authority. And in the aftermath of that triumph, he was the only conceivable choice to be the first Chief Executive of the republic.

Yet we may wonder how many of his countrymen ever caught a glimpse of him in the flesh — how many of them heard him utter a word. Only a relative handful, of course, and all too often those who did were so awed by the presence that their recorded impressions add little or nothing to our knowledge of Washington the human being. Possibly the worst disservice done him was by the mythmakers who, in the wake of his death, determined to make an unimpeachable, godlike figure of him — majestic and remote. In fact, Washington in later life was a rather distant and very private person, not given to revealing much of himself, and the result — as the historian Marcus Cunliffe has suggested, was that it became increasingly difficult to distinguish between Washington the man and Washington the monument.

The century in which we live has seen the seeds of revolution sowed by Washington and his fellows come to fruition in a multitude of ways, and what we should not forget is that the man known as the father of his country — no matter how unapproachable or ostensibly conservative — was intimately related to the liberal movement of his day. Not only was he part of it, he *led* the forces of activism through six years of struggle, literally risking his neck for a cause that had, for most of that period, little hope of success.

Accustomed as we are nowadays to having our men and events served up visually, it is difficult for us to imagine an age two centuries past; through the camera's eye we experience vicariously the triumphs and sorrows of men and mankind alike, and virtually nothing is denied us. It may be that the illustrations in this volume will bring us closer to terms with George Washington. Not since his death has an effort been made to portray the man and the world he knew entirely through paintings, drawings, prints, and the incunabula of the eighteenth century. So far as can be determined, every illustration reproduced here was made during the lifetime of George Washington or earlier; individually and collectively they reflect the stage upon which he walked, as seen through the eyes of contemporaries. Their chief virtue is less one of artistry than that of revealing the man and his century in terms familiar to him.

— Richard M. Ketchum

1

VIRGINIA
YOUTH

He described himself as one "who always walked on a straight line," which is very like the image of George Washington we retain — a one-dimensional figure of such old-fashioned rectitude as to defy understanding. The fact that he was, in the familiar phrase of Henry Lee, "first in war, first in peace, and first in the hearts of his countrymen," challenged his own and subsequent generations to know what manner of man personified the newborn nation. Yet for all the millions of words written by and about him, the portrait is filled with shadows, with depths that cannot be plumbed, and he comes down to us across the centuries as the marble man of the Houdon bust or the unbending Gilbert Stuart likeness.

There are reasons for the enigma, of course, not least of which is Washington's personality. He was naturally shy and reticent, ungiving in public, unwilling to let contemporaries perceive what he thought or felt, reluctant to reveal his emotions. Those who knew him best often remarked his approachability, but they realized that there was no crossing the line he had drawn to forbid familiarity. His life was peopled with companions but few close attachments; as an English visitor to Washington's Virginia neighborhood was told, he "never had an intimate, particular bosom friend, or an open, professed enemy in his life."

To quote Washington's self-portrait more fully, he said he was "a mind who always walked on a straight line and endeavored, as far as human frailties and perhaps strong passions would enable him, to discharge the relative duties to his Maker and fellow men without seeking any indirect or left-handed attempts to acquire popularity." And here, in this awkward but purposeful statement, we come closer to the heart of the matter. There is the admission of weakness that had to be overcome — the natural impetuosity he curbed only by forcing himself to arrive at decisions deliberately, the passions he felt he must hold in check. There is the overriding sense of duty to God and to his fellow men that prevented him, ambitious though he was, from seeking power for its own sake. All things considered, it is the picture of a "loner," resolutely going his own way along the path he had set for himself.

In his day men were highly conscious of the model

of ancient Rome, and Washington's own goal might best be described as *virtus,* connoting not only manliness and strength, but implying also the lofty attributes of patriotism, of selfless dedication to country, of magnanimity and self-mastery. Long after his death Thomas Jefferson — who had broken with him after their early friendship — wrote that "His was the singular destiny and merit of leading the armies of his country successfully through an arduous war for the establishment of its independence, of conducting its councils through the birth of a government, new in its forms and principles, until it settled down into a quiet and orderly train; and of scrupulously obeying the laws through the whole of his career, civil and military, of which the history of the world furnishes no other example." As the Romans had been his own example, so he was to serve his countrymen, and the role is not conducive to intimacy.

Another difficulty to be faced in coming to terms with George Washington is the distance between our century and his own — a distance measured more in attitudes than in time. Washington's life fell entirely within the eighteenth century and he was truly a man of his age, speaking a language whose form and shades of meaning we comprehend only dimly, following principles and an outlook on life that are current no more. Not only that. At the time of his birth every country of any consequence in the world was ruled by a monarch — France and Spain by kings, Russia by a tsarina, China by an emperor, Japan by a shogun — and the globe was marked off in terms of empires — British, French, Holy Roman, Ottoman, Swedish. All these have passed into limbo.

British America consisted of only twelve disparate colonies, struggling to survive, sprawled out along the Atlantic seaboard, populated by three or four hundred thousand souls of whom one in five was a black slave. The character of life was essentially rural, the settlements not much more than a fringe of civilization, and beyond lay unknown wilderness disturbed only by roaming tribes of Indians and occasional Frenchmen.

In two centuries the world into which George Washington was born would change beyond all recognition, yet Washington himself has to remain what he was — not a man for our time but for his own. Even in his lifetime he became a legendary figure, cast in a heroic mold by a people desperately in need of such a model. He was increasingly aware of this, although he never conceived of himself as others did; he was simply a man who met events as they came and dealt with them as best he could. But the needs of the day produce the hero, and if his contemporaries dress him in the cloak of a god, making him something more than he was in life, that is part of the mythmaking of which nations consist. In Washington's case it was no difficult feat. From the time he was twenty-two years old until the end of his life he was a hero in varying degrees to an increasing number of his countrymen; admittedly this is no easy role for a man to fill with complete objectivity — whether he seeks it or not, idolatry is bound to affect the individual, and in Washington's case it seems to have increased his wariness, making him less giving of himself, heightening his native tendency to be reserved and distant.

The age in which the American Revolution took place was one of loyalties to kings and when that war began it was a commonly held conviction among colonists that their sovereign, George III, was the best of monarchs. As time and the conflict wore on he was judged to be a conspicuously bad one, and when the Americans considered it necessary to replace him, many who had honored and respected their former king simply transferred their loyalties to George Washington, endowing him with some of the attributes formerly reserved to royalty.

Whatever qualities he possessed Washington had come by largely on his own. Surprisingly little is known about his forebears, and Washington himself is of little help to the historian: as a man for whom the present was always the most important consideration he gave little recorded thought to his ancestry (in all his surviving letters, diary entries, and memoranda, he mentions his father only three times, and then without particular emphasis or interest). But since the time and place of his birth played such a part in all that followed, his story properly begins fifty years after the founding of Jamestown.

The first Washington to land in Virginia was John, son of an English clergyman who had been thrown out of his parish by Puritans on a charge that he was "a common frequenter of ale houses" and often drunk. In 1657 John arrived in the New World aboard the ketch *Sea Horse of London,* on which he served as mate, and as the vessel stood out to sea for the homeward voyage she ran aground and sank. But for that accident, the story of the Washington family might have been altogether different.

John decided to remain in Virginia, where he met and married a young woman named Anne Pope, whose father gave him seven hundred acres of land and a cash loan, and in 1659 their first son — Lawrence Washington — was born. As time passed, John's family and land holdings increased and he received one office or appointment after another — coroner, trustee of estates, justice of the county court, and vestryman. After Anne died in 1668, John remarried — first to a twice-widowed woman who had been slanderously accused of operating a bawdy house; then to her sister, a three-time widow, who had been castigated by the same source as being the royal governor's mistress. John inherited more property from his second wife. In 1674 he and one Nicholas Spencer procured a patent for five thousand acres along Little Hunting Creek on the south side of the Potomac River. Before his death in 1677 the former mate of the *Sea Horse of London* was firmly established as a member of Virginia's landed gentry, and his son and principal heir — who would become George Washington's grandfather — was off to a respectable start in life.

For rich and poor alike in eighteenth-century America, land was the talisman of success, the way to affluence and social position, a goal in whose pursuit thousands of men and women braved the Atlantic every year in order to strike out on an unfamiliar path in a hostile, uncertain world. Land represented both capital and currency: its ownership conferred wealth and status upon the likes of John Washington, for whom substantial parcels were all but unobtainable in England; and once ownership was established, the land could be rented out to tenants or its produce marketed — in either case providing a regular source of income. By 1700 most land in tidewater Virginia was occupied or claimed by the first comers, but every new settler knew of the lands to the west, available in

undreamed of quantities to anyone with the wit, the foresight, and the courage to claim them, and in his mind's eye he could foresee the day when he and his might be as affluent as the Byrds or the Carters.

William Byrd I's Virginia domain consisted of fifteen thousand acres, John Carter owned more than that, and Robert Beverley possessed at least thirty-seven thousand acres. Although the numerically largest group of farmers in the colonies owned an average of only about 150 acres, there was always the dream that one might prosper and add to his holdings and eventually possess the kind of riches that only land might bring. Furthermore, there was readily at hand in Virginia a work force that made possible the construction of houses and outbuildings and the harvesting of crops. Prior to 1680 it had consisted largely of indentured servants; after that date it was made up increasingly of Negro slaves.

As estates increased in size the owners gave over the supervision of work to overseers and spent their days more often in politics, social affairs, military pursuits, sports (of which hunting and horse racing were the overwhelming favorites), the management of their properties, and — incessantly — land speculation. Emulating the county families of England they dispensed justice as magistrates, governed their private domains in the manner of feudal masters, and influenced the Governor's Council as best they could to prevent the passage of laws inimical to their personal interests. They were, or appeared to be, the chosen people. To the large landholders went positions of importance — church warden, vestryman, sheriff, justice, colonel of militia, membership in the councils of state — while the style of life they enjoyed was on a scale rivaling some of the great English country establishments. The planters were at the top of the pyramid of the social caste system, an aristocracy that enjoyed a virtual monopoly of economic and political benefits, and since the system favored primogeniture — by which such men left most of their land and slaves and livestock to the eldest son — the dynasties they founded were likely to increase in wealth and influence.

Lawrence, John Washington's first-born, was educated in England, after the fashion prevailing among well-to-do families, and upon his return to America he seems to have taken more interest in the law than in adding to the property left him by his father. His marriage to Mildred Warner was an advantageous one in terms of position (her father had been Speaker of Virginia's House of Burgesses and a member of the Governor's Council), and Lawrence eventually became a justice of the peace, a burgess, and a sheriff. When he died in his thirty-eighth year, leaving his property to his wife and three children, John, the eldest, received the home tract and other lands; Augustine inherited about eleven hundred acres; and Mildred, an infant, obtained twenty-five hundred of those five thousand acres her grandfather John Washington had patented on the south shore of the Potomac River.

Few eligible widows in Virginia remained that way for long, and Mildred Warner Washington was no exception. With her new husband she and the children went to England, where the boys were sent to Appleby School in Westmoreland. There, for four years, young Augustine — who was to become George Washington's father — remained, and after his mother's death he returned to America to live with a cousin. A blond six-footer, Augustine had a reputation for great physical strength and a kindly disposition, and like his paternal grandfather he was disposed to the acquisition of land and to advantageous marriage. Through inheritance he and his bride Jane Butler possessed some 1,740 acres, and on one tract near Pope's Creek and the Potomac he constructed a dwelling and a mill; on another, near Fredericksburg, iron ore was discovered; and he purchased from his sister Mildred the twenty-five hundred acres known as the "Little Hunting Creek Tract." While Augustine was on a business trip to England his wife died, leaving three small children — Lawrence, Augustine Jr., and Jane — and in 1731 their father married the woman who would give birth to George Washington.

Mary Ball was the daughter of an illiterate woman named Mary Johnson and an Englishman named Joseph Ball who migrated to Virginia. The father died when Mary was three years old, leaving the child four hundred acres of land near the falls of the Rappahannock, three slaves, fifteen head of cattle, and all the feathers in the kitchen loft, "to be put in a bed for her." By the time she was twenty-three and married to Augustine Washington, she had come into a comfortable estate through the death of other relatives and was known as an extremely self-willed woman.

Mary joined the household on the bank of Pope's Creek, took over the supervision of Augustine's motherless children, and on February 22*, 1732, at ten o'clock in the morning, gave birth to her first child. Some six weeks later he was christened George.

George could have had only the dimmest recollection of the modest Pope's Creek house in which his first three years were spent, but from then until the final hour of his life his heart was never far from the family's next home — the twenty-five-hundred-acre tract on Little Hunting Creek, forty miles up the Potomac from Pope's Creek — to which Augustine moved his wife and offspring in 1735. Portions of it were still virgin land and timber, and the site included a high flat bluff that commanded a majestic view of the river below. Sweeping around a bend from the northeast, the mile-wide Potomac passed the house under the bluff, across from the Indian village of Piscataway. Other than this, there was no sign of human habitation as far as the eye could see, and the nearest road — from Belhaven to Fredericksburg — was so distant that travelers could neither be seen nor heard.

Little is known of the origins of the house then called Epsewasson beyond the probability that a small structure, or portions of one (possibly built by George's grandfather, Lawrence) existed on the site before Augustine Washington erected a story-and-a-half house there, flanked by the cabins of his Negro slaves, and a mill on Dogue Run. Here in this sparsely settled section the family lived for three years, until Augustine purchased and leased some six hundred

---

* George Washington was born two decades before the reform of the calendar, by which all dates were moved ahead eleven days. Thus his birth date at the time of his entry into the world was February 11 (customarily designated O.S., or Old Style). According to the new calendar, which has been in use ever since, the date was February 22, 1732.

acres near his iron mine on the Rappahannock and moved in 1738 to a place called Ferry Farm.

Across the river from the new home was something George had never before seen — a town called Fredericksburg, established eleven years earlier, which now possessed a wharf, quarry, courthouse, several tobacco warehouses, a stone prison, and numerous small houses (by town ordinance they were limited to a maximum size of twenty feet square). By the time the Washingtons had lived at Ferry Farm for a year the family was complete. In addition to Augustine's two sons by his first marriage (the daughter, Jane, had died in 1735), Mary Ball Washington had given birth to George in 1732, Betty in 1733, Samuel in 1734, John Augustine in 1736, Charles in 1737, and Mildred in 1739. Of them all, George's closest relationships were with John Augustine, or Jack, whom he once described as "the intimate companion of my youth," and Lawrence, fourteen years his senior, whom he regarded with a mixture of awe and admiration.

Ferry Farm was a lively place for a boy of seven and the days of his youth were spent watching the busy life on the tidal river, where small ocean-going vessels passed the house continuously. Nearby was the ferry landing, where travelers were always landing or debarking; there was fishing, swimming, and boating, the nearby woods to be explored, and the streets and buildings of Fredericksburg to be investigated. All this was accompanied by sporadic and fairly rudimentary tutoring, from which George acquired a knowledge of arithmetic, or ciphering as it was called, and the elements of surveying, while he practiced penmanship and spelling by recording such homely syllogisms as the "Rules of Civility and Decent Behaviour" into his copybook. He was never to have what could be called a formal education — only the tutoring and possibly a brief attendance at a school — but what he learned was of a highly practical nature. In addition to arithmetic and surveying, he learned something of geography, astronomy, composition, and deportment. He wrote a good, clear hand and evidently took pride in doing so. There is some question if he ever read much for pleasure; for

him, reading was largely a pragmatic matter — something one did in response to a need for information or instruction.

It troubled some of Washington's better-schooled contemporaries that he had so little formal education. John Adams remarked unkindly, "That Washington was not a scholar was certain. That he was too illiterate, unread, unlearned for his station and reputation is equally past dispute." But the fact was that young George's education, which came to an end by the time he was fourteen or fifteen, was quite adequate for his needs. It was his nature to profit from experience and observation, and the rudiments he had acquired were sufficient groundwork on which to build. As he once wrote, "Errors once discovered are more than half amended," to which he added, "Some men will gain as much experience in the course of three or four years as some will in ten or a dozen."

The most memorable event of his boyhood involved his half-brother Lawrence, who had returned from Appleby School in England and become a soldier — a captain in a Virginia regiment raised to supplement the British army in the war with Spain. In the fall of 1740 the young officer said farewell to Ferry Farm and sailed, with four-hundred Virginians (including a number of convicts drafted for duty, since the quota could not be filled with volunteers), to join British Admiral Edward Vernon for an assault on Spanish-held Cartagena in the Caribbean. Lawrence's letters to his family told of his admiration for Vernon, his contempt for Thomas Wentworth — the British general responsible for the disastrous repulse of the British forces — his own inactivity aboard the flagship (like many another English general, Wentworth had little regard for the fighting ability of colonials, most of whom were kept aboard ship), and two years later Lawrence returned, filled with tales of war and far-off places that captivated his ten-year-old half-brother. It was well that the relationship between the two was so close and that the younger boy had a respected elder to look up to, for the following year Augustine Washington died at the age of forty-nine.

In the manner of the day Augustine had provided well for his male heirs. Lawrence, the oldest son, received the lion's share of the estate of ten thousand acres and forty-nine slaves; he got the land on Little Hunting Creek, including the house named Epsewasson, his father's interest in the iron mine, and certain other property. To Augustine, the next in line, went certain lands in Westmoreland County, twenty-five head of cattle, four slaves, and some debts due his father. George received Ferry Farm, half of a 4,360-acre tract of rather poor land, ten slaves, three lots in the town of Fredericksburg, and a share of other personal property left to the widow and her four sons.

George's bequest sounds more munificent than it proved to be, for Augustine's will provided that his widow was to administer all the property left to his minor children until they came of age, and the fact was that Mary was not only a poor administrator but extremely reluctant to part with any portion of the estate that fell within her purview. Not for three decades would George obtain actual possession of Ferry Farm.

Although it is difficult to judge, at this distance and on the basis of relatively sparse evidence, the relationship between George Washington and his mother, it seems clear that while he honored and respected her he found her a powerful, strong-willed, demanding, and extremely difficult parent. During the course of his career she resented many of the achievements that brought him increasingly into the public eye, on grounds that he was neglecting her, and although she lived into his first term as President, she seems never to have appreciated or participated in any of the honors that came to her son. How trying she could be at times is suggested by her complaints during the Revolutionary War that he was permitting her to starve, although he was in fact providing for her to the best of his ability even in the most difficult of circumstances. What is more important than the lady's personality, however, is the effect it had upon her son, for it is evident that after his father's death he had less interest in remaining at Ferry Farm with his mother than in spending his time with Lawrence or in striking out on his own — an inclination that was to have far-reaching consequences.

Another effect of Augustine's death was the dashing of George's hopes that he, like his half-brothers, would go abroad to attend school, and he wrote later of "the longing desire which for many years I have had of visiting" England. Lawrence apparently sensed the need for young George to leave home, for when the latter was fourteen he encouraged him to go to sea — an overture that was overruled by Mary Ball Washington, supported by her brother in London. Writing to his sister, Joseph Ball remarked that George would be better off apprenticed to a tinker than sailing before the mast. No possible preferment would be open to him in the navy, said Joseph, since he had no influence in the right quarters and the navy would only "cut him and staple him and use him like a Negro, or rather, like a dog." Far better to become a planter, adding to his land and slaves; in such manner he could "leave his family in better Bread, than such a master of a ship can." George had his baggage packed and was ready to go to sea when the plan had to be abandoned because of "earnest solicitations" from his mother.

When Lawrence wrote his half-brother to suggest a naval career, he was living in the "patrimonial Mansion," Epsewasson — a conventional, center-hall dwelling with two rooms on either side of the hall on both the first and second floors, and the place was renamed Mount Vernon in honor of the admiral in 1743, the year Lawrence brought a bride to share it with him. She was Anne Fairfax, daughter of Colonel William Fairfax, who was the cousin and agent of Thomas, sixth Lord Fairfax, sole proprietor of the Northern Neck of Virginia. With Anne came a considerable dowry in lands (before long, she held patents for four thousand acres) and an alliance with the most powerful and influential family of the Northern Neck, whose seat was the handsome, two-story brick house known as Belvoir, on a pleasant tract below Mount Vernon. Lawrence's connection with the Fairfaxes was to prove of the first importance to George Washington at a formative period of his life, giving him entree to a wider, more cosmopolitan milieu and introducing him to a career on the wilderness frontier of America at a crucial moment in colonial history. It was also to give him his first glimpse of a peer of the realm and produce the first love of his life.

Through a tangled interplay of marriages and inheritance, Thomas Fairfax, sixth Lord Fairfax of Cameron, came into possession of the grant made in 1649 by Charles II of a million and a half acres of land lying between the Potomac and Rappahannock Rivers, constituting what was known as the Northern Neck of Virginia. The original grantees had been given the right to build towns, sell acreage within the proprietary, collect fines, create and endow educational institutions, and collect rents—all in return for an annual payment of £6 13s. 4d. to the King of England. In the intervening years Virginia colonists had protested time and again over what they regarded as the injustice of the patent, but in 1745 Fairfax's claims were upheld, and the following year there arrived at Belvoir three foxhounds, presaging the coming of the great man himself, who wanted a pack of hounds waiting when he visited his vast fiefdom in the near future. In the summer of 1747 he arrived at Belvoir— a squat, ugly, slovenly man with a vast wardrobe of unused finery and an obsessive hatred for women that was rivaled only by his love for fox hunting.

His Lordship had business matters on his mind, and when he decided to have his lands in the Shenandoah Valley surveyed in farm-size lots, the sixteen-year-old George Washington accompanied young George William Fairfax, the colonel's son, and a surveyor when they crossed the Blue Ridge Mountains in March of 1748 and headed into the wild lands of the valley. In his first frontier experience George kept field notes, watched the surveyor as he went about his work, hunted wild turkeys, lived in a tent and cooked over an open fire for the first time, encountered a tribe of Indians, and looked on in wonder as they performed a ritual war dance. From this month-long foray into an almost unsettled wilderness that was only a few days' ride from the civilized Tidewater, he gained a love for the west that was to remain with him always, and reached a decision to make surveying his vocation.

Through the Fairfax connection he obtained his first job—assisting a surveyor who was laying out the town of Alexandria, at the head of navigation on the Potomac—and in July of 1749 he was appointed official surveyor for the new county of Culpeper. During the next two years he made surveys on the northwestern frontier of Virginia for Lord Fairfax and for the Ohio Company—a partnership formed by Lawrence Washington, some of his Northern Neck neighbors, Robert Dinwiddie, the lieutenant governor, and several influential Englishmen, who acquired a grant of two hundred thousands acres west of the Alleghenies. The pay was good (well over £1 per day) and by the spring of 1750 George had saved enough money to purchase 1,459 acres for himself on Bullskin Creek, a tributary of the Shenandoah, beyond the Blue Ridge Mountains.

During this period, he had become captivated by the bride of his neighbor, George William Fairfax. Sally Cary was eighteen when George William married her in 1748 and from the moment she arrived at Belvoir George Washington—an impressionable sixteen—found her an irresistibly lively, good-humored companion. The main evidence of his growing attachment to her dates from later periods of his life, from two surviving letters. One was written in 1758, when he was engaged to marry another woman; the other forty years later, a year and a half before his death; between the two they make a rather convincing case that George—between the time he was sixteen and twenty-six— fell in love with the unattainable wife of his good friend, George William Fairfax, and that this affection was not dimmed by the passage of time. Certainly there was never the slightest hint of scandal, which there must have been in a small social circle had there been reason for it. But the fact was that Sally's husband was a somewhat plodding, insecure young man; she a coquettish, "amiable beauty" as Washington described her, possessing "mirth, good humor, ease of mind—and what else?" Since the Fairfaxes' marriage, like so many of the time and place, involved considerations of social position and wealth, it may not have been a love match and Sally may have played somewhat carelessly on the attention and admiration she received from the gangly young man who was as much at home at Belvoir as at Mount Vernon.

In his late teens, George was strong and big—at

six feet two inches a head taller than most of his contemporaries — and a superb rider (Thomas Jefferson later said he was "the best horseman of his age and the most graceful figure that could be seen on horseback"). Clothes and appearance had become increasingly important to him: he began shaving at sixteen, attended frequent dances, and when traveling about considered it necessary to carry with him nine shirts, six linen waistcoats, a cloth waistcoat, six collars, four neck-cloths, and seven caps, according to an inventory he wrote down. He had light, grey-blue eyes, auburn hair, and — according to several contemporaries — the largest hands and feet they had seen. Through the Fairfaxes he had formed some acquaintance with the world of the landed Virginia aristocracy; he had had his first glimpse of the frontier; and now, because of Lawrence, he was to make his one and only trip beyond the continental limits of North America.

In the spring of 1749 Lawrence returned from a session of the Burgesses in Williamsburg, where he was a delegate, with a bad cough that worsened as time went on, and neither a trip to England to consult physicians nor a visit to the warm springs in western Virginia improved the condition. In September, 1751, he decided to seek a cure in the tropical climate of Barbados, and George accompanied him on the trip. During his stay there George attended the theater for the first time, exulted in the "beautiful prospects" of the island, and then was laid low with an attack of smallpox, from which he did not fully recover until mid-December. It left him with a few slight pock-marks on his face and an immunity which was to prove a blessing.

Lawrence, unhappily, was not recovering, and when he decided to see if the climate of Bermuda would improve his health George left him and returned to Virginia and his surveying in January of 1752. That spring he purchased some additional land on Bullskin Creek and met Betsy Fauntleroy, the daughter of a wealthy Richmond County planter, who turned down George's efforts to court Betsy on grounds that the young man was not suitably positioned in life to deserve her. Then Lawrence returned to Mount Vernon, his health and spirits broken, and in July he died, leaving three lots in Fredericksburg to George. There was another provision in the will that was to prove more meaningful: if George survived Lawrence's wife Anne, and if Lawrence's only child, a daughter, died without issue, then George was to receive Mount Vernon and its adjacent lands.

Among the positions Lawrence had held was that of Adjutant General in the Virginia militia, and when George learned that the office was to be divided into four districts he wrote to Lieutenant Governor Dinwiddie, applying for appointment to one of them. In December, before he had turned twenty-one, he was made Adjutant of the Southern District, which carried with it the rank of major and a salary of £100 a year. It was as a military man that his long career of service to the public began.

The earliest document at Mount Vernon relating to the Washington family is the 1601 quitclaim deed (below) to a piece of land in Sulgrave, England. A Latin manuscript inscribed on parchment, it bears the signature of Robert Washington, proprietor of Sulgrave Manor, and his son Lawrence, and the attesting seal at left retains the impression of the family coat of arms. Concerning these ancestors, George Washington knew virtually nothing and cared little. Genealogy was of "very little moment" to him; as he once wrote a nephew, "I have not the least Solicitude to trace our ancestry." At the age of sixty he replied to an inquiry from an Englishman who had been studying the family records to say that he had been told, as a child, that his forebears came from one of the northern counties of England — but he could not recall which one it was. So it is somewhat curious that the family arms, which first crossed the Atlantic with his great-grandfather John Washington in 1657,

A DISTANT ANCESTRY

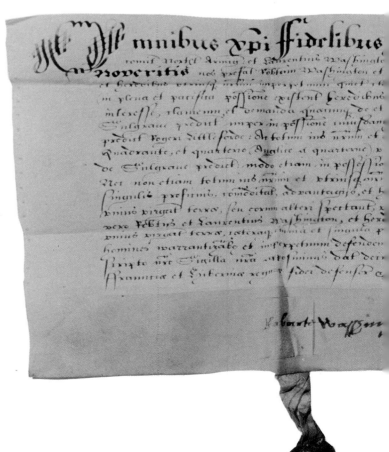

should have been prominently displayed above the
mantelpiece in the parlor at Mount Vernon,
carved in wood and painted. The ancestral home in
England dates back to Lawrence Washington, who was
born about 1500, became a successful wool
merchant and mayor of Northampton, and acquired
from Henry VIII the property of Sulgrave Manor,
where he built a small, handsome, Elizabethan
house. It was his son Robert who inherited the
estate and who, to celebrate the marriage of his own
son Lawrence, commissioned the two heraldic
stained-glass window panels shown on these pages.
Originally they were set in the kitchen windows
of the manor house. The panel at left represents
the union of John Washington with Martha Kitson;
that at right the marriage of their great-grandson
Lawrence to Margaret Butler in 1588, the year of the
Spanish Armada. Inevitably (and unsuccessfully),
efforts have been made to link the red and white
bars and the stars of the shield in the coat
of arms to the origins of the American flag.

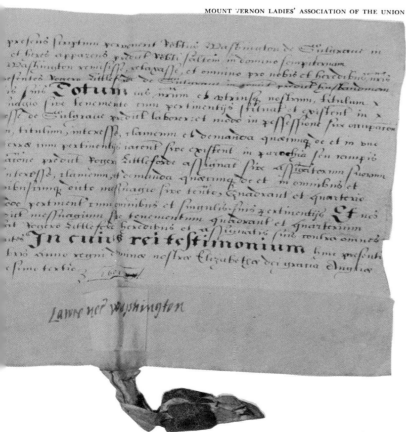

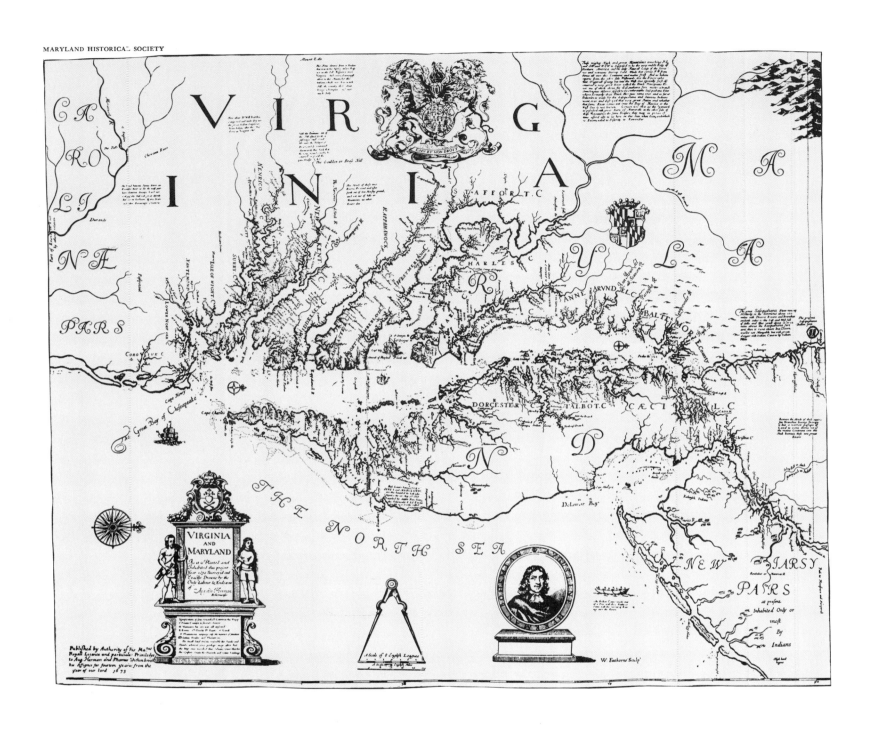

THE WASHINGTONS
IN THE NEW WORLD

Augustin Herrman's 1673 map (above) shows the colony of Virginia and parts of Maryland, New Jersey, and North Carolina a decade and a half after John Washington's arrival. He was relatively early on the scene, for not until 1640 and later had any appreciable number of immigrants filtered into what was called "the Northern Neck" between the Potomac and Rappahannock Rivers. Only a few of the people who settled along the river estuaries emptying into Chesapeake Bay could be classed as English gentlemen; most were small farmers, tradesmen, artisans, and younger sons of the middle class who sought an opportunity in the New World that was denied them in the Old, and Virginia's "first families" were mostly hard-working folk who collected "head rights," or warrants for fifty free acres of land for each person (including servants and children) they brought to the colony.

There are almost no surviving personal memorabilia of John, the great-grandfather of George Washington. One of the few is the wine bottle seal (right) bearing his name, which was found near his homesite. What proved to be far more important to his heirs than family mementos was the land John Washington acquired and left to them. The parcel that was to play the most significant role in George Washington's life was the one described below. This grant of land on the upper Potomac, bounded by Dogue and Little Hunting Creeks, consisted of five thousand acres, and was awarded to John Washington and Nicholas Spencer in 1674 by the proprietor of the Northern Neck. The grantees were required to "seat and plant" the land within three years' time and to pay an annual rent in perpetuity. Sixteen years later the land was divided between John Washington's son Lawrence and the heirs of Nicholas Spencer, and the Washington half of the property passed eventually into the hands of Augustine Washington, George's father, who moved his family here in 1735. Later the plantation established on this site was named Mount Vernon.

SPARSE
FRAGMENTS
OF
BOYHOOD

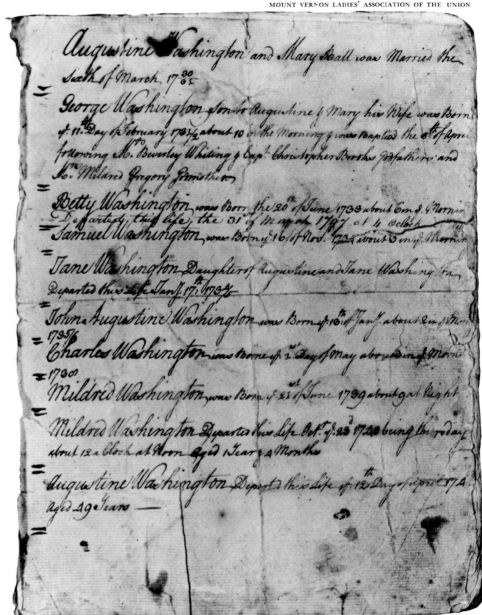

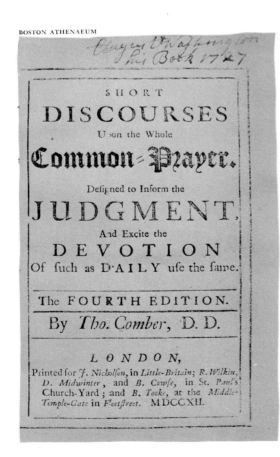

Precious few objects associated with George Washington's childhood have been found. The record of his birth, and that of his brothers and sisters, was dutifully preserved in Mary Ball Washington's Bible, on a sheet of paper affixed to one of the pages (above). The "11th Day of February 1731/2 about 10 in the Morning" refers, of course, to the Old Style calendar which was revised in 1752. A book owned by his father, which George had in his library at Mount Vernon, was the "Short Discourses" at left; on the opposite page is the title page of a religious volume owned by his mother, on which George practiced signing his name.

THE
SUFFICIENCY

Sam^t OF A *Bowman*

Standing REVELATION in General,

And of the *Bowman*

Scriptur REVELATION in Particular.

BOTH *Washington*

As to the Matter of *it*, and

As to the Proof of *it*;

George AND *Washington*

That NEW REVELATIONS

Cannot Reasonably be Desired, *and*

Would Probably be Unsuccessful.

In Eight SERMONS,

Preach'd in the

CATHEDRAL-CHURCH of St. *Paul, London*;
At the LECTURE Founded by the Honourable
ROBERT BOYLE Esq; in the Year 1700.

By *OFSPRING*, Late Lord Bishop of EXETER.

LONDON: Printed for *Jer. Batley* at the Dove, and *T. Warner*
at the *Black-Boy* in *Pater Noster-Row*, 1717.

J. D.

ADVENTURE IN MIND

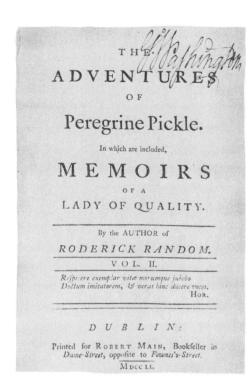

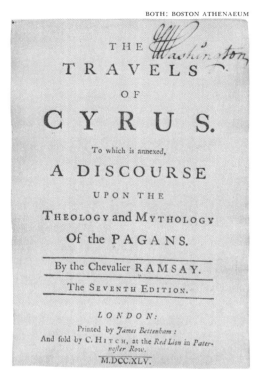

A boy's life near Fredericksburg in the eighteenth century was not much different from that in any other sleepy village on Virginia's coastline, and adventure was something one usually came by vicariously. Two books that belonged to young George Washington were *The Adventures of Peregrine Pickle* and *The Travels of Cyrus,* on whose title pages (above) he carefully inscribed his signature. Undoubtedly one of the most memorable episodes of his boyhood involved the expedition of Admiral Edward Vernon (shown at the left in a miniature portrait now at Mount Vernon), who sailed from home waters to the West Indies in July, 1739, to open hostilities against Spain. Early in the following year Virginia newspapers carried accounts of Vernon's triumphal attack on Porto Bello, on the coast of Panama, where he forced the town's surrender within two days after his arrival. The engraving (opposite) is a contemporary view of the battle. Among several hundred Virginians recruited for service in the admiral's next operation was Lawrence Washington, George's half-brother, who was commissioned a captain in an "American Regiment" and left Ferry Farm in the fall of 1740 to participate in the assault on Cartagena. That citadel, unlike Porto Bello, proved a match for the admiral and the bungling, procrastinating Brigadier Thomas Wentworth, who commanded the army, and after a month-long siege Vernon gave up the attempt and sailed away. Some six hundred troops had been killed in action and a larger number succumbed to yellow fever; to his disappointment, Lawrence saw no fighting — like most of the colonial troops, for whom Wentworth had no use, he was confined to shipboard during the siege. For all his contempt for Wentworth, Lawrence returned home with an abiding admiration for Edward Vernon, and after he inherited the land on Little Hunting Creek from his father he named the plantation after the man he revered.

A BROTHER'S

INHERITANCE

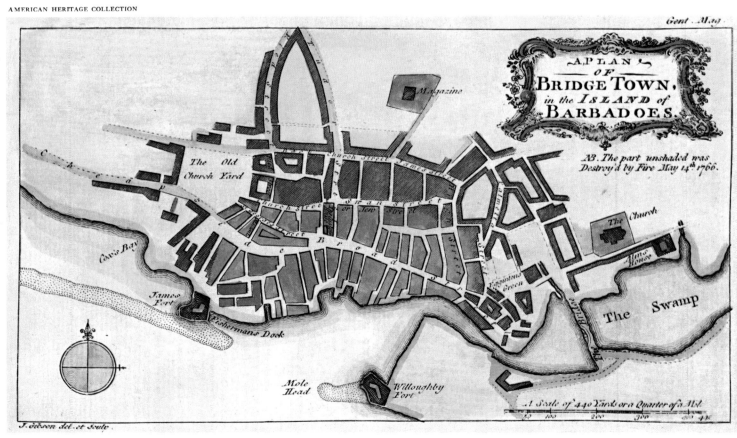

In the spring of 1749 Lawrence Washington returned from a session of the Burgesses in Williamsburg with a bad cough suggestive of consumption, and he never recovered his health. The following year he and George visited the primitive resort at Berkeley, Virginia, where the springs were reputed to have restorative properties, but Lawrence's condition did not improve. In the fall of 1751 the two made a voyage to Barbados where, it was hoped, the climate might benefit Lawrence's health. They stayed in Bridgetown (shown on the facing page in a map drawn about 1770), where George was much taken with the island's beauty and the cordiality of society. In Barbados he was "strongly attacked" with smallpox, from which he recovered in several weeks, but Lawrence was no better and so decided to go to Bermuda. George returned to Virginia and in June, 1752, Lawrence was also home, now with the look of death in his face. The following month he died. George's half-brother, fourteen years his senior and virtually a foster father to the young man, is shown opposite. While Lawrence lived, George received from him affection, tutelage, inspiration, and an introduction to the world beyond Ferry Farm. When he died, he left George three lots in Fredericksburg and a slim hope of possessing the place they both loved better than any other — Mount Vernon. Lawrence's widow remarried six months after his death, and from her and her new spouse, Colonel George Lee, Washington leased the plantation on December 17, 1754, thus becoming tenant and master of Mount Vernon. The agreement, reproduced at right, stipulated that for an annual rental of fifteen thousand pounds of tobacco he might have the use of the estate, including the grist mill, and eighteen resident slaves.

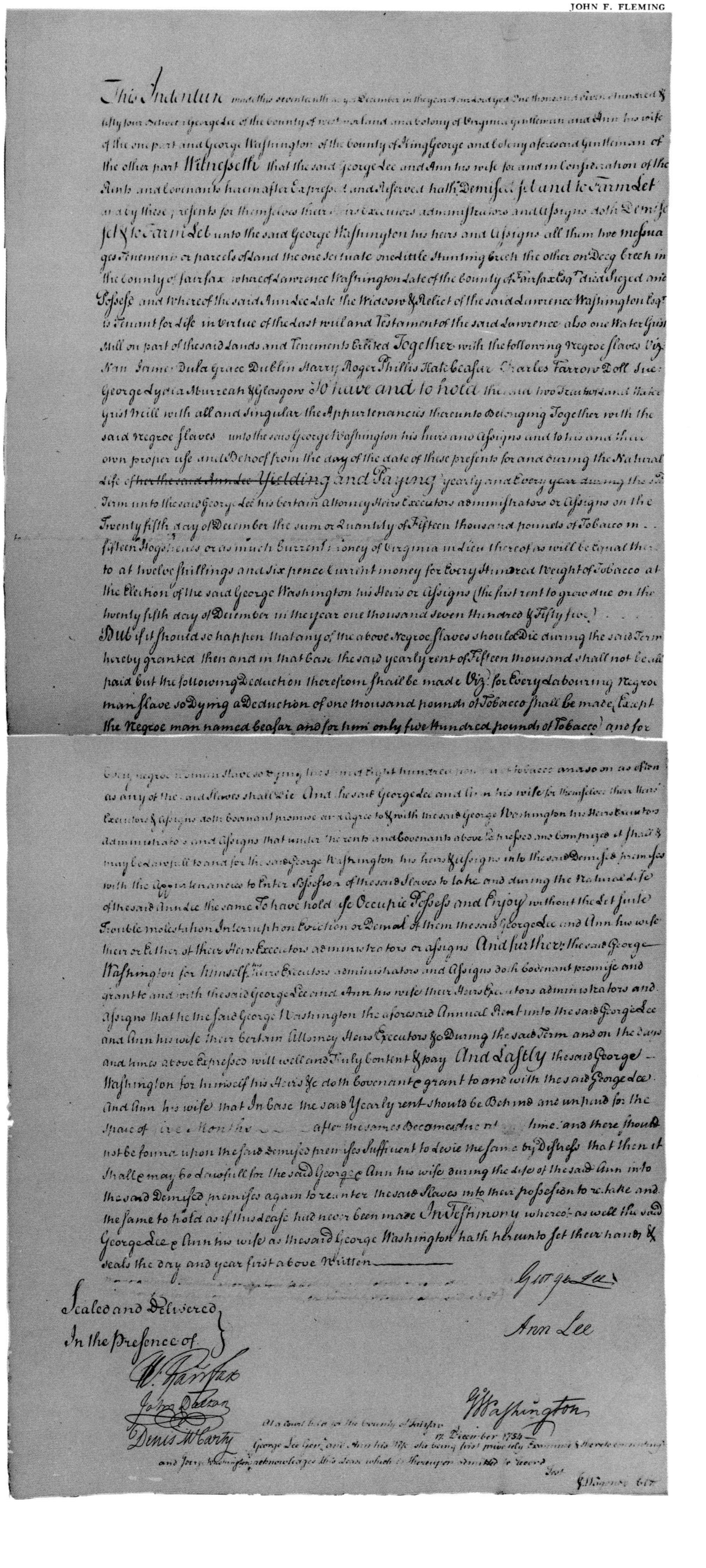

THE FAIRFAX WORLD

How vast were the lands of Thomas, Lord Fairfax, is suggested by the survey map (below) which shows that his proprietary embraced all the area between the Potomac and Rappahannock Rivers. Since it extended as far west as their headwaters, this immense, five-million-acre fiefdom also included the present West Virginia counties of Jefferson, Berkeley, Morgan, Hampshire, Mineral, and parts of Hardy, Grant, and Tucker. George's introduction to the wilderness and to his first vocation came in this region, not long after the arrival in America of the man who owned it all — Thomas, sixth Lord Fairfax of Cameron, who appears (top right) in a portrait by Sir Joshua Reynolds. When his Lordship engaged a surveyor to lay out certain of his Shenandoah Valley lands in family-sized lots, George went along, thereby acquiring his first experience of the frontier, of Indian war parties, and gaining a practical knowledge of surveying.

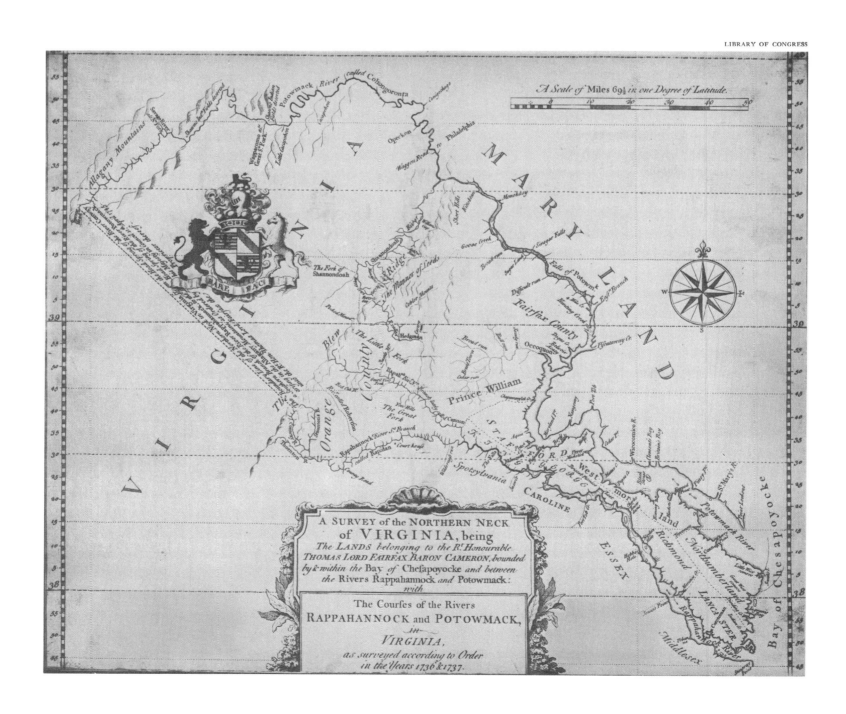

A SURVEY of the NORTHERN NECK of VIRGINIA, being The LANDS belonging to the R.t Honourable THOMAS LORD FAIRFAX BARON CAMERON, bounded by & within the Bay of Chesapoyocke and between the Rivers Rappahannock and Potowmack: with The Courses of the Rivers RAPPAHANNOCK and POTOWMACK, in VIRGINIA, as surveyed according to Order in the Years 1736 & 1737.

He was accompanied by his close friend and neighbor, George
William Fairfax (lower right), a timid young man seven years
Washington's senior, whose childhood in England had been
made miserable by wealthy relatives, who spread rumors that he was a
mulatto. In December, after their return from the surveying
expedition, George William married Sarah Cary, known as Sally.
Washington was sixteen at the time, and as Lord Fairfax had observed
in a letter to his mother, was "beginning to feel the sap rising,
being in the spring of life, and is getting ready to be the
prey of your sex, wherefore may the Lord help him . . . ." Sally
was two years older, attractive, vivacious, and high-spirited,
and it was probably inevitable that she should soon become
the most fascinating young lady in his life. Unfortunately,
the portrait of Sally Fairfax has been lost; the photograph
(below) of the original is the only likeness of her that exists.

A PROFESSION AND LIFETIME AVOCATION

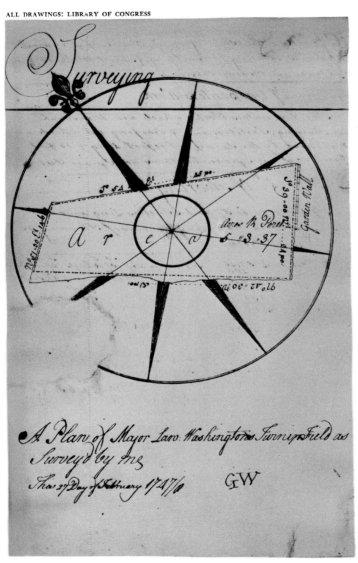

A Plan of Major Law. Washington's Turnip Field as Surveyd by me Thos 27 Day of February 1747/8 GW

In a country where land was the commodity most sought after by nearly everyone, the services of a surveyor were essential. The licensed surveyor took an oath as a government official, pledging to lay out lands according to restrictive laws; he was also a combination of explorer, planner, and agent of the landowner who employed him. For an ambitious young man like George Washington, surveying not only provided cash; it also gratified his sense of neatness and accuracy. He had learned the rudiments of surveying from tutors; he had access to his father's surveying instruments at Ferry Farm, and in Fredericksburg were knowledgeable men who taught him to use a compass and run a line. When he was fourteen he drew the chain, dividers, and scale shown below and a year later made the plan at left of his stepbrother Lawrence's turnip field. By the time he made the expedition into Lord Fairfax's western domain in 1748, George was thoroughly competent in his vocation, and at the age of seventeen he was appointed official surveyor of Culpeper County. It was to be an abiding interest: until the last year of his life he was still running lines on his own property.

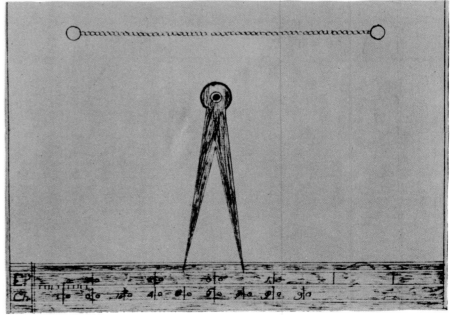

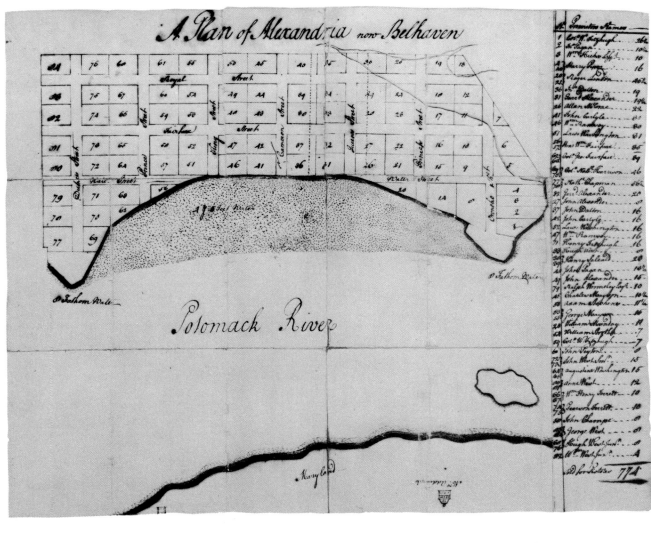

Washington's plan of the town of Alexandria (above) was made in 1749. For some time, residents of the area had been agitating for the establishment of a town at the head of navigation on the Potomac, above Hunting Creek. In 1732 a warehouse had been erected to receive goods that arrived by water, and stores of various kinds had been built in succeeding years. Originally the town was to be called Belhaven, but by legislative act the name was changed to Alexandria, in honor of the family that owned much of the tract — descendants of John Alexander, who had once surveyed the grant made to Nicholas Spencer and John Washington. As assistant to the regular surveyor employed by the town, Washington began work on May 27, and two months later had completed his part of the survey and drawn the plan of the town, which served as the basis for the public sale on July 18, when twenty-five lots were auctioned. The tripod (left) and the red morocco pocket case containing ivory scale, dividers, and pencil (right) were used by Washington.

CLARK KINNAIRD

2

FRONTIER SOLDIER

Like so many conflicts in human history, the struggle in the wilderness of North America that was to be known as the French and Indian War had its roots in a contest for power, commerce, and wealth. Although the sporadic frontier fighting gained a certain legitimacy from the fact that France and England, having endured three decades of relative peace, formally declared war in 1744, the plain truth was that French *coureurs de bois* and English traders were pitted against each other — war or no war — in the competition for land and profits from the Indian trade, and trouble had been inevitable for years. Like the French before them, Pennsylvanians and Virginians moved into the Allegheny Mountains and beyond to traffic with Indians for beaver and other furs and set up trading posts and supply depots. By the 1740's the primary occupation of many Virginia planters seemed to be land speculation, and the lieutenant governor of the province, Robert Dinwiddie, who was deeply involved in such ventures through investment in the Ohio Company, was determined that French domination of the Ohio and Mississippi valleys must not continue lest it jeopardize the stake which he, personally, and the empire he represented officially, had in western lands.

Beginning in 1749, Frenchmen quietly circulated through the great basin, burying lead plates and nailing up tin plaques signifying their claim to the territory, and in 1752 Dinwiddie learned that they were building forts as well. His efforts to arouse London to the danger fell for a time on deaf ears — most authorities there having little interest in what was going on across the Atlantic — but in October of 1753 Dinwiddie received a message that gave him an opportunity to do something about the situation himself.

His Majesty George II authorized Virginia to build forts of its own on the Ohio River and at the same time to send a mission to determine whether the French were intruding on English soil. (This was bound to be the case, so long as Virginia persisted in claiming all territory west of its dominion as far as the Pacific Ocean.) If the French were trespassing, the message continued, the emissary should "require of them peaceably to depart," and if they refused, the King proclaimed, "We do strictly command and charge you to drive them out by force of arms." No promise of active support was forthcoming, but at least Dinwiddie now had authorization to take matters into his own hands, and since the aims of empire happily coincided with his own financial interest, he acted promptly.

The newly appointed Adjutant of the Southern District of Virginia had almost certainly heard about these matters of state from his friend Colonel Fairfax, who was a member of the Governor's Council, and sensing opportunity, George Washington rode to Williamsburg and volunteered to carry the message to the French. That Dinwiddie should accept the offer of an untrained, twenty-one-year-old man to execute a delicate mission whose outcome might precipitate hostilities between Britain and France came as something of a surprise, even to his appointee. As Washington admitted years later, "It was deemed by some an extraordinary circumstance that so young and inexperienced a person should have been employed on a negotiation with which subjects of the greatest importance were involved." The governor's only explanation appears in a letter to a friend, in which he describes Washington as "a person of distinction." Beyond that, Dinwiddie of course knew that Washington had done some surveying for the Ohio Company and he realized that the mission required a knowledge of the terrain and the wilderness itself, plus stamina and intelligence — all of which the young man possessed. (In the words of a soldier who later served with Washington in the French and Indian War, he was not only "used to the woods" but was "a youth of great sobriety, diligence, and fidelity.")

In any case the die was cast, and on October 30, 1753, Dinwiddie gave George Washington orders to proceed to Logstown, downriver from the Forks of the Ohio, where he was to meet with friendly Indians and arrange for a bodyguard to escort him to meet the French commanding officer. He was to present that gentleman with a letter from Dinwiddie, await a reply, and in the meantime keep his eyes and ears open, acquiring all the information he could concerning French military strength, forts, and plans. Once he had carried out his instructions, he was to "return immediately back."

In Fredericksburg Washington enlisted the services of a young Dutchman named Jacob van Braam, who was reputed to have a fair knowledge of French (of which Washington had none). The two went on to Alexandria, purchased some supplies, and on November 14 arrived at the Ohio Company's warehouse and trading post at Wills Creek, in the Shenandoah Valley at the eastern edge of the Allegheny Mountains. Here they found the cabin of Christopher Gist, for whom Washington had a letter from Dinwiddie. Gist, forty-seven, was a frontiersman and fur trader who had an intimate knowledge of the forest and Indians. He was also a superb shot, an eternal optimist, a man of some education and strong religious principles, and as the first white American to explore the Ohio Valley and parts of what became Kentucky (anticipating Daniel Boone's travels into that region by nearly two decades) he was the man Dinwiddie wanted as guide and aide to Washington.

Gist agreed to go along; Washington hired four local fellows as hostlers or, as he called them, "servitors"; and the little party set out through the wilderness in the first snowfall of winter, trailed by a string of pack horses carrying enough baggage for a month. Crossing the Alleghenies, they entered a region entirely unfamiliar to Washington — an area described two years later by a British soldier as "a desolate country uninhabited by anything but wild Indians, bears and rattlesnakes" — made their way over Laurel and Chestnut Ridges, and followed the Youghiogheny River to Turtle Creek, at the confluence of the Monongahela River, where they gathered some intelligence at the lonely cabin of John Frazier, an Indian trader and gunsmith. Moving on, they finally arrived at the place that was to be the strategic objective of British and French throughout so many years of wilderness fighting — the Forks of the Ohio — that point of land where the Allegheny and Monongahela Rivers meet to form the Ohio. Here Washington spent two days studying the terrain and settled on a site for a fort for the Ohio Company that would provide "absolute command of both rivers."

At Logstown, an Indian settlement eighteen miles downriver from the Forks, they conferred with a chief called the Half-King and learned that although he was angry at the French, he opposed any effort by French *or* British to settle in the Ohio Valley. To Washington's annoyance, three interminably long days were spent parleying before the Half-King and several other Indians agreed to lead him to Fort Le Boeuf, the nearest French outpost, which was located on French Creek near present-day Waterford, Pennsylvania. Along the way they stopped at Venango, an old Indian town, and found some Frenchmen who let fall the information that the route between Venango and Montreal was now protected by seven forts, including Le Boeuf, sixty miles north, another one fifteen miles beyond at Lake Erie, one at Niagara, and another on Lake Ontario. These posts, they said, were garrisoned by 150 men each.

On December 12 Washington and his party reached Fort Le Boeuf, where he presented his credentials and Dinwiddie's letter to the commandant, Legardeur de St. Pierre. While the Frenchman and his aides studied the letter, Washington unobtrusively took the opportunity "of taking the Dimensions of the Fort, and making what Observations I could" — incidentally providing posterity with one of the most detailed and accurate descriptions of a French frontier fort of the period. He estimated that there were about a hundred men at the fort, and his party also counted 170 pine canoes, fifty of birch bark, and others under construction.

St. Pierre reacted predictably. His written reply indicated that he would deliver Dinwiddie's request to the Marquis Duquesne, governor of Canada, but in the meantime, "As to the summons you send me to retire, I do not think myself obliged to obey it." It was all very polite, but unmistakably clear: the challenge issued by Dinwiddie, acting for George II, was about to be taken up.

It was snowing hard when Washington left Fort Le Boeuf, and he sent the hostlers ahead with the horses while he, Van Braam, Gist, and the Indians traveled by canoe until the river froze so hard it was impossible to proceed. When they rejoined the hostlers they had to carry packs laden with food and other supplies, since the going was too difficult for the animals in the deep snow, crusted ice, and almost unbearable cold. For three days they trudged through the drifts, making so little progress that Washington — who was "uneasy to get back, to make Report of my Proceedings to his Honour the Governor" — announced that he could make better time alone. Fortunately Gist insisted on accompanying him and the two set off, leaving Van Braam and the others to make their way as best they could with the horses and baggage.

After encountering a group of "French Indians," Washington and Gist had a narrow escape when one of the red men shot at them from a distance of fifteen paces and narrowly missed; the next day Washington almost lost his life again when he slipped from a raft they had built in order to cross to the east bank of the Allegheny, fell into the icy water, and barely avoided being swept downstream. Gist's fingers and toes were frozen, but they made it at last to John Frazier's trading post and on New Year's Day of 1754 Washington was crossing the mountains again, headed for home. He stopped off at Belvoir for a day's visit with the Fairfaxes, and on January 16 was in Williamsburg to deliver his report to the governor.

Under any circumstances it would have been an arduous, demanding trip, but as Washington recorded in his journal there had been only one day between December 1 and 15 when it did not rain or snow incessantly, "and throughout the whole Journey we met with nothing but one continued Series of cold wet Weather" — not to mention hostile Indians and French and a near-drowning. Despite all the difficulties, however, the mission was extraordinarily successful. The young Virginian had delivered his important message and received a reply; he had collected quantities of useful intelligence concerning the Forks of the Ohio, the Indians, and the French military garrisons; and on the basis of notes he kept, he prepared an admirable map of the region. Dinwiddie forwarded copies of Washington's journal (which the latter wrote in twenty-four hours from "the rough minutes" he kept on the trip) to the Secretary of State for the Southern District and the Board of Trade in London, and to colonial governors throughout America. *The Journal of Major George Washington* was also published as a pamphlet and reprinted in newspapers in the colonies and in the *London Magazine* for June, 1754, as a consequence of which the young man became widely and favorably known on both sides of the Atlantic when he was only twenty-two years old. In the course of the next four years he would retrace his steps across the Alleghenies three more times; by then the name Washington would be almost a household word in the colonies and in London.

In April, 1754, Washington was on his way west again, as a lieutenant colonel of Virginia militia, in command of about 140 officers and men who marched out of Alexandria bound for the Ohio country. Dinwiddie had persuaded the House of Burgesses to appropriate £10,000 for the defense of the Ohio Valley, and while Washington was nominally under the command of Joshua Fry, a fat, elderly Burgess who had been appointed colonel of the expedition, Fry never did catch up with the advance detachment, and the young man was entirely on his own. Late in April Washington, riding ahead of the rangers who were chopping a road through the forest to accommodate wagons and cannon, encountered some thirty Virginians under the command of Ensign Edward Ward, who had been chased away from the Ohio by the French. Ward had been sent to the Forks by Dinwiddie to construct a fort on the site chosen by Washington, and one day his men looked up from their work to see the Allegheny River alive with boats — sixty bateaux and three hundred canoes — carrying eighteen cannon and six hundred Frenchmen. When the commander of this armada landed and ordered them to pick up their tools and go back to Virginia they had no choice. It was clear to Washington that he had no chance of taking on a French force four times the size of his own, so he elected to continue his road-building, clearing a way to the Ohio Company's storehouse at the mouth of Redstone Creek on the Monongahela, about thirty-seven miles from the Forks, where he would strengthen the building and await reinforcements. Impatient as always, he was thoroughly disgusted with his woodsmen's slow progress (two to four miles a day was about all they could do), but the accomplishment was far more significant than

he realized. They were making a continuous clearing through the virgin timber that covered the Allegheny Mountains, opening up the Ohio country for the first time to wheeled vehicles.

There was, in all these excursions and alarums, a certain element of irony. After all, Britain and France were not at war now — had not been, in fact, since 1748, when the Treaty of Aix-la-Chapelle ended the so-called War of the Austrian Succession in Europe and brought an uneasy truce to America. Yet here, in the wilderness of the Alleghenies, two tiny armies were jockeying for position, each aware of the other's presence, each under instructions that would almost certainly lead to bloodshed. In carrying out Dinwiddie's instructions to complete the fort at the Forks, Washington was supposed to "act on the Defensive" if an attempt was made to obstruct the work or "interrupt our Settlements," but he was also expected to "restrain all such Offenders; and in Case of resistance to make Prisoners of or kill and destroy them." Similarly the French. Captain Claude Pecaudy de Contrecoeur, who commanded the force that ousted Ward from the Forks, had learned of Washington's approach and sent Ensign Joseph Coulon Sieur de Jumonville with an interpreter and thirty-three men to find out what the Englishmen were doing. When he found them he was to order them to withdraw, and if they refused he was to "repousser la force par la force" — meet force with force.

The Half-King, who had accompanied him to Fort Le Boeuf, and Gist, his former guide, warned Washington that the French were on the way to intercept him, and on May 28 the Virginian and forty men, plus some of the Half-King's Indians, spotted fresh tracks and discovered the French party camped in a hollow. In this, his first battle, Washington set a pattern he was to repeat on a number of occasions in the Revolution, dividing his force and sending the Indians around the enemy's rear while his Virginians approached the French on both flanks. At the moment the French spotted him, he ordered his men to fire without warning, and the Indians immediately attacked from the opposite side of the hollow. Most of the French fire was directed at the Virginians, since the Indians were well-concealed, and as Washington wrote later to his brother Jack, "I heard the bullets whistle, and, believe me, there is something charming in the sound."

One of his men was killed and several wounded, but the French were in an impossible predicament and after the firing continued for about a quarter of an hour they threw down their arms. Total confusion followed — Indians racing in to scalp the dead and wounded, Frenchmen waving frantically to Washington trying to tell him something in a language he could not comprehend, interpreters attempting to make sense of the babel of French, English, and Indian tongues — but finally things quieted down sufficiently for Washington to get some inkling of what was happening. Ten of the Frenchmen, including Jumonville, had been killed, and the gist of what the survivors seemed to be saying was that the Virginians and their Indian allies had murdered a number of men who were in fact carrying diplomatic messages. Their mission had been simply to warn the English off lands belonging to France.

As a result of his eagerness to surprise the French and carry out Dinwiddie's instructions, Washington was to find himself — and, through his actions, the King of England — charged with the crime of murdering an ambassador. From this little skirmish in the wilds of America the repercussions were felt in the seats of European empires, and although he could not have guessed it at the time, Washington had spilled the first blood of the Seven Years' War, a conflict that would eventually become global in scope, waged in Europe and India as well as North America, involving France, Austria, Russia, Saxony, Sweden, Spain, Prussia, Hanover, and Great Britain, and costing nearly one million lives. As Horace Walpole described the event, "The volley fired by a young Virginian in the backwoods of America set the world on fire."

George Washington was not, just then, troubled by such awesome thoughts about the future; what he had on his mind in the camp at the Great Meadows immediately after the attack on Jumonville was the fear that he might be overwhelmed at any moment by a superior force, and he decided to share his uneasiness with Dinwiddie, in a letter doubtless sent to prepare the latter for the bad news that would almost surely follow. If the governor should learn that Washington's men had been defeated, he wrote, he should know that they had done their duty as long as there was any hope of holding out. As for himself, "I have a constitution hardy enough to encounter and undergo the most severe trials, and, I flatter myself, the resolution to face what any man durst." His troops were busy erecting a "small palisaded fort" — a structure made of logs fixed upright in the ground — and he concluded that Fort Necessity, as he called it, would withstand an attack by five hundred men.

Meanwhile, the man under whom Washington was supposedly serving — Joshua Fry — had died, and Dinwiddie appointed the young man Colonel of the Virginia Regiment in his stead. Washington was also reinforced by some Virginians and an "Independent Company" of South Carolinians under Captain James Mackay, and the latter's arrival precipitated a dispute over who was to be in overall command — Mackay arguing that since he held a commission as captain in the British regular army that dated to a time when Washington was only a few years old, there was no question of the latter exercising jurisdiction over those South Carolina troops. This nettlesome problem would recur again and again in Washington's early military career, leading to his determination to obtain a commission in the British army, but before anyone in authority had the opportunity to adjudicate the question at the Great Meadows, the French had attacked Fort Necessity and the matter became quite academic.

On the morning of July 3, 1754, Washington's scouts raced into camp shouting that the enemy — "a heavy, numerous body, all naked!" — was only four miles off, and shortly after nine o'clock they appeared in an open field beyond the fort. The Virginians and Carolinians opened fire, swivel guns booming with the muskets, and the French and Indians disappeared immediately into the forest. But almost at once the little fort was pelted with gunfire from all directions, musket balls pouring into the walls, gunsmoke appearing from "every little rising, tree, stump, stone, and bush," as Washington described it, and before he knew what was happening his men were falling, horses and cattle were screaming in pain, and the young commander, trying to move around the fort to encourage his troops, found himself slipping on their blood. For hours the attack continued — a "constant galling fire" made worse by a sudden cloudburst that drenched the men's ammunition and ruined the powder in the magazine of the open fort. Not until darkness was falling, by which time one-third of Washington's command was dead or wounded, did the enemy fire slacken; then the defenders heard a voice calling, "Voulez-vous parler?" Washington instructed Van Braam to give them a refusal in French, and a reply came back: the French were willing to receive an emissary. Van Braam was the obvious spokesman and he walked into the pelting rain under a white flag, disappeared, and then returned with what sounded like good news: the French commander, Coulon de Villiers, brother of the slain Jumonville, was offering surprisingly lenient terms for a man who had come to avenge his kinsman's death. All he required was that the Englishmen sign a surrender document, march out of the fort with the honors of war, carry off their wounded and their baggage, and go home. It all seemed very simple, and it was quickly done the next morning. With seventy wounded, the beaten Virginians and Carolinians limped out of Fort Necessity and headed east across the mountains after abandoning their one remaining cannon as soon as they were out of sight of the French.

Not until he returned to Williamsburg and capitulation terms were examined and published there and abroad did Washington realize the folly of his act. He was criticized for having signed a document, written in French, stating that he and others involved in "l'assassinat" or murder of Jumonville were being released by De Villiers since no state of war then existed between England and France. What this meant was that Jumonville's death could only be viewed as murder and that Washington, in signing the paper, virtually admitted that he and his men were responsible for that unlawful act. Dinwiddie criticized him obliquely in a letter to the government voicing concern over "the late action with the French." His orders to the commanding officer,

he said, "were by no means to attack the enemy till all of the forces were joined." In London a writer stated that the terms were the most infamous a British subject had ever signed; in Paris the death of Jumonville was called "a monument of perfidy that ought to enrage eternity"; and the British ambassador to France, General Lord Albemarle, who needed no convincing that colonial troops were not worth their salt, declared sourly that "*Washington* & many *Such,* may have courage & resolution, but they have no Knowledge or Experience in our Profession; consequently there can be no dependence on them! Officers, & good ones must be sent to Discipline the Militia, & to Lead them on."

Washington defended himself by stating somewhat lamely that his interpreter, Van Braam, had mistranslated the articles of capitulation as referring to the "death" or "loss" of Jumonville, not his murder, but in fact Washington had had no complaints about Van Braam's linguistic skills on his earlier trip to Fort Le Boeuf and had urged Dinwiddie to give the man a captaincy in the Virginia Regiment where, surely, he would not have been suited if he was so "little acquainted with the English tongue," as Washington now maintained.

It was a dark hour for the ambitious militia colonel. On the heels of his humiliation came word that the governors of Virginia, Maryland, and North Carolina had decided to combine their separate military forces into one army commanded by Governor Horatio Sharpe of Maryland and that one effect of the reorganization was to be the breaking up of Virginia's regimental organization into companies, with captain as the highest rank. Rather than accept what he viewed as a demeaning reduction, in which he would be outranked by "every Captain, bearing the King's commission, every half-pay officer, or other, appearing with such a commission," Washington resigned from the army and took up residence at Mount Vernon.

Under terms of his brother Lawrence's will, George was to receive that property on two conditions: if Lawrence's widow Anne died, and if their daughter Sarah died without issue. Sarah had followed her father to the grave in 1754, Anne had remarried, and now she offered to lease Mount Vernon to George for the remainder of her life (in 1761, when she died, he fell heir to the property). So, in return for an annual payment of fifteen thousand pounds of tobacco or, at his option, about £80 in Virginia currency, George became master of the plantation that was to be his home for the remainder of his days.

In the meantime the military pot continued to boil. As if in response to Albemarle's demand that good officers be sent to lead the raw colonial militia, the British government had dispatched Major General Edward Braddock and two regiments of regulars to America and in February, 1755, they landed in Virginia. Braddock, a short, stout man of sixty, had spent forty-five of those years in the British army, acquiring a thorough knowledge of military life and regulations but almost no combat experience. He had a quick temper, a blunt, direct manner, and, as George Washington would observe, was seemingly incapable of yielding a point in any discussion, "let it be ever so incompatible with Reason." Before meeting Braddock, Washington read or heard almost daily about the preparations going forward in Williamsburg — the recruiting of troops to fill out the British regiments, the hiring of carpenters, cavalrymen, and rangers, and the letting of contracts on a scale beyond anything the provincial capital had seen — including a call for two hundred wagons and twenty-five hundred horses. Braddock's orders from the King were secret, but it took very little imagination by anyone familiar with the existing state of affairs to guess that he was expected to drive the French from their forts on the Ohio; build a fort at the Forks; and then push the enemy out of all outposts on the Great Lakes, Lake Champlain, and wherever else in North America Frenchmen were trespassing on lands claimed by George II. The thought of what he might be missing while tending his plantation was too much for the former militia colonel. While he could not bring himself to request an appointment with the coming expedition, he wrote to Braddock, congratulating him on his arrival in America, thus informing that exalted personage of the existence of George Washington. On March 14, 1755, he received a reply from Robert Orme, Braddock's aide-de-camp, indicating that the general had made inquiries about Washington in Williamsburg and, having been impressed by what he heard, was suggesting a means by which the tricky business of rank might be solved to Washington's satisfaction. What Orme proposed was that Washington join Braddock's official family, "by which all inconveniences of that kind [i.e., rank] will be obviated."

On March 26 Braddock and his officers, along with a vast number of troops, weapons, and baggage, debarked from vessels at Alexandria, Virginia, and the sleepy little town was suddenly transformed into a staging area for the English army's expedition into the wilderness. At one of the numerous functions held to welcome the distinguished Britishers to the neighborhood, Washington was introduced to the general and soon afterward was offered a brevet captaincy, which he declined as a matter of pride, preferring to serve as a volunteer aide in hopes that something more rewarding would come of that. Amid all the preparations for departure, Mary Ball Washington arrived in Alexandria from Ferry Farm to say that she was "alarmed with the report" that he planned to accompany Braddock and had come to prevent him from going. A long argument ensued — she complaining that he was neglecting his duty to her, he protesting that it was duty to King and country that called — and finally he rode off to join Braddock's army in Frederick, Maryland, after leaving his brother Jack in charge at Mount Vernon.

In the British camp, Washington made the acquaintance of Braddock's staff — among them Lieutenant Charles Lee, Captain Horatio Gates, and Major Thomas Gage, with whom he would come in contact in entirely different circumstances two decades later — and he sensed immediately that his friendship with these regular officers in the British military establishment would be highly useful. As he wrote his brother Jack, his present "oppertunity" ought to be "serviceable hereafter, if I can find it worthwhile pushing my Fortune in the Military way." By early June Braddock had assembled about eighteen hundred regulars of the 44th and 48th regiments, plus three independent companies, a detachment of British artillery, and about five hundred provincial troops, mostly from Virginia, with a company each from Maryland and North Carolina. But the difficulties he encountered in getting these men moving toward their destination had the general in a mood ranging from despair to rage. The colony of Pennsylvania, it appeared, would do nothing to assist his expedition; the various provincial legislatures were dragging their feet in the matter of providing funds; he could not obtain adequate transport (instead of two hundred wagons, only twenty-five were available to him at Wills Creek); and he stormed about the sloth and indifference of the colonials who seemed so oblivious to a campaign undertaken for their own defense. In Philadelphia, Benjamin Franklin persuaded some farmers to make their wagons available, and when he wrote the general he took the occasion to warn him that once his long, encumbered column made its way into the deep forest there was a good chance that it would be cut to bits by hostile Indians. But Braddock would hear none of that: "These savages may be a formidable enemy to raw American militia," he observed, "but upon the King's regular and disciplined troops they can make no impression."

The rangers slowly chopped a lane into the wilderness. Braddock glimpsed the "Endless Mountains" and the difficulties that lay ahead, and Washington urged him to leave the supply wagons behind to facilitate the movement of troops; the baggage, he argued, could be packed on horses and the only rolling stock required would be cannon. But Braddock was a wheeled-vehicle man and turned aside the suggestion abruptly. On June 14 Washington fell ill with a fever and was forced to travel in one of the wagons bumping its way along the crude road. Two days later, surveying the virtually impenetrable tangle of brush and trees with which his men were attempting to cope, Braddock realized that at their present rate they would not reach the Forks of the Ohio for a month or more, and summoned his officers to ask for suggestions. He also requested Washington's private opinion of their situation, and the answer he received was the basis of the plan adopted. A picked division of twelve hundred men, with a minimum of wagons, would go on ahead, leaving the impedimenta

to follow as soon as additional horses could be obtained. This plan took effect on June 19, when Braddock and his men headed off into the forest, but by then Washington was so ill that he had to remain behind with the baggage. Even under a revised order of March, the advance party did not make much headway; word came back that they had progressed only twelve miles in four days and had had several men scalped by roving Indians.

For a week Washington suffered in camp, then boarded a wagon and was taken to the Great Crossing of the Youghiogheny, where his fever grew worse. Not for seventeen days was he able to climb into a wagon, in which he rumbled past the site of Fort Necessity and onward, finally rejoining Braddock on July 8, at a point near the Monongahela River and about twelve miles from the Forks. At dawn the next morning he tied pillows to the saddle to ease the agony of riding and painfully made his way to the head of the long column, where Braddock and his officers were discussing a dangerous movement that was getting under way. They had to ford the Monongahela twice, and Gage had led an advance party to secure the river crossings against surprise attack; now the main body was heading into the slow-moving water, accompanied by cattle, horse-drawn wagons, and artillery, after learning that Gage had beaten off a few Indians and seized the high banks at the second ford. Ahead lay the forest, dark and silent except for the sound of axemen felling trees to make a road precisely twelve feet wide — just enough to accommodate guns and wagons. From the advance guard to the extreme rear, the army was strung out for nearly a mile.

About two-thirty in the afternoon, while Gage's men were moving into dense underbrush on the opposite side of the river and Braddock and his officers were splashing across the second ford, the crack of a gun was heard. Someone up ahead spotted a uniformed French officer motioning with his arms as if to direct troops into position, and suddenly a volley of musket fire and the bloodcurdling sound of Indian war whoops echoed through the forest, followed by steady firing that indicated a general engagement. Braddock, accompanied by Washington, got his men moving forward on the double, but as they came within range of the fighting a confused mass of terrified redcoats from Gage's advance party, who could see no signs whatever of the enemy that was attacking from ahead and along both sides of their narrow road, pelted headlong into the main body, creating absolute chaos. Braddock and other officers tried to rally the frantic soldiers, but the fugitives could think of nothing but reaching safety as quickly as possible, and there was no stopping them. As Washington wrote later, he might as easily have tried to halt the wild bears of the mountains. The precipitate flight of the advance party threw the main body into a state of utter confusion and the raw path through the woods was suddenly clogged with a mass of panicked, uncomprehending men, many of them firing willy-nilly at anything that moved, often hitting their comrades in the back. When the colonial troops realized what was happening a number tried to get into the undergrowth, out of the line of fire, where they could fight the way they were accustomed to do, but the regulars, thinking they were French troops, opened fire on them too, while some of the British officers, assuming they were retreating, refused to let the regulars follow them.

From the woods poured volley after volley and the conspicuously mounted British officers, trying to rally their troops, were shot down one after another. Washington's horse was knocked from under him, his coat was pierced by bullets, and he grabbed the reins of a riderless horse and joined the apoplectic Braddock just as the general ordered a charge on some of the enemy who were visible off to the right. But the redcoats, who had lost all semblance of the discipline on which Braddock counted so heavily, refused to rush the French and Indians, and Braddock, Orme, and another officer who had ridden ahead to lead the men, fell to the ground wounded. Again, Washington's horse was shot from under him, his hat was knocked off by a bullet, and as he saw the terrible carnage on all sides he was suddenly aware of "the miraculous care of Providence that protected me beyond all human expectation."

Braddock, grievously wounded, had sunk into a coma, his second in command was dead, the two lieutenant colonels were wounded, and Washington realized that he was "the only person then left to distribute the general's orders, which I was scarcely able to do" in the aftermath of his illness. The troops were in a state of terrible confusion, incapable of fighting any more, and Washington helped some men place the general in a small covered cart and managed to get him across the Monongahela just ahead of some Indian pursuers, who emerged from cover and began scalping wounded and exhausted soldiers who had fallen in the water. The Virginian then reformed the shattered regiments as best he could and Braddock roused from his coma long enough to order Washington to alert the second division to cover the retreat. The young man, so sick and spent he could hardly sit his horse, rode off through the forest to find help, some forty miles away.

He never forgot the sights and sounds of that night, and three decades later he recalled that "The dead, the dying, the groans, lamentations, and cries along the road of the wounded for help . . . were enough to pierce a heart of adamant, the gloom and horror of which was not a little increased by the impervious darkness occasioned by the close shade of thick woods." To add to the horror, the night was so black his two guides had to walk ahead of him on all fours, groping for the track with their hands.

Word of the catastrophe had already reached the second division by the time Washington arrived next morning, and when Colonel Thomas Dunbar ordered the troops to arms a number of them ran off in a panic. Finally a relief column moved up the road toward Braddock's command and Washington collapsed, utterly spent. Hours later Braddock and the remnants of his army appeared; the general had been moved from the cart to a litter, but when the soldiers refused to carry him he somehow managed to mount a horse for the rest of the journey. On the agonizing ride one of his men heard him mutter, "Who would have thought it?" and, again, "We shall know better how to deal with them another time," but for the moment his only thought was to get out of the endless forest and he ordered the destruction of everything that would slow down the army — cannon, wagons, ammunition, and anything that had to be hauled. Mercifully, Braddock died not far from the site of Fort Necessity, and Washington had a trench dug in the road, buried the general, and had the troops and wagons march over the grave to conceal it from the enemy.

The disaster was almost total. Of a force of 1,459, some 914 men and sixty-three officers had been killed or wounded, and Washington was Braddock's only aide to escape unscathed. Four bullets had torn through his coat and two horses had been shot from under him, but he had a humorous word for his brother Jack when he wrote him from Fort Cumberland on July 18: "As I have heard since my arriv'l at this place, a circumstantial acct. of my death and dying speech, I take this oppertunity of contradicting the first and assuring you that I have not as yet composed the latter." All things considered, it was one of the worst defeats in British colonial history and a humiliating one, as Washington realized when he wrote, "We have been most scandalously beaten by a trifling body of men." The immediate result was to lay open the frontier to attack by French and Indians as far east as fifty miles from Baltimore, and as the Marquis de Vaudreuil could boast in 1756, "Messengers no longer come any further than Winchester [Virginia] because of our savages who are always in the field."

A fascinating sidelight of the battle was the roster of participants who later achieved some fame in one capacity or another. They included, in addition to Washington, Daniel Boone, Horatio Gates, Thomas Gage, Christopher Gist, Dr. James Craik (who would be at Washington's bedside when he died), Daniel Morgan, Captain Roger Morris (who married a woman named Polly Philipse, whom Washington wooed a year after the battle), George Croghan the Indian trader, who was one of the most important men on the frontier, Adam Stephen and Charles Lee, who became generals in the Revolution, and — possibly — the Indian chieftain Pontiac. As historian Robert C. Alberts writes in a discussion of the Braddock alumni, four of these men "had been at the Battle of Fort Necessity . . . six were with General Forbes at the taking of Fort Duquesne . . . four fought [with Wolfe] at Quebec . . . six were intimately involved in Pontiac's conspiracy . . . eight became general officers in the American Revolution . . . one became commander in chief of British forces . . . two were considered for the post of commander in chief of the Revolutionary forces . . . one entered the U.S. Congress . . . and one became President of the United States."

Shortly after his return to the peaceful countryside of Mount Vernon, Washington learned that whatever might be said about Braddock and his other officers, he himself was the subject of almost universal acclaim. Orme had praised the Virginian's behavior in battle as an example of "the greatest courage and resolution," the famous Benjamin Franklin had commended him highly, and Virginia's governor and assembly were said to be equally enthusiastic about his performance — confirmation of which came when Dinwiddie reestablished the Virginia Regiment and offered Washington the colonelcy.

For two years — 1755 and 1756 — Washington was engaged in an effort to secure Virginia's frontiers against raids by the triumphant French and Indians. Neither colonies nor mother country had the stomach or the resources to mount another attack on Fort Duquesne, as the French named the outpost they had built at the Forks, and since he could not get at the enemy's base of operations Washington limited his activities to establishing a chain of forts at the edge of the wilderness. Although it proved a frustrating task, since he was hampered by continual shortages of men and supplies, the experience was invaluable, giving him real insight into the problems of maintaining an army, building defensive works, administering a complex military project, and acquiring an understanding of how to work with officers and men. He was, it appears, a rather strict disciplinarian — despite criticism from some civilians to the contrary — and according to a man who served under him was held in considerable esteem. "Our colonel," Robert Munford wrote, "is an example of fortitude in either danger or hardships, and by his easy, polite behavior, has gained not only the regard but affection of both officers and soldiers."

In the meantime he was still trying his best to

secure a commission in the regular army. He had undoubtedly hoped that Braddock would aid him in this, but with Braddock gone there was no influential patron to help him overcome the deficiencies of youth, relatively short service, lack of political support, and the expense of purchasing a commission It is doubtful that he could have aimed as high as a lieutenant-colonelcy; more likely he hoped to be made a major — but the going price in the British army for a majority at that time was about £2,000 sterling, an enormous figure for one of Washington's fairly limited means.

A galling reminder of his situation was a Maryland officer named Captain John Dagworthy, who moved into Fort Cumberland, where some of Washington's Virginians were garrisoned, and insisted — since he had held a commission from the King — that he was in command of the Virginians. Washington argued the point vigorously but without success, considered resigning, and finally appealed to Dinwiddie to allow him to petition General William Shirley, who had succeeded Braddock as commander in chief in North America. To see Shirley, Washington made a trip to Boston, traveling via New York, in February, 1756, accompanied by his aide-de-camp, George Mercer, a friend named Robert Stewart, and two servants (one of whom, named Bishop, had served as orderly to Braddock until his death and then attached himself permanently to the young Virginia colonel). This was his first glimpse of two cities on the eastern seaboard with which he would be closely associated during the Revolution, and the occasion also furnished posterity with the earliest personal description of George Washington of which there is any record. A British officer named Captain David Kennedy, who accompanied him on part of the journey, wrote that his companion was "about 6 foot high of a Black Complection, Black hair which he then wore in a Bag, looks like a Forrener, a Strong Man . . . his uniform . . . Bleau faced with Red and Laced."

Beyond providing a first impression of the country between Virginia and Massachusetts, the trip was unproductive; no commission was forthcoming and Washington again thought of resigning. Then hope arose momentarily in another quarter. In May, 1756, Great Britain had formally declared war on France and Lord Loudoun was sent to America to succeed Shirley, bringing with him General James Abercromby as his second in command. Dinwiddie knew Abercromby and recommended Washington to him, but to no avail. Washington made a personal visit to Loudoun's headquarters in Philadelphia, was rebuffed and dismissed, and returned to Virginia empty-handed to resume the work of fort building and to while away the hours taking fencing lessons.

Militarily, the year 1757 was an unhappy one for the colonies. The frontiers were aflame, under constant harassment from Indian and French raiding parties; an expedition the incompetent Lord Loudoun mounted against Louisbourg was a fiasco; and the French captured Fort William Henry on Lake George. Personally, Washington suffered an equal lack of success: he was unable to bring his regiment up to strength, his men were deserting, he thought of himself as an exile faced with an impossible task in the wilderness, and there were accusations of misconduct against him that led to a misunderstanding with his irascible old patron, Governor Dinwiddie, with whom he finally had a falling out. It is impossible to say whether Washington's poor health during this period resulted from his unhappiness at being unable to procure the regular army commission that meant so much, but considering the fact that he was remarkably healthy during the entire eight years of the Revolutionary War — remaining constantly with his troops except for a ten-day stopover at Mount Vernon just before the battle of Yorktown — it may be supposed that his state of mind had something to do with the physical afflictions that now plagued him.

He suffered considerable difficulty with his teeth despite the use of "sponge" toothbrushes and various dentifrices, and his diary is filled with references to aching teeth and swollen gums, for which the usual recourse was extraction. In August of 1757 he had a serious bout of dysentery and by November, when he began to experience a high fever and violent pain, he was so weak he was scarcely able to walk. Dr. James Craik, who attended him, was perplexed as to what to do; his condition was grave, and the physician recommended that his best chance of recovering was to get a change of air and complete rest. (Craik, who was to remain a lifelong friend, seems to have perceived that Washington was destined for some great task. "The fate of your Friends and Country are in a manner dependent on your recovery," he wrote his patient later.) Washington turned over his command at Winchester to Captain Robert Stewart and painfully made his way to Mount Vernon. Until March of the next year he was under the care of doctors, worrying constantly about his condition, which he feared to be the tuberculosis that had killed Lawrence. Some nights as his fever mounted he felt he would not live until morning; he was increasingly depressed; and not until April of 1758 did he return to duty, just in time to participate in his last expedition to the Forks of the Ohio.

In London, Prime Minister William Pitt had reshaped Britain's colonial war effort, and was now furnishing arms, provisions, and troops with which three major campaigns were to be launched: one against Fort Ticonderoga on Lake Champlain; one against the French bastion at Louisbourg; and a third against Fort Duquesne. To Washington's delight, Pitt had resolved the long-simmering dispute over rank by announcing that colonial field officers would have seniority over all regular officers of lower rank. This meant that Washington, as a provincial colonel, could only be commanded by a regular officer with the rank of colonel or higher.

The expedition against Fort Duquesne was placed in the hands of Brigadier John Forbes, a tough, methodical Scot who avoided the mistakes Braddock had made by leaving nothing to chance, but who was no improvement over Braddock when it came to heeding the advice of colonial officers. Almost at once he and his second in command, Henry Bouquet, a Swiss soldier of fortune, had a dispute with George Washington that was to persist throughout the expedition, thoroughly embittering the Virginian. The British general and Bouquet decided to use Phila-

delphia, not Alexandria, as their base of operations; and against Washington's continued and unavailing urging, began constructing a new road directly west across the Alleghenies from Philadelphia rather than using the route followed by Washington on two earlier occasions. Since the road avoided a crossing of the Youghiogheny River and was at least forty miles shorter than the route taken by Braddock, their reasons were justified, but Washington saw it as a trick by Pennsylvanians to protect their own frontier at the expense of Virginia's and Maryland's. While rangers hacked his "Great Road" across the mountains Forbes was so ill he had to be carried in a litter hung between two horses (he was, in fact, in the final stages of the disease that would kill him), and he became convinced that Washington was scheming against him. The Virginian was a somewhat grudging participant in a campaign he thought would fail; he was suffering from a recurrence of dysentery; and the triumph he should have felt when word came that the French had evacuated and burned Fort Duquesne was a sour one. On Christmas morning of 1758 he reached the triangular piece of land near the spot where he had almost lost his life on a raft five years before, and what he saw was not a vision of the new English fort that would rise there, to be named Fort Pitt in honor of the statesman who had recognized its significance, but the smoldering ruins of a small log fort and, across the river, the burned out remains of a French village.

To the dismay of his men, Washington announced his intention to resign and return to Mount Vernon. He was still sick when he received an affectionate "humble address" signed by twenty-seven officers, begging him to reconsider, but his mind was made up. He responded with equal affection, bidding farewell to the men who had been his comrades in arms during the French and Indian War, and after five grueling years of wilderness service turned his back on the military life and returned to his plantation. Not for seventeen years would he take up the sword again.

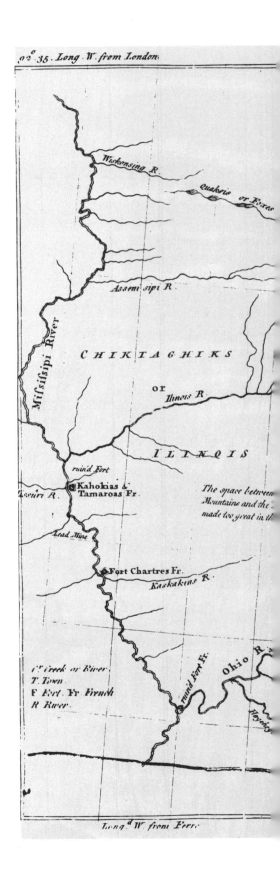

The man who gave George Washington his first major opportunity was Robert Dinwiddie, lieutenant governor of Virginia, portrayed here by an unknown artist. When Washington met him in 1753 Dinwiddie was sixty and had served as collector of customs in Bermuda and surveyor-general for the southern colonies before taking office in Virginia. Not a man of much intellect, he was nonetheless an honest, active public servant and an early advocate of intercolonial cooperation, who had the wit to see that the French must be driven from the Ohio. Considering his admitted ignorance of military matters, it was ironic that he should have recognized young Washington's military talents and precipitated the conflict that resulted in the downfall of New France.

COLONIAL WILLIAMSBURG

The only known contemporary view of colonial Williamsburg is the so-called Bodleian Plate, a copperplate engraving made between 1732 and 1747 and found in the Bodleian Library at Oxford University. This detail shows the Governor's Palace as Washington knew it.

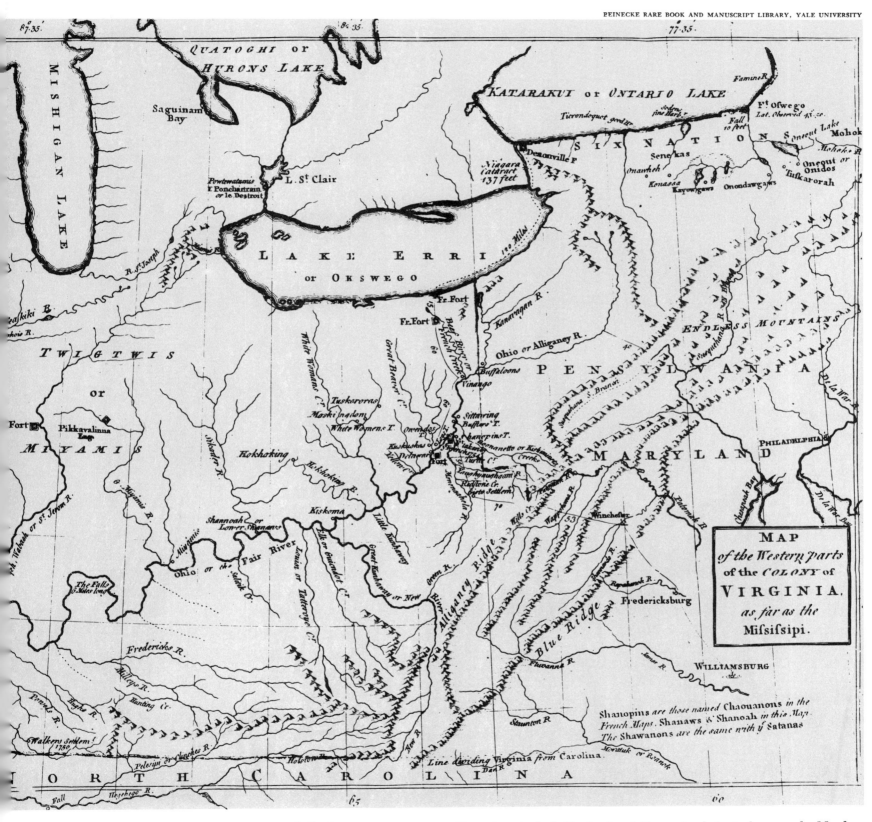

A disadvantage common to policymakers in both England and France in their rivalry over the North American continent was a lack of accurate maps. This one, made by Thomas Jefferys and published in London in 1753, indicates a rather general knowledge of the Great Lakes and some confusion over the names and location of Indian tribes. The French fort at the mouth of the Wabash did not exist.

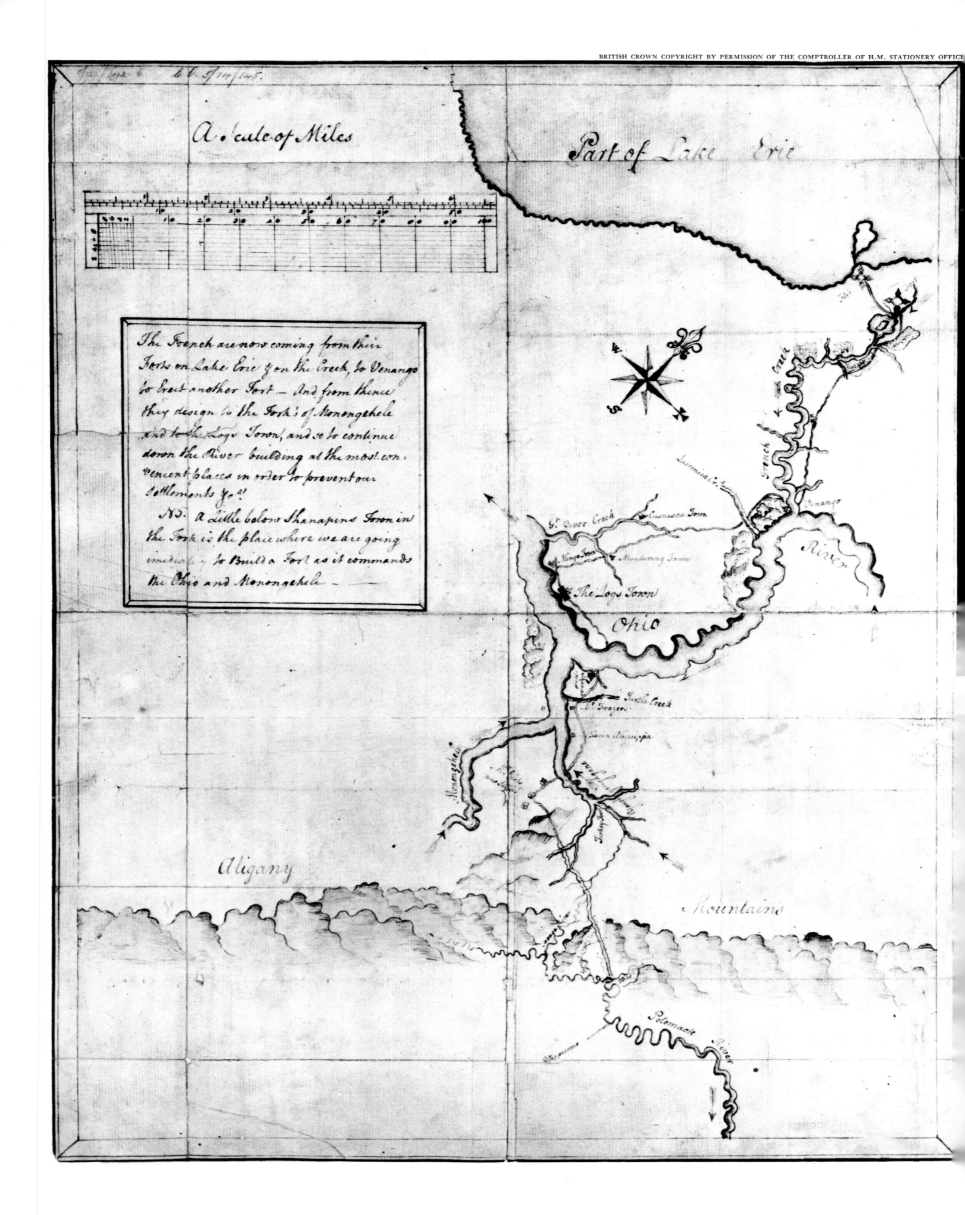

A Scale of Miles

Part of Lake Erie

The French are now coming from their
Forts on Lake Erie & on the Creek, to Venango
to Erect another Fort — And from thence
they design to the Fork's of Monongehele
and to the Logs Town, and so to continue
down the River building at the most con:
venient places in order to prevent our
Settlements &c.

NB. A little below Shanapins Town in
the Fork is the place where we are going
imediately to Build a Fort as it commands
the Ohio and Monongehele —

Venango

River

Gt. Beaver Creek   Kuskuska Town

Kinge Town   Murdering Town

The Logs Town

Ohio

Turtle Creek

Mr. Frazer.

Queen Aliquippa

Monongehele

Aligany

Mountains

Potomack River

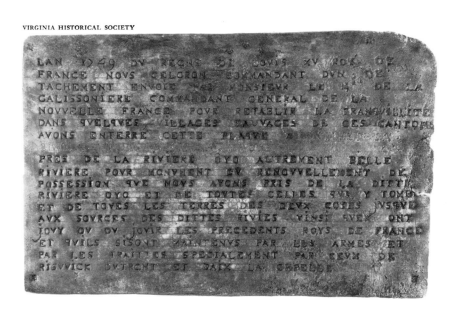

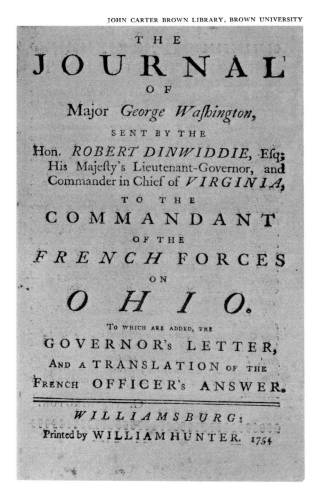

THE
JOURNAL
OF

Major *George Washington*,

SENT BY THE

Hon. *ROBERT DINWIDDIE*, Efq;
His Majefty's Lieutenant-Governor, and
Commander in Chief of *VIRGINIA*,

TO THE

COMMANDANT

OF THE

FRENCH FORCES

ON

OHIO.

TO WHICH ARE ADDED, THE

GOVERNOR's LETTER,

AND A TRANSLATION OF THE

FRENCH OFFICER's ANSWER.

WILLIAMSBURG:
Printed by WILLIAM HUNTER. 1754.

One factor behind Dinwiddie's decision to send Washington to the Ohio country was the information that the French were depositing lead plates like the one above throughout the great basin, claiming it in the name of Louis XV. France and Britain coveted the immense territory for itself and for its rich fur trade. Until English traders arrived on the scene, Frenchmen had been able to demand almost any price in pelts for the goods they exchanged — nine beaver skins for a blanket, three for a pound of gunpowder — with the result, one Indian chief remarked, that "With the French, a man must hunt a year to clothe himself." When Washington returned to Williamsburg in January of 1754, Dinwiddie requested that he submit a report on his mission to Fort Le Boeuf which the governor could show his Council to prove France's intentions. Given a twenty-four-hour deadline, Washington transcribed the rough notes he had made on the trip, drew a remarkably accurate map (opposite) showing the principal geographical features of the terrain he had covered, marked on it his route and the places he had seen, and delivered the report to Dinwiddie. The latter ordered it printed as a pamphlet, in which form it appeared in Williamsburg and London, after which it was reprinted in periodicals in America and England. In the document, whose title page appears at right, Washington stated modestly that there was nothing to recommend his account but this: "Those things which came under the notice of my own observation, I have been explicit and just in a recital of. Those which I have gathered from report, I have been particularly cautious not to augment, but collected the opinions of the several intelligencers, and selected from the whole the most probable and consistent account."

The musket shots fired by Washington's band of men at what became known as Jumonville Glen began the final stage of a century-long struggle between France and Great Britain for control of the North American continent. Symbolizing the rival empires were the coat of arms of Britain (above left) that graced Boston's Old State House and that of France (above right) on the gates of Quebec. At the same time Washington ambushed Jumonville's party in the wilderness, commissioners from seven colonies were meeting in Albany with chiefs of the Six Nations to secure their support against France. Out of that meeting came Benjamin Franklin's "Albany Plan," represented by the device (below) he drew for the Pennsylvania *Gazette*. Although it was not adopted, the proposal was the first to call for voluntary union of the colonies and as such was the forerunner of the Stamp Act Congress of 1765 and the First Continental Congress in 1774.

CLASH OF EMPIRES

On July 3, 1754, just over a month after he had surprised Jumonville, Washington was attacked by a superior French force at the Great Meadows, where he had built Fort Necessity. The surrender document signed by him and a rival, Captain James Mackay of South Carolina, and Coulon de Villiers, the French commander, created an international incident because of a word appearing in the fourth line of the second paragraph below. (Here it reads "l'assassin"; elsewhere in the agreement it is "l'assassinat.") As a result of what he maintained was a faulty translation, Washington was accused — in England, France, and America — of admitting to the murder of Jumonville, who the French claimed was carrying a diplomatic message at the time of his demise.

THE BRADDOCK CAMPAIGN IS LAUNCHED

Final preparations for the expedition to be led by
General Edward Braddock were complete by late September,
1754; £50,000 was appropriated for the operation;
and anyone who read the London papers knew about the
government's plan to drive the French from the Forks
of the Ohio and then seize their forts from Niagara to
Nova Scotia. As one English nobleman remarked, "I
don't think a little war would do us any harm."
Braddock viewed the adventure fatalistically: on his
last night in London he told a young woman friend he
would never see her again. "We are sent like lambs
to the altar," he observed, and before departing
pressed his will into her hand. As this portrait by
an unknown artist suggests. Braddock was a good-
looking man with regular features; short and stout,
he had the erect bearing of a soldier who had spent
forty years in the Coldstream Guards.

Although Washington did not solicit an appointment to Braddock's command, he let it be known that he was available, and on March 2, 1755, the general's aide Robert Orme wrote him this letter, saying that Braddock "will be very glad of your company in his family" — i.e., as a member of his staff. Replying, Washington noted his desire to serve King and country, adding, "I wish for nothing more earnestly than to attain a small degree of knowledge in the military art." Sir Joshua Reynolds' lush portrait (right) is of Captain Robert Orme, Braddock's favorite aide, who was cordially disliked by many of the other English officers, who were jealous of his influence on the general. One went so far as to say that Orme "really directed everything and may justly be said to have commanded the expedition and the army." Washington liked Orme and got on well with him, although the captain's confidence — given his inexperience in wilderness warfare — made him extremely uneasy. Three of Washington's souvenirs from the Braddock campaign appear at left; the heavy leather pack bag may also have served him during the Revolution. The three-foot sword, of French origin, was imported into England in 1753 or 1754 and acquired by Washington the year he joined Braddock. The red silk sash, bearing the date 1709, is said to have formed part of the litter used to carry the wounded general; just before his death, Braddock gave it to Washington, his only unwounded aide.

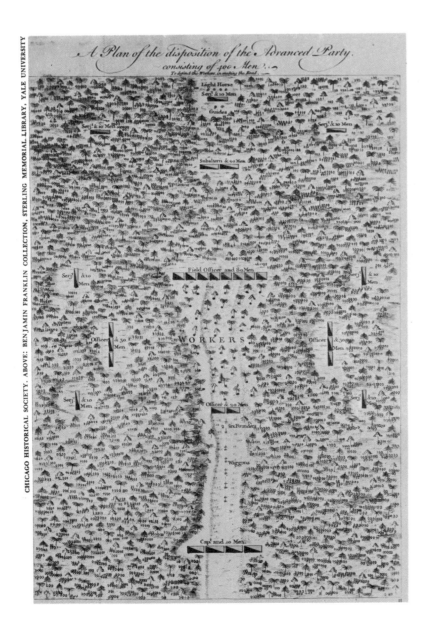

DISASTER ON THE MONONGAHELA

Newly in command of the French fort at the Forks of the Ohio was forty-year-old Captain Daniel Hyacinthe Marie Lienard de Beaujeu, the Canadian-born son of a former mayor of Quebec. Not until Braddock was six leagues away did the Frenchman decide to ambush the British. After receiving communion, he stripped to the waist, led about two hundred French and Canadians from the fort, and exhorted the Indians camped nearby to follow (they had refused the night before on grounds that the British outnumbered them). Some four hundred changed their minds and on the morning of July 9, 1755, Beaujeu led his war party to meet Braddock, hoping to intercept him as he crossed the Monongahela River near Turtle Creek. What is often lost sight of is Braddock's remarkable achievement of forging a road through unbroken forests and across mountains, opening a 110-mile lane for wheeled vehicles over a path once traveled only by Indians and English traders. The plan of march, as suggested in the 1758 map at left, was for three hundred workers to cut and clear a road twelve feet wide (for the wagons), while the army marched two men deep on either side of the road, their baggage in the middle, with advance and rear guards and flanking parties to watch for surprise attacks. The cutting of the road advanced at a frustratingly slow pace; Braddock's anger mounted when the wagons, horses, and provisions which had been pledged by colonists were not supplied in the quantities promised. Only one colonist, Benjamin Franklin of Pennsylvania, came through with his full pledge, thanks in part to the advertisement at left, above. On the morning of July 9 Braddock's army forded the Monongahela just above Turtle Creek (lower right in the contemporary map, opposite) where the river was no more than knee deep. Since the French had not attacked here, where the British expected them, "There Never was an Army in the World in more Spirits then we where," one soldier wrote; the band began playing the Grenadiers' March, the "grand Army" swung off into the woods, and Fort Duquesne (upper left), only five miles off, seemed an easy mark. When Beaujeu struck the British advance (A, B, and C on the map), the rear guard had just cleared the ford — 1,900 yards to the rear — and the British, strung out along their narrow, exposed road, had no chance as the French and Indians cut them down from front and both sides.

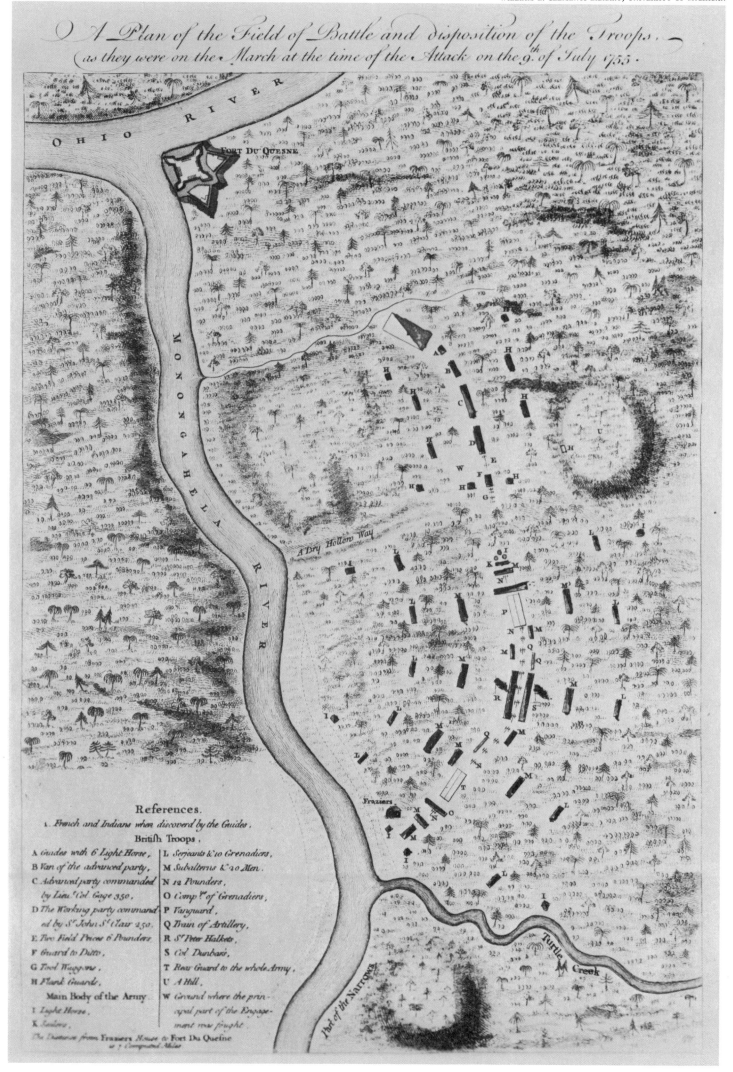

A Plan of the Field of Battle and disposition of the Troops, as they were on the March at the time of the Attack on the 9th of July 1755.

OHIO RIVER

FORT DU QUESNE

MONONGAHELA RIVER

Fraziers

A Dry Hollow Way

Turtle Creek

Part of the Narrows

References.

1. French and Indians when discover'd by the Guides.

British Troops.

A Guides with 6 Light Horse,
B Van of the advanced party,
C Advanced party commanded by Lieut Col. Gage 350,
D The Working party commanded by St John St Clair 250,
E Two Field Pieces 6 Pounders,
F Guard to Ditto,
G Tool Waggons,
H Flank Guards,
  Main Body of the Army.
I Light Horse,
K Sailors,

L Serjeants & 10 Grenadiers,
M Subalterns & 20 Men,
N 12 Pounders,
O Comp.s of Grenadiers,
P Vanguard,
Q Train of Artillery,
R St Peter Halkets,
S Col. Dunbars,
T Rear Guard to the whole Army,
U A Hill,
W Ground where the principal part of the Engagement was fought

The Distance from Fraziers House to Fort Du Quesne is 7 Computed Miles

On Washington's 1756 visit to New York he
met Mary Eliza Philipse, known as Polly, and
squired her to an exhibit called "The Microcosm,
or World in Miniature." Among Polly's attractions
were the 51,000 acres of New York land she
owned. This portrait was painted by John Singleton
Copley, who spent his early years in Boston
and made trips to Philadelphia and New York in
1771–1772 to execute commissions. In 1774
he left for Europe and settled the following year
in London, where he remained until his death.
This painting of New York as seen from the
Brooklyn shore was probably done the year
after Washington's sojourn in the city. By then
there were "2 or 3,000 houses and 16 or
17,000 inhabitants," many of whom lived in
the gabled houses dating to the period of Dutch
possession. At the extreme left of the British
ships in the East River is a French vessel captured
by the English. In the center, below the steeple
of Trinity Church, a militia company parades.

A MATTER OF RANK: BOSTON

One of the most popular colonial officials was William Shirley, governor of Massachusetts and Braddock's successor as commander of British forces in America, on whom Washington called in 1756 to settle the question of his rank. Shirley, who had planned the successful attack on French-held Louisbourg in 1745, had a sound grasp of military matters but his ideas seldom bore fruit because of intercolonial bickering and lack of support. Apart from trimming Washington at cards, he treated the Virginian courteously and supported him in his command dispute with Captain Dagworthy. This portrait of the governor was made by Thomas Hudson in 1750. This view of Boston, painted in 1764 by a British officer named Richard Byron (a great-uncle of the English poet) shows the port as Washington first saw it. Visitors considered it more like an English town than any other American city, and Washington took advantage of its shops' low prices to purchase a new hat, some clothing, a quantity of silver lace, and two pairs of gloves. The first settlers had been quick to see the site as a natural port, and in 1719 one Daniel Neal wrote that "The Bay of Boston is spacious enough to contain in a manner the Navy of *England*. The Masts of Ships here . . . make a kind of Wood of Trees," as may be seen along the famous Long Wharf (far right) which Neal described as "a noble Pier, 1800 or 2000 Foot long, with a Row of Warehouses on the North Side, for the Use of Merchants."

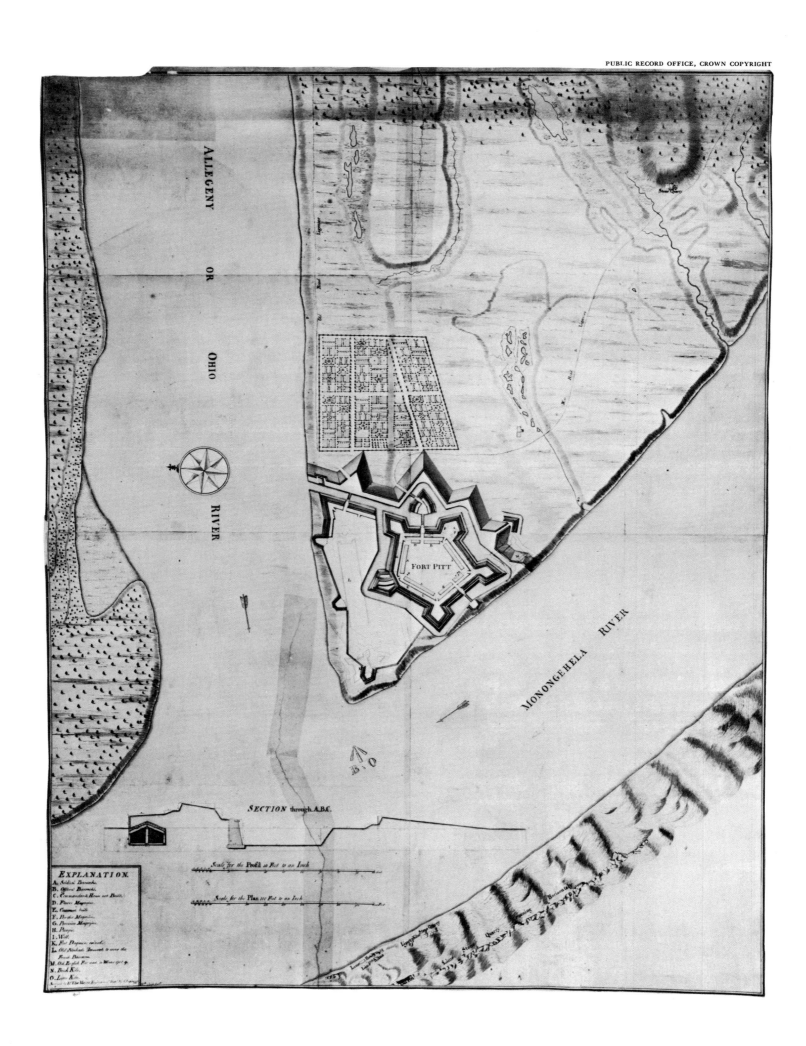

ALLEGENY OR OHIO RIVER

FORT PITT

MONONGEHELA RIVER

SECTION through A.B.C.

Scale for the Profil 20 Feet to an Inch

Scale for the Plan 100 Feet to an Inch

EXPLANATION.

A. Soldiers Barracks.
B. Officers Barracks.
C. Commandants House not Built.
D. Pieces Magazin.
E. Casemat Vault.
F. Bomb Magazin.
G. Provision Magazin.
H. Pumps.
I. Well.
K. Fort Draguin ruined.
L. Old Stockado Barracks to cover the
    Forces Retreation.
M. Old English Fort now in Water 9 or 4.
N. Brick Kiln.
O. Lime Kiln.

56

Three years after Braddock's defeat an army led by Brigadier John Forbes (right) was heading west from Philadelphia, its objective the capture of Fort Duquesne at the Forks of the Ohio. Forbes elected to cut a new road across the mountains instead of taking the old Braddock route Washington urged on him, and not only was the army's progress painfully slow, but Forbes was so ill he had to be carried in a crude litter, slung between two horses. Convinced that the British would not strike before winter set in, the French commandant at the fort sent most of his men back to Canada. The French had not reckoned on John Forbes' determination, and when it became evident that his superior force would take the fort, they destroyed its cannon and evacuated the place. On November 26, 1758, Forbes wrote William Pitt from the place he named "Pittsbourgh," saying, "I do myself the Honour of acquainting you that it has pleased God to crown His Majesty's Arms with Success over all His Enemies upon the Ohio." A few months later Forbes was dead, but four years afterward, when Elias Meyer made the map on the facing page, the fort he had taken and renamed was still in British hands, and the town of Pittsburgh was beginning to take shape beyond its walls. During a visit to America in 1796, a French explorer and soldier named George Henri Victor Collot, who had served with Rochambeau during the American Revolution, made the watercolor sketch of Pittsburgh (below), showing the new town rising where the Allegheny and Monongahela Rivers join to form the Ohio.

SUCCESS AT THE FORKS OF THE OHIO

George's return from the wars brought relief to his mother, Mary
Ball Washington, as this letter of July 26, 1759, to her brother
Joseph reveals. "There was no end to my troble while George was
in the army," she complained, "butt he has now given it up."

PORTRAIT OF THE VIRGINIA MILITIA COLONEL

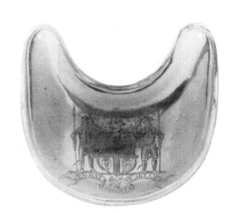

The earliest known portrait of George Washington was done in 1772 by
Charles Willson Peale, a 31-year-old former saddler and wood carver who
had studied art in London with the American Benjamin West. Although
Washington commissioned the likeness (along with miniatures of Martha,
Jack, and Patsy), he was self-conscious about posing and said that he was
in "so grave [and] so sullen a mood" that the artist would be hard put
to describe "to the world what manner of man I am." He was forty years
old when the painting was made but decided to have it done in the uniform
he had worn during the French and Indian War, including the gilded brass
gorget (right) signifying that he was an officer, and the sword (above)
believed also to have been worn at his presidential inauguration. During
Peale's stay at Mount Vernon, the artist and some other young men were
pitching the bar — a popular pastime of the day — when Washington
appeared and asked to be shown "the pegs that marked the bounds of our
effort; then, smiling, and without putting off his coat, held out his hand for
the missile. No sooner did the heavy iron bar feel the grasp of his mighty
hand than it lost the power of gravitation, and whizzed through the air,
striking the ground far, very far, beyond our utmost limits. We were
indeed amazed, as we stood around all stripped to the buff, with shirt
sleeves rolled up . . . while the Colonel, on retiring, pleasantly
observed, 'When you beat my pitch, young gentlemen, I'll try again.' "

3

TIDEWATER PLANTER

George Washington's search for domestic tranquillity might be said to have begun when the state of his mind and health were at low ebb, during the winter of 1757–58 when he returned from the frontier, desperately ill, to Mount Vernon. In the extended convalescence that followed, his thoughts turned increasingly toward Sally Fairfax, the wife of his friend and neighbor. A local doctor had put Washington on a diet of "jellies and such kinds of foods" and Sally may have come to the rescue with them after George wrote her to say that no one at Mount Vernon was capable of preparing such fare. William Fairfax had recently died; Sally's husband, George William, was in England to settle the estate; and it is probable that Sally visited the patient from time to time while he was recuperating. Whether she did or not, when he emerged from his sickroom he was in love with her, as a letter he wrote from Fort Cumberland on September 12, 1758, indicates.

He had written on several earlier occasions — notably from the road west with Braddock in 1755, when Sally responded by insisting that he observe certain proprieties: he should not correspond with her directly, she said, but should send news through someone else. While it is virtually impossible to judge the true nature of her feelings for him, since George invariably destroyed her letters, the fact that she retained his correspondence suggests an interested, affectionate attitude at least. And from that correspondence retained by her one can surmise the tone of voice, if not the contents, of Sally's letters to which George was responding. Apparently they were lengthy, at times coy, saucy, or teasing (to the frequent despair of her admirer); then — if his reply was too warm — they turned evasive and rather distant (to his further chagrin).

Answering a brief note from Sally, Washington wrote from Fort Cumberland "joyfully . . . at the happy occasion of renewing a Corrispondance which I feard was disrelished on your part." In a passage filled with significant pauses and innuendo, he affirmed his love for her while at the same time referring to his apparent engagement to Martha Custis. "If you allow that any honour can be derivd from my opposition to Our present System of management," he wrote, "you destroy the merit of it entirely in me by attributing my anxiety to the annimating prospect of possessing Mrs. Custis. — When — I need not name it. — guess yourself. — Shoud not my own Honour and Country's welfare be the excitement? 'Tis true, I profess myself a Votary to Love. I acknowledge that a Lady is in the case — and I further confess, that this Lady is known to you. — Yes Madam, as well as she is to one who is too sensible of her Charms to deny the Power, whose Influence he feels and must ever Submit to. I feel the force of her amiable beauties in the recollection of a thousand tender passages that I coud wish to obliterate, till I am bid to revive them. — but experience, alas! sadly reminds me how Impossible this is. — and evinces an Opinion which I have long entertaind, that there is a Destiny, which has the Sovereign countroul of our Actions — not to be resisted by the strongest efforts of Human Nature. —

"You have drawn me my dear Madam, or rather have I drawn myself, into an honest confession of a Simple Fact — misconstrue not my meaning — 'tis obvious — doubt [it] not, nor expose it, — the World has no business to know the object of my Love, — declard in this manner to — you, when I want to conceal it — One thing, above all things in this World I wish to know, and only one person of your Acquaintance can solve that, or guess my meaning. — but adieu to this, till happier times, if I ever shall see them. . . ."

Sally's response to this has never been found, but evidently she did reply, for on September 25 George was writing again, "Dear Madam: Do we still misunderstand the true meaning of each other's Letters? I think it must appear so, tho' I would feign hope the contrary as I cannot speak plainer without, — But I'll say no more, and leave you to guess the rest. . . ."

Sally might be forever out of reach, but that she was never entirely forgotten is plain from the letter Washington wrote her toward the end of his life, long after her husband's death and twenty-five years after she and George William Fairfax had moved to England. In 1798 he referred to the earth-shaking events and changes that had occurred since their last meeting in 1773, adding, "None of [these] events, however, nor all of them together, have been able to eradicate from my mind, the recollection of those happy moments, the happiest in my life, which I have enjoyed in your company."

The woman who was to supplant Sally in his life was a different personality altogether. One year George's senior and a widow, she was at the time of their courtship one of the wealthiest unmarried women in Virginia. Martha Dandridge had been eighteen when she married Daniel Parke Custis, the son of a rich, eccentric miser, and they made their home at White House Plantation on the Pamunkey River, maintained in grand style by the revenues from some seventeen thousand acres of Virginia land owned by Daniel. Martha's own origins were modest, but she had little difficulty adapting to a life that provided elegant imported clothing and furniture, a chariot and sedan chair, and a sunny place in the ranks of Tidewater society. She was, as she described herself, "a fine, healthy girl," slightly plump, with dark hair, hazel eyes, and fine teeth, with a quiet, gentle nature and an unerring instinct for getting along with people. By the time her husband died in 1757 she had borne four children, of whom only two — John Parke Custis and Martha Parke Custis — survived. George probably met her at one of the Williamsburg assemblies they both attended, and on March 16, 1758, after recovering from his illness, he paid a call on the delightful and wealthy widow at White House on the Pamunkey. A little more than a week later he returned, and when he left for Williamsburg this time he had her promise to marry him — or at least to consider his proposal. Early in April he ordered from London "as much of the best superfine blue cotton velvet as will make a coat, a waistcoat and breeches for a tall man, with a fine silk button to suit it . . . six pairs of the very latest shoes . . . [and] six pair gloves." On May 4 he sent to Philadelphia for a ring and on January 6, 1759 — shortly after Washington's return from Fort Pitt — he and Martha were married.

Seemingly, it was a whirlwind courtship, yet it is difficult to judge what the real nature of the relationship between the two was, since — of all the correspondence that passed between them during almost four decades of marriage — only two letters from him and a postscript from her escaped being burned by Martha after his death. Washington was to say that their marriage was based not on "enamoured love" but on "friendship," and it was, in the manner of the day, a union that brought advantages to both parties. Certainly the handsome frontier hero and proprietor of Mount Vernon would have been regarded as a good catch. From Washington's standpoint, Martha's assets substantially enhanced his own wealth and property. At the time he and Martha's attorney appeared before the General Court in Williamsburg to request that George be named to administer the estate, a valuation was made, indicating that her personal property — three hundred slaves, livestock, bonds, accounts receivable, and other items — amounted to almost £20,000 sterling, or the rough equivalent of half a million dollars in twentieth-century terms. Nor was that all of it: her land, which was not included in the appraisal, consisted of 17,438 acres. Under provisions of the common law, Martha's bridegroom received the estate and could control it as his own, so long as he did not encumber her lands in such a way as to prejudice her rights or those of her heirs. Martha's three-year-old daughter "Patsy" was awarded a substantial portion of the bonds and securities; Martha was assigned one-third of the Negro slaves, two-thirds of the cattle, and one-third of the sheep and hogs; while the five-year-old "Jackie" was given the remainder of the slaves and livestock for use on the plantations he inherited (he and his new stepfather divided the land equally between them). Most of Daniel Parke Custis' library of 450 books went also to Jack, while George retained in his wife's name certain volumes on business, agriculture, and history. In sum, Washington acquired through his marriage to Martha Custis a direct interest in more than eighty-five hundred acres of land, and personal property worth nearly £7,000 sterling. During the minority of Martha's children, their expenses were to be paid out of the residue of the large Custis estate.

Washington also acquired a ready-made family, and as time went on and he realized that he was to have no children of his own, he discovered how difficult it was to be a surrogate father for two young people over whom his wife worried incessantly. Washington believed that a stepfather's duty was to be "generous and attentive," and when Jack was seven he engaged a tutor for him (the man lived with the family at Mount Vernon until Jack was thirteen) while taking a constant interest in what the boy was studying. Then Jack was placed in a school conducted by the Reverend Jonathan Boucher, and by the time he had been there for two years the schoolmaster was obliged to write Washington to complain of the lad's laziness. Never, said Boucher, had he known a youth "so exceedingly indolent, or so surprisingly voluptuous." Jack had "a Propensity to the [other] Sex, which I am at a loss how to judge of, much more how to describe,"

and as for his taste in other matters, "one would suppose Nature had intended him for some Asiatic Prince." In 1773 Jack left the uneasy care of Reverend Boucher to head for King's College (later Columbia University) and without first consulting his parents became engaged to Nelly Calvert, the daughter of an illegitimate son of the fifth Lord Baltimore. This news was not received enthusiastically at Mount Vernon, but Jack's stepfather put the best face on it he could, wrote a stiff letter to Mr. Calvert informing him that Jack should go to college before the marriage took place, and hurried the young man off to New York. En route they stopped in Annapolis with Governor Robert Eden, in Philadelphia with Governor Richard Penn, and in Basking Ridge, New Jersey, with William Alexander, the self-styled Lord Stirling. In New York, Washington renewed an old acquaintance when he called on Thomas Gage, commander in chief of the British army in North America, with whom he had served in Braddock's expedition. Then he departed, leaving Jack to cut a rather grand swath at King's College. The young man had a horse, a valet and groom, a suite of three rooms, and was the one student privileged to dine with the faculty. Jack, in fact, seemed determined to live up to that "Asiatic Prince" reputation: after marrying at nineteen, the only "son" of George Washington spent the remaining seven years of his life as a wealthy idler, concerned mostly with dogs, horses, and fine clothes. His death came in 1781, soon after the battle of Yorktown, where Jack contracted "camp fever" while serving as an aide to his illustrious stepfather.

If Martha's two children were pampered by their parents, perhaps it was as well in Patsy's case, since her life was both short and tragic. Each child had a personal, liveried slave at Mount Vernon; each had the best clothes from England and imported toys, but these proved of little comfort to Patsy after the age of twelve, when she cried out and fell and it was discovered that she was an epileptic. From then on, doctors took the place of playmates and dancing partners, "fit drops" the place of sweets, and in June, 1773, she was suddenly stricken with a seizure and died in less than two minutes. She was then seventeen years old. At the time this shattering blow fell, Washington had been planning a trip to the Ohio country with Virginia's Governor Dunmore, but this had to be postponed indefinitely so that he could devote his full attention to Patsy's grief-stricken mother. And now, as at other troubled times in his life, Mount Vernon was to exert its profound restorative powers upon him.

We are so accustomed to think of George Washington as the man of history that his dossier as frontier soldier, leader of the Revolution, and first President tends to obscure what was, for him, a more deeply satisfying existence — squire of Mount Vernon. All told, the public service kept him away from the place he loved best for over two decades; but even so, twenty-three years of his mature life were spent in residence at Mount Vernon. While it was not without its frustrations, the plantation was his source of greatest enjoyment and a release from the awesome burdens he assumed in behalf of the country. At times it seemed as if Mount Vernon were his only link with sanity; no matter where he was or what his preoccupation, his land and home remained in his mind's eye, and throughout the war and the Presidency long, detailed letters went from him to his cousin Lund Washington and to Lund's successors as farm managers — letters filled with instructions concerning additions to the house, or the planting of crops and trees, or about slaves, craftsmen, and livestock. During the long years of absence, Mount Vernon was never out of his thoughts for long.

The summer before his marriage to Martha, Washington had begun enlarging the house in anticipation of his new family's arrival. The roof was raised, making the rather modest one-and-a-half story farmhouse into a more imposing two-and-a-half story dwelling. Since there was no room sufficiently elegant for visitors, the West Parlor was remodeled. In it were placed a marble chimney piece and an overmantel painting (described by Washington when he ordered it in 1757 from London, as a "neat landskip"); the walls were paneled, and pedimented columns added to the door frames. To give the exterior the appearance of a stone edifice Washington had the horizontal siding grooved vertically and coated with a mixture of sand and paint to create the illusion of a rough surface. Four outbuildings were also connected to the main house by palisades and brick walls.

For this, as for further alterations made in 1774 and later, Washington was his own architect, and the eminently pleasing results testify to his observant, practical nature and his sure eye for proportion and style. Eventually one end of the house was enlarged by the addition of private living quarters for the master and his wife (their bedroom suite could be reached only by means of a separate, private stairway); a matching wing at the other side became a large, two-story parlor. A high, columned porch that ran the entire length of the house was added on the river side; outbuildings set at a diagonal to the main dwelling were joined to the latter by means of curved arcades; a triangular-shaped pediment was erected above the eaves over the front door; and a windowed cupola was placed in the center of the roof.

This simple, gracious mansion was the heart of a self-contained community of more than three hundred people that would become more self-sufficient as the owner concluded that it must be less dependent on English imports. Martha oversaw the health and training of domestic slaves (of whom there were thirteen in the house); she supervised the preparation of food, the smoking of meat, soap-making, sewing and weaving, and a staggering array of other household tasks.

The stereotype of the eighteenth-century Virginia planter is a man whose days were spent fox-hunting, attending cockfights, and breeding and riding fine horses, and whose nights were a round of dancing, card-playing, and drinking imported wines. It was a world of the privileged few, but along with those privileges went a long catalogue of responsibilities. Washington thoroughly enjoyed the pleasures and excelled at hunting, riding, and dancing; but by far the greatest portion of his time was devoted to planning and superintending the demanding, complex affairs of the plantation. In order to do so, he had to be a combination of farmer, horticulturist, inventor, builder, businessman, and bookkeeper. And other, more specific skills were needed: he constructed and operated a grist mill, raised grapes to be made into wine, grafted his numerous fruit trees, bred horses, studied the latest books on agriculture, experimented with crops and farming techniques in an effort to improve the land's fertility, operated an extensive commercial fishery in the Potomac, and oversaw the activities of blacksmiths, weavers, tanners, carpenters, and bricklayers, among other craftsmen. (He even considered domesticating bison — a dream that evidently died hard, since a buffalo cow was at Mount Vernon at the time of his death.)

His self-imposed obligations were heavy ones, as a letter written to Lund during the war reveals so expressively: "Let the Hospitality of the House, with respect to the Poor, be kept up; Let no one go hungry away — if any of these kind of People should be in want of Corn, supply their necessities, provided it does not encourage them in Idleness; and I have no objections to your giving my Money in Charity, to the Amount of Forty or Fifty Pounds a Year, when you think it well bestowd. — What I mean by having no objections is, that it is my desire that it should be done. — you are to consider that neither myself or Wife are now in the way to do these good Offices. — In all other respects, I recommend it to you, and have no doubts of your observing the greatest economy and frugality; as I suppose you know that I do not get a farthing for my Services here any more than my Expenses; and it becomes necessary, therefore, for me to be saving at home. —

"The above is copied, not only to remind myself of my promises and requests; but other also, if any mischance happens to G. Washington."

Like most other plantations in Virginia, Mount Vernon's principal crop was tobacco, and the system followed by planters was to employ a London agent, or factor, to receive and sell their tobacco and act as banker and purchasing agent for the myriad of manufactured goods not obtainable in the colonies. Washington engaged the firm of Robert Cary & Co. for this purpose, and his correspondence with them is a case-book on the problems endured by so many of his fellow Virginians. They failed to get an adequate price for his tobacco; they overcharged him for the goods he ordered; they delivered shoddy or inferior merchandise; they hectored him for money he did not have and charged exorbitant rates of interest on what he owed them.

Of course, the curse of tobacco was that it wore out the land. Traditionally, the good Virginia land was worked until its fertility was gone; then the owner would open up new fields, leaving the old to grow up to brush and weeds, and eventually this prodigality could destroy a plantation. In Washington's case, the dilemma was made more difficult by the fact that Mount Vernon did not have good soil to begin with; at best it might be described as mediocre land, whose heavy clay subsoil caused the topsoil to run off in heavy spring rains and retained the moisture in the spring long after the time for planting had passed. To compound the problem of single-crop agriculture, Virginia suffered from a serious imbalance of trade. There was never enough specie in circulation and the local currency, which was a combination of mixed coin and tobacco certificates, could only be exchanged for sterling at a premium. Planters typically over-extended themselves and ran up debts beyond their ability to pay off, and their troubles multiplied as a result of having to pay a high export duty on their sole crop, tobacco, while having to purchase with inferior currency everything their acreage could not furnish.

In 1764, after purchasing additional land around Mount Vernon and buying more slaves to till it, Washington discovered that his account with Robert Cary & Co. no longer showed a credit, but a debit balance. Faced with this problem, he took a step that was to have a profound effect on his thinking vis à vis the mother country. Realizing the extent of his dependence upon England, he began in 1765 to decrease his tobacco acreage in order to raise crops that could be sold locally. An effort to grow hemp and flax proved only that they were not suited to his land; then he turned to new crops, planted "7,000 bushels of wheat and 10,000 of Indian corn, which was more the staple of the farm," and by 1766 abandoned tobacco altogether. By 1770 his wheat crop was even larger; he had discovered that he could harvest it more economically than tobacco and he was adding further to the plantation's revenues through an enlarged fishing operation in the Potomac. His men built a schooner and he was soon selling shad and herring at a substantial profit. His mill was grinding flour for local customers and he was disposing of woven goods in the neighborhood. He had discovered that "The nature of a Virginia estate is such that without close application it never fails bringing the proprietors into debt annually" — and close application aptly described his attention to Mount Vernon.

As a slaveholder, Washington's attitude toward ownership of Negroes was consistent with that of most Virginia planters. The system was one he had always known; it was the accepted practice; and it was, moreover, essential to the maintenance and productivity of his plantation. In common with other slaveowners he viewed slaves as property, customarily calling them his "people" and doing his best to keep them healthy (humanitarian considerations aside, it was a matter of maintaining a valuable asset in proper operating condition). He was strict with them, largely on grounds that since they had no hope of improving their lot, they would do as little work as possible when left to their own devices; but the record bears out the fact that he was good to them, and fair. He followed a practice of refusing to sell a slave unless the slave was willing to be sold, and since few wanted to leave Mount Vernon it may be assumed that they considered themselves well-treated — or at least better so than they might be elsewhere. In addition to the slaves he had acquired through marriage to Martha, he had inherited ten of his own from his father, and added another eighteen when Mount Vernon became his in 1761. By 1770 he owned eighty-seven Negroes and two years later stopped buying slaves altogether. How much this decision owed to altruism is not clear: this came at a time when he was trying hard to cut down expenses at Mount Vernon in order to reduce his debts, and there had been natural increases in the work force since births exceeded deaths (by 1775 his slaves numbered 135 even though none had been purchased for three years), so the result was that he eventually had more slaves than he could employ — a situation that reduced the profitability of his estate. Yet by 1774 he had adopted what can only be described as an enlightened attitude for the day. One of the clauses in the so-called Fairfax Resolutions, which Washington helped to write, urged that "during our present difficulties and distresses, no slaves ought to be imported, . . . and we take this opportunity of declaring our earnest wishes to see an entire stop forever put to such wicked, cruel, and unnatural trade." A decade later his position in the subject had hardened considerably; as he wrote to Robert Morris, "there is not a man living who wishes more sincerely than I do, to see a plan adopted for the abolition of it." By then he had concluded that the practice must be abolished by "Legislative authority" — it would not go away of its own accord, nor would slaveowners willingly abandon it since their chattels represented a large portion of their property and wealth. Sadly, Washington concluded, "it introduces more evils than it can cure."

Despite the relative isolation of Mount Vernon, social life was full and gay. The Washingtons exchanged frequent visits with the Fairfaxes of Belvoir, to the south of their land. Farther downriver was Gunston Hall, the gracious mansion built by George Mason, who was becoming widely known as a master of public law and with whom Washington conducted a fairly regular correspondence (Mason preferred not to leave his beloved home and family, and for Washington a visit meant an eleven-mile ride over poor roads). Eight miles upstream was the town of Alexandria, where a county courthouse attracted visitors from the entire area and whose port was the center of all shipping activities on the Potomac.

Beginning in 1748 Washington made a practice of recording how he spent his time, and his diaries in the late seventeen-sixties and early 'seventies suggest a leisured succession of enjoyable days. In January of 1768, for example, he speaks again and again of fox hunting, of surveying, of visits to Mount Vernon by relatives and friends (most often the Fairfaxes), of shooting expeditions, of trips to neighboring plantations, and of card playing and other diversions.

In 1758, while stationed at Fort Cumberland, Washington had introduced a new dimension to his life: he had been elected to the House of Burgesses from Winchester, and later he changed his constituency to Fairfax County. Attendance at sessions of the House meant a four-day journey over the 160 miles between Mount Vernon and Williamsburg, and as the years passed Washington found that he had less and less interest in making the arduous trip and tended to spend as much time as possible close to home. By and large the issues discussed in the House had little interest for him unless they touched on matters of local importance, and until 1767 he played no significant role in the legislative body. He was not a man who took pleasure in debate, nor did he enjoy public speaking. As one Virginian described him, he was "a modest man, but sensible, and speaks little." Some years later, writing to a nephew, Washington revealed his attitude toward public address: "Speak seldom," he urged, "but to important subjects, except such as particularly relate to your constituents, and in the former case make yourself *perfectly* master of the subject. Never exceed a *decent* warmth, and submit your sentiments with diffidence. A dictatorial style, though it may carry conviction, is always accompanied with disgust."

He came to be known as a man who held his own counsel during debates, preferring to reserve his public expression of attitude for important subjects, when he would speak briefly and directly. Thomas Jefferson recalled that he never heard Washington speak for more than ten minutes in the House of Burgesses, and then it was to "the main point which was to decide the question." In Jefferson's phrase, he would lay his shoulder "to the great points, knowing that the little ones would follow of themselves." And until 1767, in Washington's opinion, few "great points" came before the Burgesses.

Other honors came his way, indicating his rank in the community and the respect people had for him: he was made a trustee of the town of Alexandria, a justice of the county court, and a vestryman of Truro Parish. But these activities never won his wholehearted or divided interest, nor distracted him from his most consuming passion during this period — the acquisition of land.

In addition to buying various parcels adjacent to Mount Vernon, Washington in 1763 turned his attention to the affairs of a company that he and others had formed to secure rights in 148,000 acres of Crown land in southeastern Virginia. "Land," he once wrote, "is the most permanent estate and the most likely to increase in value," and he concluded that an opportunity for profit lay in an unlikely direction — in the drowned lands between the lower James River and Albemarle Sound that had been characterized accurately as the Great Dismal Swamp. Washington and his partners in the Dismal Swamp Company petitioned successfully for a seven-year option to improve the land, which involved an immensely difficult and ambitious operation of draining the swamp by means of a huge ditch that would not only siphon off the water but also serve as a canal southward from Norfolk. Between 1763 and 1768 Washington visited the swamp on seven or more occasions, exploring, determining where the outlet should be, and supplying his own slaves to dig the ditch. (Although the project was never completed during his lifetime, his optimism was finally confirmed when a canal was completed in 1828 and the swamp reduced from over two thousand square miles to less than six hundred.)

Another land venture on which he embarked in 1763 was even more ambitious. He and eighteen others organized a Mississippi Company in an effort to secure an immense tract of Crown land east of the Mississippi River. In all, it encompassed 2,500,000 acres, reaching from the Mississippi eastward over much of the richest land in the present states of Illinois, Indiana, Ohio, Kentucky, and Tennessee. In return for their option on the land and an exemption from quitrents and taxes, the members of the company agreed to encourage settlement in the region by at least two hundred families — "if not interrupted by the Savages or any foreign enemy." But the project came to naught: a Royal Proclamation of October 7, 1763, reserved these and other lands west of the Alleghenies for the Indians, thus precluding any further legitimate settlement by Americans, and in 1771 Washington wrote off his investment of £27 13s. 5d. in the venture as a loss.

While neither the Dismal Swamp nor Mississippi Companies fulfilled his expectations, still another effort to acquire western lands did — at least to the extent that his claim to them became one of the principal assets in his estate at the time of his death. The origin of these claims went back to 1754 and to Governor Dinwiddie's efforts to encourage enlistment in the Virginia Regiment during the French and Indian War. At that time the governor proclaimed that two hundred thousand acres south and east of the Ohio River would be made available to men enlisting for service. The war and the King's Proclamation of 1763 prevented anyone from taking advantage of the offer, but in 1768, in the wake of several treaties with the Indians, the area was opened for settlement. The following year Washington presented a petition to Dinwiddie's successor, Lord Botetourt, and his Council requesting that the two hundred thousand acres promised by Dinwiddie be alloted to the "Officers and Soldiers who first Imbarked in the Service of this Colony," and he followed this up by offering to assume responsibility for surveying the lands. He recommended his friend William Crawford, who had done some work for him on the Mississippi Company project, as the surveyor, and after the governor approved his request, Washington and his friend Dr. Craik set out in October of 1770 for Ohio country.

Following once again the familiar route, he took Braddock's Road past the site of Fort Necessity and on to Fort Pitt at the Forks of the Ohio, where he picked up Crawford, some other frontiersmen, and a few Indians, and drifted down-river in two canoes. Ten days later they reached a place that seemed like the promised land—so beautiful that it was to have a lifelong hold on him. At the point where the Great Kanawha River flows into the Ohio was a ten-mile-wide peninsula—rich bottomland bounded on three sides by water. Covered with oak, hickory, walnut, and other hardwoods, it was filled with birds and game of all descriptions, and Washington at once began his survey, blazing trees as boundary markers while his mind filled with the thought of tenants occupying this wondrous spot by the majestic river.

By the first of December, 1770, Washington was back at Mount Vernon and the following March he met with a small group of Virginia Regiment veterans who elected him to supervise their claims and agreed to share in the cost of surveying the land. In November the governor and his Council ordered distribution of the proclamation land to eighty-one claimants, awarding the maximum of fifteen thousand acres each to Washington and two other field officers (privates were to receive four hundred acres apiece). Thirty thousand acres were held in reserve for soldiers who had not yet filed claims, with the proviso that any unclaimed land was to be divided among those claimants who shared the cost of the survey and other expenses. By fall of 1772 Crawford had surveyed some 128,000 acres, constituting thirteen tracts, and he brought his drawings to Mount Vernon where Washington made up a plan for the allotment.

Although there were no immediate complaints about the manner in which he divided the land, they were to come. Certain officers talked to Crawford, who reported that they were "a good deal shagereened" to learn that Washington and Craik had appropriated the best bottomland. With some justification Washington argued that he had borne the greatest part of the expense of having the land surveyed and stated that "if it had not been for my unremitting attention to every favorable circumstance, not a single acre of land would ever have been obtained." Eventually he secured title to thirty thousand acres—of which five thousand were awarded him by the then governor of Virginia, Dunmore, on the basis of a dubious claim that he was entitled to them by provisions of the Royal Proclamation of 1763. This document had promised land to officers who had honorably retired from active service when their regiments disbanded, but Washington, of course, had voluntarily resigned some time before that event actually occurred. As two of his biographers, James Flexner and Bernhard Knollenberg, point out, Washington was not by nature a greedy man, but in this instance of the western lands these writers tend to accept the characterization of him published in London in 1779 by a man who wrote that he was "avaritious under the specious appearance of disinterestedness—particularly eager in engrossing large tracts of land."

While Washington was engrossed in the affairs of Mount Vernon and efforts to obtain land in the West, the political scene in Williamsburg and other provincial capitals along the Atlantic seaboard had altered drastically. Similarly, London. A decade and more earlier, Englishmen had characterized 1759 as "the year of miracles" to describe the triumphs of British arms over the French and Spanish, but in the following year the incompetent George III succeeded to the throne and from that moment the relationship between Britain and her North American colonies began to worsen. Once he had ousted William Pitt as prime minister the King turned to one bad ministry after another, and every change of leaders brought further deterioration in the stability of government, further exacerbation of the once-harmonious relations between colonies and mother country. For several decades the British government had pursued a policy of benevolent neglect toward America, until few colonists gave much thought to the ties that bound them to London. Despite their obligatory economic and political dependence on England, Americans exhibited a growing self-sufficiency, and when the wars with the French and Indians ended, the habit extended to local control of legislative assemblies, avoidance of unwelcome foreign authority, and resentment of the commercial exploitation by London bankers and merchants that was the handmaiden of mercantilism.

On the other side of the sea Englishmen were increasingly aware of what the Seven Years' War, which had begun in America, had cost them. Britain's debt was two and a half times what it had been before the war; taxes, particularly those on land, had become exasperatingly high; and the average man of property, knowing that the colonists depended upon the mother country for military security and financial support, felt that those colonists ought to pay their share of the cost of empire. Taxation appeared to be the sensible answer.

After the government prohibited westward migration by the colonists in 1763, it reorganized the colonial customs system, clamped down on smuggling activities, and introduced a spate of revenue bills — taxes on sugar, coffee, indigo, wine, and other commodities, and in 1765 a stamp duty on legal transactions. The last led to a collective uproar in every colonial port and capital, the passage of a set of resolves by Virginia's House of Burgesses (followed by similar resolutions in most other colonies) to the effect that only Virginians could tax Virginians; and in the fall of 1765 delegates from nine of the thirteen colonies met in New York to consider unified action against this move by Parliament. The Stamp Act Congress was, one of its members wrote, "an Assembly of the Greatest Ability I ever yet saw," and it was only a foretaste of what was to come. Mobs went into action in Boston, New York, and Charleston, destroying private and public property, harassing tax collectors, demonstrating to the authorities in London that the Americans intended to resist Parliamentary authority.

For the moment, England backed down, but in 1766 a Declaratory Act was passed, asserting the right of Parliament to control the colonies through legislation, and in 1767 the so-called Townshend Acts (which levied new duties on paper, paint, glass, lead, and tea) made clear the government's determination to raise revenues in America. More violence ensued in colonial towns; British troops landed in Boston in 1768 to keep order there; the colonies passed non-importation agreements; there were riots, the ugly "massacre" in Boston; and perhaps most significant of all — a widening pattern of resistance and revolutionary organization.

At first George Washington seems not to have been overly concerned with matters involving constitutional issues; his mind was occupied with problems concerning his plantation, his land speculations, and local issues. But in 1769, after reading several opinions on the subject of non-importation agreements, he wrote his friend and neighbor George Mason to express his views, indicating that he had devoted serious thought not only to the problems but to the possible solutions. It was the first evidence in writing that Washington had taken a long step toward formulating an attitude that was to put him on the side of America's independence movement. "At a time when our lordly masters in Great Britain will be satisfied with nothing less than the depreciation of American freedom," he wrote, "it seems highly necessary that something should be done to avert the stroke and maintain the liberty which we have derived from our ancestors; but the manner of doing it to answer the purpose effectively is the point in question."

The use of arms, he believed, should be the last resort. But since petitions to King and Parliament had proved ineffective, it was certainly worth trying a method by which Britain's trade and manufactures might be hurt. What was more, he liked it for practical reasons quite apart from the political considerations; he had already moved on his own to lessen his farm's dependence upon the mother country and he advocated it as a good thing for others to do, to "emerge the country from the distress it at present labors under."

As he began assisting Mason to draw up a list of items that should not be imported by Virginians, Washington was profoundly influenced by his wise neighbor's political philosophy, and at the spring, 1769, session of the House of Burgesses he voted with all other delegates to petition the King, "praying the royal interposition in favor of the violated rights of America." That was too much for the governor, Lord Botetourt, who angrily dissolved the assembly. Later, Washington's and Mason's draft of a non-importation agreement was accepted by a committee of delegates and Washington returned home to ensure that Mount Vernon followed the spirit of that agreement insofar as it was possible to do so. The result, as a contemporary wrote, was that "he carried the scheme of manufacturing to a greater height than almost any man" in the colony.

In 1770 Parliament repealed most of the Townshend duties except the one on tea, colonial non-importation agreements were relaxed, and for three years after the Boston Massacre relations between Britain and the colonies were relatively untroubled, marred only by occasional outbursts. What damaged that uneasy truce irreparably was the decision of Parliament, in 1773, to grant the East India Company a monopoly on tea sold to the colonies, with prices pegged so as to undersell tea smuggled into America. When a party of Liberty Boys boarded three ships in Boston harbor and dumped 342 chests of tea into the bay, the result in London was an initial cry of outrage over this wanton destruction, followed by the punitive measures known in America as the "Intolerable Acts" which virtually annulled the charter of Massachusetts and closed the port of Boston. In Williamsburg, where Washington was attending a session of the Burgesses, Parliament's act was condemned as "a hostile invasion of Boston" and Lord Dunmore dissolved the legislature again. Although Washington and others disapproved the lawlessness of the Boston Tea Party, the members met in an impromptu, extralegal session to declare the Boston Port Act "a most dangerous attempt to destroy the constitutional liberty and rights of all North America," and called it "an attack made on all British America."

During this trying period, Washington was slowly turning the issues over in his mind, balancing one argument against another, moving ever closer to a stance of strong opposition to the government. He hoped that solutions to the dispute separating mother country and colonies might be left to posterity to determine, for he was not yet prepared to accept the necessity or inevitability of violent resistance unless the government demonstrated a wilful, unlawful determination "to overthrow our constitutional rights and liberties." But by July of 1774, when he wrote to Bryan Fairfax, the son of his former patron William Fairfax, he had concluded that there was little likelihood of appealing successfully to King or Parliament for the redress of American grievances. "Does it not appear," he asked, "as clear as the sun in its meridian brightness, that there is a regular, systematic plan formed to fix the right and practice of taxation upon us? . . . Is there any thing to be expected from petitioning after this?" And later that month, on July 18, he presided at a meeting of residents of Fairfax County in Alexandria, where a set of resolutions was adopted expressing common cause with the citizens of Boston and backing the declaration issued by the extralegal session of the Burgesses. One of the more interesting clauses of the Fairfax Resolutions was the one already alluded to—urging that no further importation of slaves be permitted and that the "wicked, cruel, and unnatural trade" should stop "forever."

Washington and his neighbors were beginning to realize, as did other colonists, that they could scarcely advocate liberty and condemn tyranny while perpetuating a system that held their fellow men in bonds of slavery.

By now, colonial assemblies had expressed the need for a general congress composed of delegates from all the provinces to discuss their problems, and in June the speaker of the Massachusetts House sent out a circular letter proposing that representatives meet in Philadelphia on September 1. When Virginia's Burgesses assembled again, it was to elect seven delegates to the forthcoming congress, and it was a measure of Washington's standing—a result of his military career and long service in the assembly—that he received the third highest number of votes. What was involved was more than a journey to Philadelphia; it was a turning point in the life of Washington and all the others accompanying him—Peyton Randolph, speaker of the Virginia House, Richard Henry Lee, Patrick Henry, Richard Bland, Benjamin Harrison, and Edmund Pendleton. Before departing, Washington attended a sad function that must have brought back a flood of memories. George William and Sally Fairfax had decided to go to England to consult physicians about their assorted ailments and to unravel the complicated Fairfax inheritance, and they asked Washington to rent their home, Belvoir, for them and auction its furnishings. It is interesting to note that he purchased £169 worth of their possessions, including the bolster and pillows from Sally's bedroom. Then he left for Philadelphia.

Instead of the State House, which Pennsylvania's conservative Speaker Joseph Galloway had recommended as the site for the intercolonial congress, Carpenters' Hall was the choice, probably because it bore no sign of royal authority, and here on September 5, 1774, there convened fifty-six delegates from twelve colonies (Georgia sent no representatives) in what was to be known as the First Continental Congress. There was general agreement that the most illustrious delegation present was Virginia's: one of its members, Peyton Randolph, was elected president; two others, Henry and Lee, were widely known for their oratory; and Washington was immediately recognized as the colonel who had fought with Braddock and met French and Indians in battle. The group as a whole,

John Adams observed, represented "fortunes, ability, learning, eloquence, acuteness, equal to any I ever met with in my life."

Washington seems neither to have spoken much nor played any conspicuous role in the proceedings, but his reputation was known to most other delegates, and to judge from letters they wrote, he was a subject of considerable interest, cutting a rather glamourous figure. One South Carolinian informed John Adams that Washington had "made the most eloquent Speech at the Virginia Convention that ever was made. Says he, 'I will raise 1000 Men, subsist them at my own Expence, and march my self at their Head for the Relief of Boston.'" Another man wrote that Washington was "generally beloved," and Silas Deane of Connecticut remarked that the Virginian showed himself "a tolerable speaker . . . who speaks very modestly in a cool but determined style and accent."

At first the Congress appeared to be divided about evenly between moderates, who preferred petitions to the King and Parliament, and radicals, who wanted action. Then a bombshell dropped into their midst, altering the complexion of their deliberations and insuring the triumph of the radicals. Washington's old comrade in arms, General Thomas Gage, who was now commanding the British troops in Boston, had sent an expedition to seize gunpowder from the provincials on Quarry Hill outside Boston, and this foray resulted in a meeting of outraged delegates from every town in Suffolk County. They passed a series of resolutions declaring the Intolerable Acts unconstitutional, recommended that Massachusetts withhold taxes from the Crown until the Acts were repealed, advised their constituents to arm themselves, and promptly rushed these Suffolk Resolves to Philadelphia in care of the Boston post rider, Paul Revere. After a lively debate on the radical proposals, Congress endorsed them with an enthusiasm, John Adams said, that convinced him "that America will support Massachusetts or perish with her." Congress rejected a moderate Plan of Union put forth by Pennsylvania's Joseph Galloway — a proposal that would have given the colonies dominion status within the empire — and then passed a declaration of rights, approved a doctrine of nonimportation, advocated cessation of the slave trade, and agreed on several notable petitions — to George III, to the people of Great Britain, and to the inhabitants of neighboring Quebec. With all this behind them,

the delegates adjourned and headed for home. Whatever else they had accomplished, they had convinced themselves that they must hang together in this crisis; of the twelve colonies represented, only New York subsequently failed to ratify the work of the Congress.

Upon his return to Virginia, Washington immersed himself in the sort of business he had set aside seventeen years before. Two veterans of the Braddock expedition visited him to talk strategy—Charles Lee and Horatio Gates, both former British officers. He presided over a meeting of Fairfax County men that recommended the stockpiling of ammunition and decided to form and train local militia companies. (The uniform they adopted, with a blue coat, "turned up with buff, with plain yellow buttons, buff waistcoat and breeches, and white stockings," was probably the forerunner of the Continental Army's colors.) He rode about the countryside, teaching raw citizen soldiers something of the rudiments of drill and the manual of arms; he served on a committee to put Virginia "immediately . . . in a position of defence." And in the face of all these preparations he could hardly help but wonder where it would all lead. He was certainly aware that he, as Virginia's most prominent military man, would be chosen to lead that colony's forces in case of hostilities; the public press was openly speculating on that eventuality, as a bit of doggerel in the Virginia *Gazette* for January 12, 1775, indicated:

> *In spite of Gage's flaming sword*
> *And Carleton's Canadian troop*
> *Brave Washington shall give the word,*
> *And we'll make them howl and whoop.*

Whether or not he was flattered to be singled out in such a manner, there was no blinking the fact that he, as a known opponent of British policies, and as a conspicuous member of the First Continental Congress, would have the most to lose in the event of war with the mother country. And certainly as an insurrectionist he could expect no clemency from British authorities, either in terms of life or property. It was an extraordinary dilemma and a particularly acute one for Washington, who must have envisioned his beloved Mount Vernon and all it represented in his life confiscated by a British army or reduced to rubble by a fleet that could sail up the Potomac within short range of the mansion. "Things wear a disagreeable aspect," he observed dourly, "and the minds of men are exceedingly disturbed." Even so, as he wrote his brother John Augustine, he had decided that "it is my full intention to devote my Life and Fortune in the cause we are engaged in, if need be." Whatever the future might hold, his mind was firmly and finally made up.

More disturbing than anything that had come before were the tidings that reached Mount Vernon on April 27, 1775, telling of blood shed at Lexington and Concord, outside Boston. To prevent a similar occurrence in Virginia, British marines landed at Williamsburg and seized the powder stored there by the colonials and suddenly soldiers of Washington's militia companies turned up at Mount Vernon, assuring him that they were ready to march on the capital. He ordered them to disband when he learned that Governor Dunmore would return the powder, but there were indications that moderate counsel of this kind was not universally desired. Some of Patrick Henry's companies did march on Williamsburg and forced the governor to pay for the powder that had been seized; there was some grumbling about Washington's failure to act and it was said that he had failed to do so for fear of possible retaliation against himself or his property.

I n the meantime he had been elected to serve as a delegate to the Second Continental Congress and on May 4, 1775, he kissed Martha goodbye, climbed into his coach with Richard Henry Lee, who was accompanying him, and rode away, passing little knots of neighboring farmers who took off their hats and cheered. Along the way they were joined by other Virginia delegates and when they were about six miles from Philadelphia a party of five hundred cavalrymen rode up to greet them. Farther along they were joined by a military band and several companies of infantrymen, and as the center of attention of this brave little parade, they rattled into the city to help decide the future of their country.

The gravity of the situation had increased geometrically since the meeting of the First Continental Congress, and delegates to the Second knew that no matter was more pressing than the question of what was to be done about their fellow-countrymen in the army outside Boston. After the battles of Lexington and Concord the British had been driven back into the city, where they were now besieged by some nine thousand armed provincials. To suggest that the latter comprised an army in the strict sense of the word was to miss the point that they were without housing or cover, lacked food and clothing and adequate weapons, had little organization or discipline, and were no better trained than might be expected of farmers and tradesmen whose experience in military matters extended only to occasional militia musters and drill or to hunting. But the fact was that they were there — and on a scale which neither the British nor the rebel leaders had imagined possible. They had, moreover, driven the British regulars into the city of Boston after a day-long fight that cost the British 244 casualties, and if some duly constituted authority did not soon decide what was to be done with them, and how, there was a good chance that they would vanish as quickly as they had assembled. So the question before Congress was: what to do? Should that body adopt the army presently commanded by a relatively unknown Massachusetts man named Artemas Ward; should it take steps to make his volunteer soldiers into a permanent force of some kind; and if it was to be an army, who should lead it? As Ward remarked in a letter to the Congress, unless such steps were taken promptly, "I shall be left all alone."

Like most other delegates, Washington had mixed feelings on the subject. There was no question that a state of hostilities now existed between colonies and mother country, but how tragic it was that the situation should have reached this pass. To complicate matters, word came that Ethan Allen, of the New Hampshire Grants, and a Connecticut soldier named Benedict Arnold had led a party of men on Fort Ticonderoga and captured it. The Massachusetts legislators were petitioning Congress to take hold of the reins and solve the question of what to do with the army besieging Boston, and at last the delegates in Philadelphia resolved their inner doubts and took a step from which there would be no turning back. On June 14 they voted to enlist ten companies of riflemen to serve in an "American continental army" for one year, and on the following day resolved that "a General be appointed to command all the continental forces, raised, or to be raised, for the defence of American liberty." For his services, the general would receive $500 a month for pay and expenses.

There appeared to be several likely candidates for the post. John Hancock of Boston, who was now president of the Congress, fancied himself in the role. There was much justification for giving the position to Artemas Ward, who was actively commanding the forces outside Boston. A favorite with many delegates was Charles Lee, who made no bones about his own availability and had impressed numerous Americans with the fact that his experience as a British officer made him an obvious choice. Israel Putnam, a veteran fighter from Connecticut, was a possibility. And there was George Washington.

The matter was decided, in the end, on the basis of political considerations. Hancock and Ward were ruled out because they were Massachusetts men; if Massachusetts needed anything just now it was help from outside its own borders and such aid would come more readily if a man from another colony were named as commander in chief. Putnam was too old and was, in any case, another New Englander. And Lee, for all his experience, was not a native-born American.

John Adams perceived that the selection of Washington had the advantage of placing a man from the most populous southern colony in charge of the New England army, and if this were coupled with congressional adoption of that army it would have a very salutary effect indeed. It would tend to unite the disparate colonies as well as compel their representatives in the Congress "to declare themselves for or against something," which was no easy matter to accomplish.

Although Washington later wrote that "no desire or insinuation of mine" led to his selection as commander in chief, he nevertheless appeared at sessions of Congress attired in the uniform of a Virginia colonel, which must have indicated his availability as a military leader and reminded other delegates of his past services in such a capacity. Yet there is no suggestion that he actively sought the command; apart from his own word for this, there is the fact that he persuaded at least one Virginia delegate to advocate the selection of Ward.

Whatever Washington's wishes might be, John Adams moved quickly. Immediately following the adoption of the resolution that a commander of the armed forces be chosen, he rose to put a name in nomination. Most delegates were doubtless prepared for the suggestion of a New Englander — probably Ward — but Adams stated that he had "but one gentleman in mind for that important command, and that was a gentleman from Virginia." (As Adams wrote later, he noted a "sudden and sinking change of countenance" on the part of the eager John Hancock and heard a movement behind him as George Washington slipped out of the room.) His nominee, Adams went on, was one "whose skill as an officer, whose independent fortune, great talents and universal character would command the respect of America and unite the full exertions of the Colonies better than any other person alive." And on June 15, 1775, Congress "proceeded to the choice of a general by ballot, when George Washington, Esq., was unanimously elected."

The next day the new commander in chief, dressed as usual in uniform, rose at his seat, took a piece of paper from his pocket, and read:

Mr. President, Tho' I am truly sensible of the high Honour done me in this Appointment, yet I feel great distress from a consciousness that my abilities and Military experience may not be equal to the extensive and important Trust: However, as the Congress desires I will enter upon the momentous duty, and exert every power I Possess In their Service for the Support of the glorious Cause: I beg they will accept my most cordial thanks for this distinguished testimony of their Approbation . . . .

As to pay, Sir, I beg leave to Assure the Congress that as no pecuniary consideration could have tempted me to have accepted this Arduous employment I do not wish to make any profit from it: I will keep an exact Account of my expences; those I doubt not they will discharge and that is all I desire.

As significant as this speech was for its modesty and humility and for its candid appraisal of his abilities, it was equally so for the expression of his willingness to serve without pay — a spirit that characterized his entire future conduct as one of dedication to the public service and to the ideals for which the war was to be fought. It was an attitude that counted as much with the world beyond America as with his own countrymen — one of whom, Eliphalet Dyer of Connecticut, wrote, "He seems discreet and virtuous, no harum Starum ranting Swearing fellow but Sober, steady and Calm." Dyer believed that such a man was humble enough to seek always the counsel of others in running the army and his assumption certainly proved accurate.

Whatever inner doubts Washington had, he was entitled to them. It was several days before he could bring himself to write to Martha about "a subject which fills me with inexpressible concern" — a concern "greatly aggravated and increased when I reflect upon the uneasiness I know it will cause you." As he told her, he regarded his appointment as "a trust too great for my capacity"; as he wrote another, the job was "too boundless for my abilities and far, very far beyond my experience." One of the most touching incidents in his career occurred shortly after he was named to lead the army. About twenty delegates to Congress met one evening at Peg Mullen's Beefsteak House and when dinner was over one of them rose to propose a toast "To the Commander in Chief of the American Armies!" Until that instant it had been a gay, relaxed affair, but when Washington slowly got to his feet to respond his friends noticed that he did so with reluctance — even "with some confusion," as one of them remarked. And suddenly what had been a purely social occasion became a moment of great solemnity, when it dawned on all those present that they had thrust a terrifying and awesome responsibility on their fellow delegate, forcing him to undertake almost single-handedly a task that could have tragic consequences for himself and all those present. As Washington himself wrote to John Augustine, "I am now to bid adieu to you, and to every kind of domestic ease for a while. I am Imbarked on a wide Ocean, boundless in its prospect, and from whence, perhaps no safe harbour is to be found."

On June 22, as he was preparing to depart for Massachusetts, word reached Philadelphia of another bloody clash on the outskirts of Boston. Details were sketchy, but it appeared that the rebels and British had both suffered substantial losses in a battle near Bunker Hill on June 17. Not knowing what he would find there upon his arrival, Washington — accompanied by Major Generals Charles Lee and Philip Schuyler and two aides, Thomas Mifflin and Joseph Reed — set out on the long road to Cambridge, Massachusetts. Just before departing he urged John Augustine to spend as much of the summer as possible at Mount Vernon with Martha, for whom news of his destination would be "a cutting stroke," and to Martha went a tender note affirming his deep affection for her. "My Dearest," he wrote, "I go fully trusting in that Providence, which has been more bountiful to me than I deserve and in full confidence of a happy meeting with you some time in the Fall. . . . I retain an unalterable affection for you which neither time or distance can change. . . . Your entire." There was no signature.

He spent several days in New York and then rode on toward the scene of combat, arriving in Cambridge on July 2, 1775.

Martha Dandridge's first husband was Daniel Parke Custis (above), a wealthy man twenty years her senior who died intestate, which meant that she had full dower right to a large inheritance. At right is the Custis coat of arms that was engraved on the family silver.

George Washington's new family included John Parke Custis and Martha Parke Custis — "Jacky" and "Patsy" — aged three and two. The portrait at left and the others on these pages were painted shortly before Daniel Custis' death in 1757 by John Wollaston, an Englishman who came to America in 1749 and executed some three hundred portraits during the ten years he was here. Two other Custis children died in infancy and Jacky and Patsy were to have tragically short lives — hers the result of epilepsy, at eighteen; his from a fever contracted during the siege of Yorktown, when he was twenty-seven.

74

Martha Dandridge Custis was regarded as a catch when George
Washington wooed her in 1758. Among the wealthiest widows
in Virginia, she was twenty-seven years old and pretty,
with a high forehead, large, slightly slanting eyes, firm
chin, and a soft, rounded figure. Toward the end of his life
Washington wrote a stepgranddaughter that a good marriage
partner should possess "good sense, a good disposition, a
good reputation, and financial means" — all of which Martha
had in abundance. The gold necklace at right is thought to
have been given her by Washington on their first anniversary.

A SWEEPING POTOMAC VISTA

In 1759 Andrew Burnaby, a vicar of Greenwich, England, paid a visit to Mount Vernon and recorded his impression of the spectacular view from the front of the mansion. "The house is most beautifully situated upon a high hill on the banks of the Potomac," he wrote, "and commands a noble prospect of water, of cliffs, of woods, and plantations. The river is nearly two miles broad, though two hundred [miles] from the mouth, and divides the dominions of Virginia from Maryland." It was indeed a noble prospect, which had not altered four decades later when Benjamin Henry Latrobe made this watercolor, looking southeastward across the river to the Maryland bank.

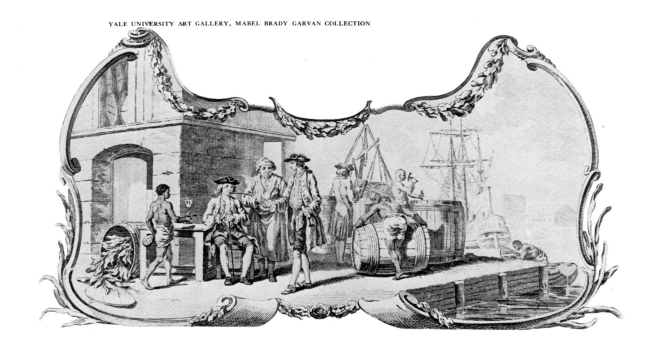

The importance of tobacco to the region was underscored in a cartouche (above) drawn in 1751 for a "Map of Inhabited Parts of Virginia" by Peter Jefferson, the father of Thomas, and Joshua Fry, a mathematics professor at William and Mary College. Below is George Washington's survey of the fields that lay along Little Hunting Creek and the Potomac River at the Mount Vernon plantation.

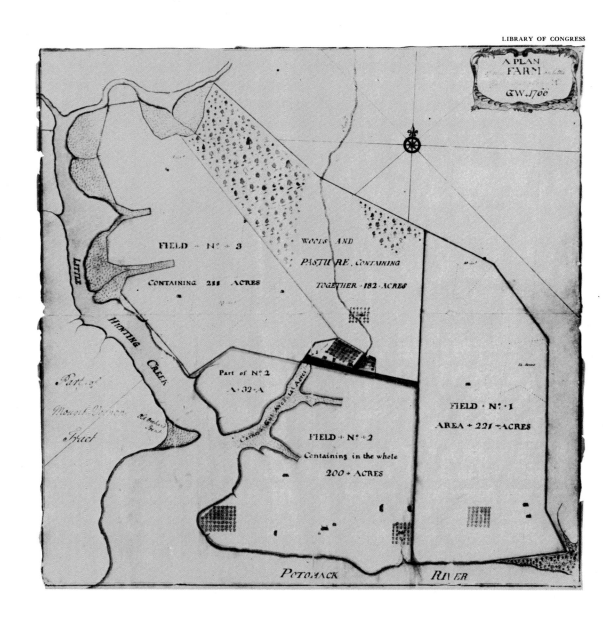

THE LAND WHERE TOBACCO REIGNED

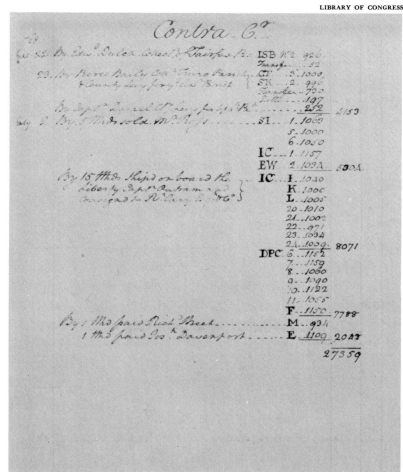

Although Washington professed to "little proficiency" in agriculture he was in fact well in advance of most contemporaries. By the time the survey on the opposite page was made he had already observed the damaging effects of continuous cultivation of tobacco and begun a system of crop rotation designed to conserve the soil. Throughout his life he kept meticulous accounts for the farm, listing income and expenditures in minute detail, as in the page shown at right. Although reliance upon slave labor was virtually forced upon him by circumstances of the time and place, he came to loathe the practice, and before the end of his life was one of the South's more progressive thinkers on the issue. "Nothing but the rooting out of slavery can perpetuate the existence of our union," he concluded, and one of his friends wrote that he seriously considered moving to the North, should the nation split over slavery. The sketch below, of "An Overseer Doing His Duty," is by Benjamin Latrobe.

THE
BRITISH CARPENTER:
OR, A
TREATISE
ON
CARPENTRY.

Containing the moſt Conc:ſe and Authentick
RULES of that ART,

A more Uſeful and Extenſive
made p...

The SIXTH ED...
And illuſtrated with Sixty...

By FRANC...

Late Surveyor to the Cathedral Church...
of Obſervations on tha...

LON...
Printed for A. PALLADIO, J. JONES...

E G Washington

THE
Compleat Tutor
For the
VIOLIN
Containing

The Beſt and Eaſieſt Inſtructions
for Learners to Obtain a Proficiency.
To which is Added
A Choice Collection of the moſt Celebrated
Italian, Engliſh, and Scotch Tunes.
with Several Choice Pieces for 2 VIOLINS.

Printed for & Sold by John Simpſon,
at the Baſs Viol & Flute, in Sweetings Alley,
oppoſite y:e Eaſt Door of the Royal Exchange.
London.

Where Books of Inſtructions for any Single Inſtruments may be had.
Price 1s:6d

The Goddeſs CERES in her Chariot drawn by Dragons
Teaches MANKIND the Art of Huſbandry.

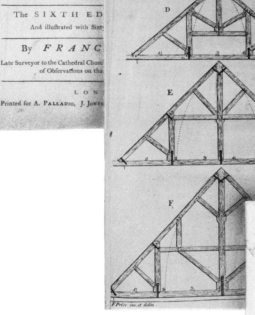

Plate H

D

E

F

P. Price inv. et delin.

THE
FIELD
ENGINEER.

Translated from the FRENCH of
M. le Chevalier DE CLAIRAC,
BY
Captain CHARLES VALLANCEY.

To which are added,

REMARKS
ON
Marſhal SAXE's new Syſtem of
FORTIFICATION

Proposed in his REVERIES, or Memoirs on the
ART of WAR.

Fas eſt et ab Hoſte doceri.

DUBLIN:
Printed for JOHN SMITH, at the Philoſophers Head
on the Blind-Quay. MDCCLVIII.

G Washington

Plate 4   Chaps of Sup.

Attack of Fortified Places

Plan of a Sap

Profile of a finiſhed Sap

Back of a Sap

Profile repreſenting the excavation
of four Sappers

Front of a Sap

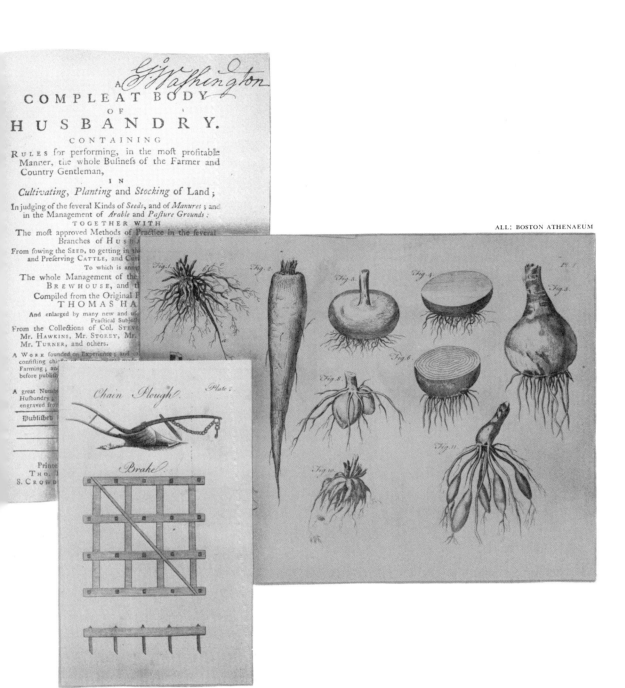

IN SEARCH OF KNOWLEDGE

When there was nothing else to guide him, a Virginia planter turned to books, and Washington's library reveals the search for knowledge and information that caused him to order volumes from London on numerous subjects. There was a *Treatise on Carpentry* (far left), "containing the most concise and authentick Rules of that Art," from which the plate showing the framing of a roof is taken. The musically inclined John Augustine Washington owned *The Compleat Tutor for the Violin*, and his brother George referred to Clairac's *Field Engineer* and to Guillaume Le Blond's treatise on "the Attack and Defence of all kinds of fortified places," from which the plate at bottom left is reproduced. Above it is an illustration from *The Compleat Horseman*, written by Jacques de Soleysell, "Querry to the late King of France." Washington ordered Thomas Hale's *Compleat Body of Husbandry* (above) from his London agents, Robert Cary and Company, in 1760, and the plate above right comes from one of his favorite guides in developing the farm at Mount Vernon — Henry Home's *The Gentleman Farmer*. So fond was he of this volume that he transcribed extensive portions of it. The page showing the plow is from Philip Miller's *English Gardener*, which described "what Works are necessary to be performed Every Month in the Kitchen, Fruit, and Pleasure-Gardens, as also in the Conservatory and Nursery."

81

THE TASTES OF AFFLUENCE

Although Washington is commonly assumed to have been a wealthy planter, what profits he made from farming were frequently exceeded by the cost of maintaining the mansion and the style of life he enjoyed. As the Marquis de Chastellux observed in 1781, "The chief magnificence of the Virginians consists in furniture, linen, and silver plate," and these and other decorative objects for the home usually came from England, from shipping depots like the Custom House Quay on the Thames (opposite) where vessels from East and West loaded and unloaded their exotic cargoes. The Washingtons' punch bowl of Chinese export porcelain (below) was decorated in a tobacco leaf pattern. The "neat landskip" (above) ordered by George for the mantelpiece in the west parlor came from London in 1757; and in 1759 he was ordering finery for his stepchildren through his London agents (right), including the children's toys and Patsy's fashionably dressed dolls.

RETURNING FROM THE CHACE. | RETOUR DE CHASSE.

JOYS OF THE CHASE

Washington's introduction to fox hunting, English style, dates
to the arrival in Virginia of Lord Fairfax, whose interest in the
sport can only be described as passionate. It became one of
Washington's favorite amusements, and his diary is filled with
references to days spent riding across the countryside in pursuit
of a fox, frequently followed by a leisurely dinner with a group
of neighbors. The primitive painting at right is an unknown artist's
conception of the chase in eighteenth-century Virginia. Washington
himself owned a number of English prints on this subject, including
the one reproduced above. The brass horn below belonged to
him, and is believed to have been purchased in 1769 or 1773. On
one of the few occasions during the Revolution when he saw an
enemy in full flight across an open field, Washington could not
resist the chase: spurring his horse in pursuit of the British
fleeing from Princeton in 1777, he cantered along beside his
troops, shouting, "It's a fine fox chase, boys!"

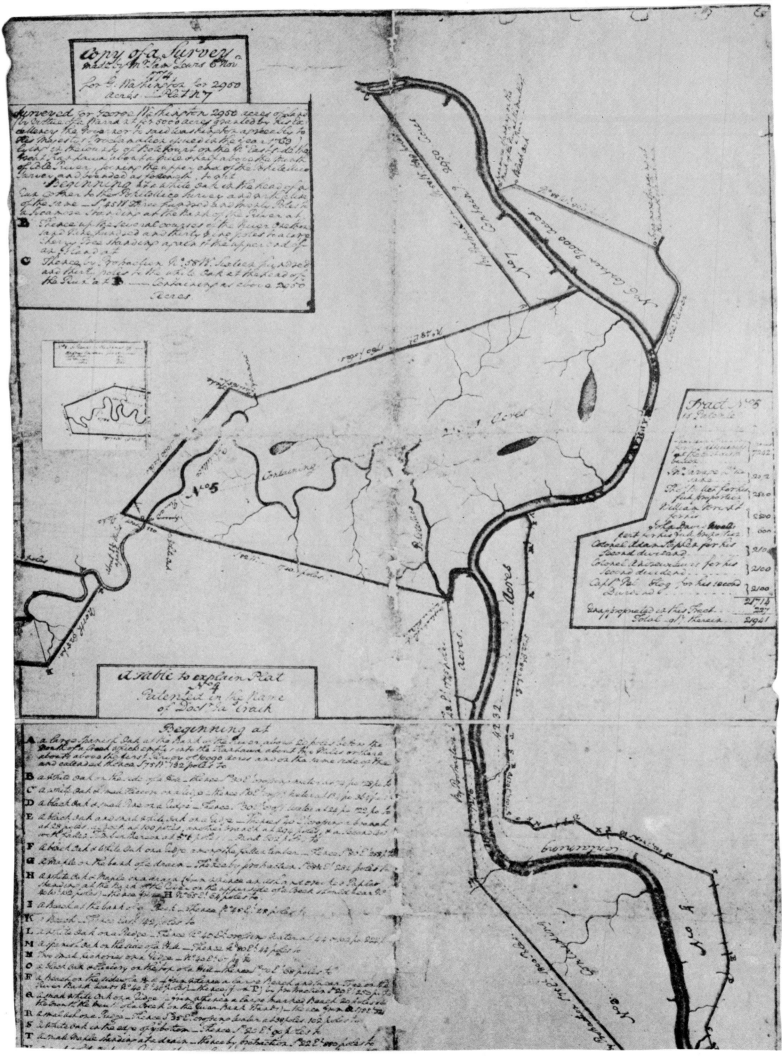

A HUNGER FOR LAND

From the time he purchased his first tract of land on Bullskin Creek, a tributary of the Shenandoah, in 1750, the desire for acquiring property never lost its hold on Washington. "Land," he wrote, "is the most permanent estate and the most likely to increase in value," and the knowledge that the great Virginia fortunes had been created by purchasing rich lands at low prices was not lost on him. He was shrewd enough to recognize that many of these acquisitions were highly speculative, but they undoubtedly appealed to the gambling instinct that was part of his nature. He and a group of friends cast their eyes covetously on an enormous parcel of drowned lands that lay between the James River and Albemarle Sound, called the Dismal Swamp, and in 1763 Washington set out to explore it, believing that if it could be drained — thus creating a profitable canal from Norfolk southward — thousands of acres of saleable land would enrich himself and his partners. Benjamin Latrobe's sketch above shows part of the region through which Washington paddled on this visionary quest. Another dream lay westward, and in 1770 Washington and his lifelong friend Dr. James Craik — shown at right in a contemporary silhouette — traveled 250 miles down the Ohio from Fort Pitt to the Great Kanawha, where they laid claim to a magnificent tract of "low-grounds of the first quality." Eventually they secured title to thirty thousand acres there, and in 1774 Washington drew the map at left, showing 2,950 acres he owned, basing it on surveys made by William Crawford, Samuel Lewis, and John Floyd.

SURROGATE PARENTS

No one can say with certainty when George Washington may have concluded that he was to be forever childless. Even after the Revolution ended, he was writing to Congress, requesting that they return his commission as commander in chief of the army, which "may serve my *grandchildren* some fifty or a hundred years hence as a theme to ruminate upon." There was, unhappily, no denying the facts of the matter: Martha had borne her first husband four children in seven years; none resulted from her union with Washington. Her two surviving children were, therefore, substitutes for the ones he could not have, so it was doubly tragic for the couple that the lives of Jacky and Patsy were cut so short. On the facing page are Charles Willson Peale's miniature portraits of Martha and her offspring: Jacky, aged seventeen, who behaved as if "nature had intended him for some Asiatic prince," in the words of his schoolmaster; Patsy, a year younger, shown as she looked the year before her death. Martha's portrait is one of the few to show her without the caps she affected in later years, the only one that suggests her agreeable appearance. This is the likeness her husband carried with him throughout the Revolution, in a gold locket worn around his neck. Below is a view of King's College in New York, drawn by a British artillery officer and engraved for a book published in 1768. In May, 1773, Washington took his stepson to New York to enter him at the institution, whose building had been opened in 1760 for faculty and students "to Lodge and Diet" in.

A CAPITAL'S
AMUSEMENTS

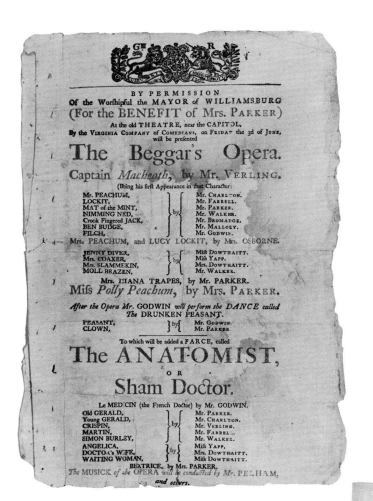

Williamsburg offered numerous diversions to delegates in the hours when they were not preoccupied with legislative matters, but social life was highly segregated (in 1769, when the Washington family spent nearly a fortnight in the capital, fifteen-year-old Jackie attended more parties with his stepfather than Martha did). Ever after attending his first theatrical performance with Lawrence in Barbados in 1751, Washington had a passion for the theater, which he attended at every opportunity. During one week in Williamsburg he went to plays five nights out of seven, to see such performers as Nancy Hallam in the Douglass Company's version of *Cymbelline*. (She is shown on the facing page in the cave scene, as painted by Charles Willson Peale.) A 1768 playbill for Gay's *Beggar's Opera* and Ravenscroft's farce, *The Anatomist*, advertised another performance he may have seen (the music for the opera was conducted by Williamsburg's Peter Pelham, who doubled as organist and jailor). Although cautious about losses, Washington had an "infatuation" for cards and gambling, was forever buying lottery tickets like the one shown on the opposite page, and liked cockfights and similar entertainments, as well as billiards (in the scene below, sketched by Benjamin Latrobe, a group of men are playing in a Virginia tavern).

Edmund Pendleton, viewed by many as a conservative for his opposition to Patrick Henry's radicalism, emerged as one of Virginia's leaders in the pre-Revolution days. He was a delegate to the First Continental Congress, helped draw up Virginia's own constitution, and headed the Committee of Safety.

Richard Henry Lee, above, shared with Patrick Henry the reputation of leading radical and orator in the House of Burgesses. He was an early advocate of the Committees of Correspondence and, as a delegate to Congress, was chosen in 1776 to introduce the motion that led to the Declaration of Independence.

FERMENT
IN WILLIAMSBURG

Despite its small size, Virginia's capital exerted a profound influence on the political thinking of colonial America. As seen in the 1780 map on the facing page, drawn by Louis Alexandre Berthier of Rochambeau's staff, the village centered on Duke of Gloucester Street, which ran the entire length of town from William and Mary College to the Capitol (the Governor's Palace is at left center). As a student at William and Mary, Thomas Jefferson — shown at left in a pencil drawing by Benjamin Latrobe — met such outstanding men as George Wythe and delighted in the capital's intellectual evenings. "At these dinners," he later wrote, "I have heard more good sense, more rational and philosophical conversations, than in all my life besides."

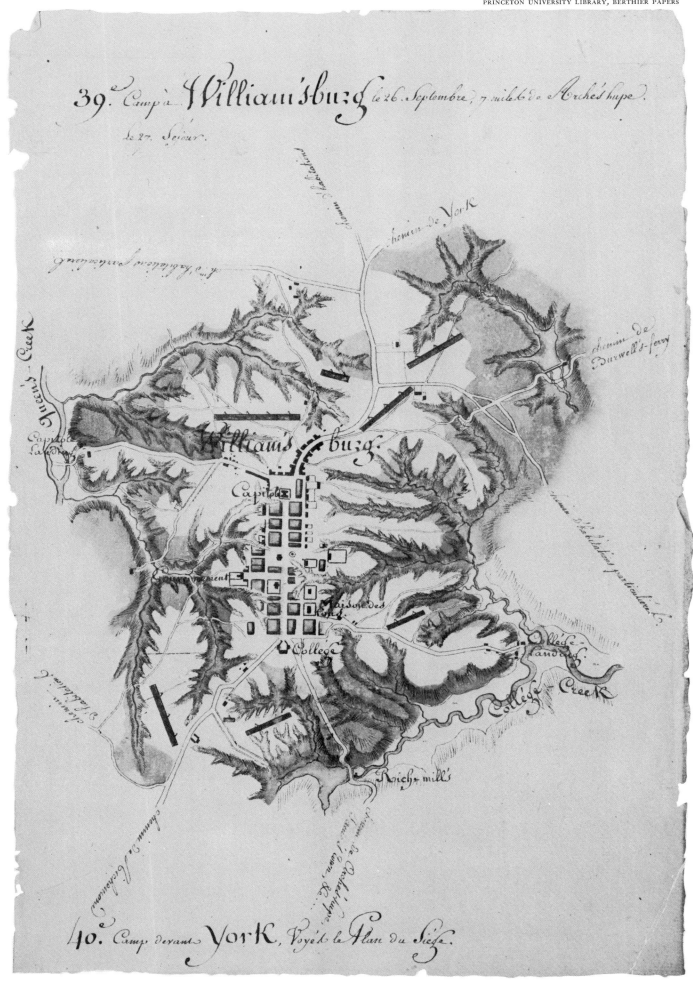

39.ᵉ Camp à **William'sburg** le 26. Septembre, 7 miles de Arché's hupe.
le 27. Séjour.

40.ᵉ Camp devant **York**, Voyé le Plan du Siège.

A VIEW OF PART OF THE TOWN OF BOSTON IN NEW-ENGLAND AND BRITTISH SHI

A BRITISH ARMY LAND.

A palpable sign of what the future might produce occurred on September 30, 1768, when a British fleet anchored in Boston harbor and proceeded to disgorge soldiers of the 14th and 29th regiments on Long Wharf. This illustration of the ominous event was "Engraved Printed, & Sold by Paul Revere, Boston," whose sympathies lay on the side of the so-called Sons of Liberty. The King's men "marched with insolent Parade" up King Street, Revere reported, and those who were refused lodging by outraged Bostonians pitched their tents on the Common in front of John Hancock's mansion. In the course of that fall some four thousand troops arrived in the city — an occupation force whose presence aroused the emotions of the residents to a point where violence was virtually inevitable, while enlisting the sympathies of all the other colonies in Massachusetts' plight. Suddenly, Virginians were aware that the problems of a sister colony were theirs, and one outgrowth of this sense of common purpose were the Committees of Correspondence, initiated in 1772 by such men as Samuel Adams of Boston and Patrick Henry and Thomas Jefferson of Virginia in order to coordinate the activities of colonial agitators and rally public opinion against British policies. Below is a covering letter sent by the Boston Committee of Correspondence to other Massachusetts towns, calling attention to the actions of friends in "the ancient and patriotic Province of Virginia," where "the earliest Resolves against the detestable Stamp-Act" had been voted.

From the Adams Papers

BOSTON, APRIL 9, 1773.

SIR,

THE Committee of Correspondence of this Town have received the following Intelligence, communicated to them by a Person of Character in this Place. We congratulate you upon the Acquisition of such respectable Aid as the ancient and patriotic Province of *Virginia*, the earliest Resolvers against the detestable Stamp-Act, in Opposition to the unconstitutional Measures of the present Administration. The Authenticity of this Advice you may depend upon, as it was immediately received from one of the Honorable Gentlemen appointed to communicate with the other Colonies. We are,

Your Friends and humble Servants,

Signed by Direction of the Committee for Correspondence in *Boston*,

} *Town-Clerk.*

To the Town-Clerk of   , to be immediately delivered to the Committee of Correspondence for your Town, if such a Committee is chosen, otherwise to the Gentlemen the Selectmen, to be communicated to the Town.

N BOSTON

an Account of a late Military Maſſacre at Boſton, or the Conſequences of Quartering Troops in a populous well-regulated Town, taken from the Boſton-Gazette, of March 12, 1770.

BOSTON, March 12, 1770.

THE Town of Boſton affords a recent and melancholy Demonſtration of the deſtructive Conſequences of quartering Troops among Citizens in a Time of Peace, under a Pretence of ſupporting the Laws and aiding Civil Authority; every conſiderate and unprejudic'd Perſon among us was deeply impreſt with the Apprehenſion of theſe Conſequences when it was known that a Number of Regiments were ordered to this Town under ſuch a Pretext, but in Reality to inforce oppreſſive Meaſures; to awe and controul the legiſlative as well as executive Power of the Province, and to quell a Spirit of Liberty, which however it may have been baſely oppos'd and even ridicul'd by ſome, would do Honor to any Age or Country. A few Perſons amongſt us had determin'd to uſe all their Influence to procure ſo deſtructive a Meaſure with a View to their ſecurely enjoying the Profits of an American Revenue, and unhappily both for Britain and this Country they found Means to effect it.

It is to Governor Bernard, the Commiſſioners, their Confidents and Coadjutors, that we are indebted as the procuring Cauſe of a military Power in this Capital—The Boſton Journal of Occurrences, as printed in Mr. Holt's York Gazette, from Time to Time, afforded many ſtriking Inſtances of the Diſtreſſes brought upon the Inhabitants by this Meaſure; and ſince thoſe Journals have been diſcontinued, our Troubles from that Quarter have been growing upon us: We have known a Party of Soldiers in the face of Day fire off a loaden Muſket upon the Inhabitants, others have been prick'd with their Bayonets, and even our Magiſtrates aſſaulted and put in Danger of their Lives, when Offenders brought before them have been reſcued; and why thoſe and other bold and baſe Criminals have as yet eſcaped the Puniſhment due to their Crimes, may be ſoon Matter of Enquiry by the Repreſentative Body of this People—It is natural to ſuppoſe that when the Inhabitants of this Town ſaw thoſe Laws which had been enacted for their Security, and which they were ambitious of holding up to the Soldiery, eluded, they ſhould more commonly reſent for themſelves—and accordingly it has ſo happened; many have been the Squabbles between them and the Soldiery; but it ſeems their being often worſted by our Youth in thoſe Rencounters, has only ſerv'd to irritate the former—What paſſed at Mr. Gray's Rope-walk, has already been given the Public, and may be ſaid to have led the Way to the late Cataſtrophe—That the Rope-walk Lads when attaked by ſuperior Numbers ſhould defend themſelves with ſo much Spirit and Succeſs in the Club-way, was too mortifying, and perhaps it may hereafter appear, that even ſome of their Officers were *unhappily* affected with this Circumſtance: Divers Stories were propagated among the Soldiery, that ſerv'd to agitate their Spirits; particularly on the Sabbath, that one Chambers, a Serjeant, repreſented as a ſober Man, had been miſſing the preceeding Day, and muſt therefore have been murdered by the Townſmen; an Officer of Diſtinction ſo far credited this Report, that he enter'd Mr. Gray's Rope-walk that Sabbath; and when required of by that Gentleman as ſoon as he could meet him, the Occaſion of his ſo doing, the Officer reply'd, that it was to look if the Sergeant ſaid to be murdered had not been hid there; this ſober Sergeant was found on the Monday unhurt, in a Houſe of Pleaſure—The Evidences already collected ſhew, that many Threatnings had been thrown out by the Soldiery, but we do not pretend to ſay that there was any preconcerted Plan, when the Evidences are publiſhed, the World will judge—We may however venture to declare, that it appears too probable from their Conduct, that ſome of the Soldiery aimed to draw and provoke the Townſmen into Squabbles, and that they then intended to make Uſe of other Weapons than Canes, Clubs or Bludgeons.

Our Readers will doubtleſs expect a circumſtantial Account of the tragical Affair on Monday Night laſt; but we hope they will excuſe our being ſo particular as we ſhould have been, had we not ſeen that the Town was intending an Enquiry and full Repreſentation thereof.

On the Evening of Monday, being the 5th Current, ſeveral Soldiers of the 29th Regiment were ſeen parading the Streets with their drawn Cutlaſſes and Bayonets, abuſing and wounding Numbers of the Inhabitants.

A few minutes after nine o'clock, four youths, named Edward Archbald, William Merchant, Francis Archbald, and John Leech, jun. came down Cornhill together, and ſeperating at Doctor Loring's corner, the two former were paſſing the narrow alley leading to Murray's barrack, in which was a ſoldier brandiſhing a broad ſword of an uncommon ſize againſt the walls out of which he ſtruck fire plentifully. A perſon of a mean countenance armed with a large cudgel bore him company. Edward Archbald admoniſhed Mr. Merchant to take care of the ſword, on which the ſoldier turned round and ſtruck Archbald on the arm, then puſhed at Merchant and pierced thro' his cloaths inſide the arm cloſe to the arm-pit and grazed the ſkin. Merchant then ſtruck the ſoldier with a ſhort ſtick he had, and the other Perſon ran to the barrack and bro't with him two ſoldiers, one armed with a pair of tongs the other with a ſhovel: he with the tongs purſued Archbald back thro' the alley, collar'd and laid him over the head with the tongs. The noiſe bro't people together, and John Hicks, a young lad, coming up, knock'd the ſoldier down, but let him get up again; and more lads gathering, drove them back to the barrack, where the boys ſtood ſome time as it were to keep them in. In leſs than a minute 10 or 12 of them came out with drawn cutlaſſes, clubs & bayonets, and ſet upon the unarmed boys and young folks, who ſtood them a little while, but finding the inequality of their equipment diſperſed.—On hearing the noiſe, one Samuel Atwood, came up to ſee what was the matter, and entering the alley from dock-ſquare, heard the latter part of the combat and when the boys had diſperſed he met the 10 or 12 ſoldiers aforeſaid ruſhing down the alley towards the ſquare, and asked them if they intended to murder people? They anſwered Yes, by G—d, root and branch! With that one of them ſtruck Mr. Atwood with a club, which was repeated by another, and being unarmed he turned to go off, and received a wound on the left ſhoulder which

The BLOODY MASSACRE perpetrated in King-Street BOSTON on March 5th 1770 by a party of the 29th REGt

Unhappy BOSTON! ſee thy Sons deplore,
Thy hallow'd Walks beſmear'd with guiltleſs Gore:
While faithleſs P—n and his ſavage Bands,
With murd'rous Rancour ſtretch their bloody Hands;
Like fierce Barbarians grinning o'er their Prey,
Approve the Carnage, and enjoy the Day.

If ſcalding drops from Rage from Anguiſh Wrung,
If ſpeechleſs Sorrows lab'ring for a Tongue,
Or if a weeping World can ought appeaſe
The plaintive Ghoſts of Victims ſuch as theſe;
The Patriot's copious Tears for each are ſhed,
A glorious Tribute which embalms the Dead.

But know, FATE ſummons to that awful Goal,
Where JUSTICE ſtrips the Murd'rer of his Soul:
Should venal C—ts the ſcandal of the Land,
Snatch the relentleſs Villain from her Hand,
Keen Execrations on this Plate inſcrib'd,
Shall reach a JUDGE who never can be brib'd.

The unhappy Sufferers were Meſs.rs SAM.L GRAY, SAM.L MAVERICK, JAM.S CALDWELL, CRISPUS ATTUCKS & PAT.K CARR *Killed. Six wounded; two of them* (CHRIST.R MONK & JOHN CLARK) *Mortally*

reached the bone and gave him much pain. Retreating a few ſteps, Mr. Atwood met two officers and ſaid, Gentlemen, what is the matter? They anſwered, you'll ſee by and by. Immediately after, thoſe heroes appeared in the ſquare, aſking where were the boogers? where were the cowards? But notwithſtanding their fierceneſs to naked men, one of them advanced towards a youth who had a ſplit of a raw ſtave in his hand, and ſaid damn them here is one of them; but the young man ſeeing a perſon near him with a drawn ſword and good cane ready to ſupport him, held up his ſtave in defiance, and they quietly paſſed by him up the little alley by Mr. Silsby's to Kingſtreet, where they attacked ſingle and unarmed perſons till they raiſed much clamor, and then turned down Cornhill ſtreet, inſulting all they met in like manner, and purſuing ſome to their very doors. Thirty or forty perſons mostly lads, being by this means gathered in King ſtreet, Capt. Preſton, with a party of men with charged bayonets, came from the main guard to the commiſſioners houſe, the ſoldiers puſhing their bayonets, crying, Make way! They took place by the cuſtom-houſe, and continuing to puſh to drive the people off, pricked ſome in ſeveral places; on which they were clamorous, and, it is ſaid, threw ſnow-balls. On this, the Captain commanded them to fire, and more ſnow-balls coming, he again ſaid, Damn you, Fire, be the conſequence what it will! One ſoldier then fired, and a townſman with a cudgel ſtruck him over the hands with ſuch force that he dropt his firelock; and ruſhing forward aimed a blow at the Captain's head, which graz'd his hat and fell pretty heavy upon his arm: However, the ſoldiers continued the fire, ſucceſſively, till 7 or 8, or as ſome ſay 11 guns were diſcharged.

By this fatal manœuvre, three men were laid dead on the ſpot, and two more ſtruggling for life; but what ſhewed a degree of cruelty unknown to Britiſh troops, at leaſt ſince the houſe of Hanover has directed their operations, was an attempt to fire upon or puſh with their bayonets the perſons who undertook to remove the ſlain and wounded!

Mr. Benjamin Leigh, now undertaker in the Delph Manufactory, came up, and after ſome converſation with Capt. Preſton, relative to his conduct in this affair, adviſed him to draw off his men, with which he complied.

The dead are Mr. Samuel Gray, killed on the ſpot, the ball entering his head and beating off a large portion of his ſkull.

A mulatto man, named Criſpus Attucks, who was born in Framingham, but lately belonged to New-Providence, and was here in order to go for North-Carolina, alſo killed inſtantly; two balls entering his breaſt, one of them in ſpecial goring the right lobe of the lungs, and a great part of the liver moſt horribly.

Mr. James Caldwell, mate of Capt. Morton's veſſel, in like manner killed by two balls entering his back.

Mr. Samuel Maverick, a promiſing youth of 17 years of age, ſon of the Widow Maverick, and an apprentice to Mr. Greenwood, Ivory-Turner, mortally wounded, a ball went through his belly, and was cut out at his back: He died the next morning.

A lad named Chriſtopher Monk, about 17 years of age, an apprentice to Mr. Walker, Shipwright; wounded a ball entered his back about 4 inches above the left kidney, near the ſpine, and was cut out of the breaſt on the ſame ſide; apprehended he will die.

A lad named John Clark, about 17 years of age, whoſe parents live at Medford, and an apprentice to Capt. Samuel Howard of this town; wounded, a ball entered juſt above his groin and came out at his hip, on the oppoſite ſide, apprehended he will die.

Mr. Edward Payne, of this town, Merchant, ſtanding at his entry-door, received a ball in his arm, ſhattered ſome of the bones.

Mr. John Green, Taylor, coming up Leverett's Lane, received a ball juſt under his hip, and lodged in the under part of his thigh, which was extracted.

Mr. Robert Patterſon, a ſeafaring man, who was the perſon that had his trowſers ſhot through in Richardſon's affair, wounded; a ball went thro' his right arm, and he ſuffered great loſs of blood.

Mr. Patrick Carr, about 30 years of age, who work'd with Mr. Field, Leather-Breeches-maker in Queen-ſtreet, wounded, a ball enter'd near his hip and went out at his ſide.

A lad named David Parker, an apprentice to Mr. Eddy the Wheelwright, wounded, a ball entered in his thigh.

The People were immediately alarmed with the Report of this horrid Maſſacre, the Bells were ſet a Ringing, and great Numbers ſoon aſſembled at the Place where this tragical Scene had been acted; their Feelings may be better conceived than expreſs'd; and while ſome were taking Care of the Dead and Wounded, the Reſt were in Conſultation what to do in thoſe dreadful Circumſtances.—But ſo little intimidated where they, notwithſtanding their being within a few Yards of the Main-Guard, and ſeeing the 29th Regiment under Arms, and drawn up in King-Street; that they kept their Station and appear'd as an Officer of Rank expreſs'd it, ready to run upon the very Muzzles of their Muſkets.—The Lieut. Governor ſoon came into the Town-Houſe, and there met ſome of his Majeſty's Council, and a Number of Civil Magiſtrates; a conſiderable Body of the People immediately entered the Council Chamber, and expreſſed themſelves to his Honor with a Freedom and Warmth becoming the occaſion. He uſed his utmoſt Endeavours to pacify them, requeſting that they would let the Matter ſubſide for the Night, and promiſing to do all in his Power that Juſtice ſhould be done, and the Law have its Courſe; Men of Influence and Weight with the People were not wanting on their part to procure their Compliance with his Honor's Requeſt by repreſenting the horrible Conſequences of a promiſcuous and raſh Engagement in the Night, and aſſuring them that ſuch Meaſures ſhould be entered upon in the Morning as would be agreeable to their Dignity, and a more likely way of obtaining the beſt Satiſfaction for the Blood of their Fellow-Townſmen.—The Inhabitants attended to theſe Suggeſtions, and the Regiment under Arms being ordered to their Barracks, which was inſiſted upon by the People, they then ſeparated and returned to their Dwellings by One o'Clock, at 3 o'Clock Capt. Preſton was committed, as were the Soldiers who fir'd, a few Hours after him.

Tueſday Morning preſented a moſt ſhocking Scene, the Blood of our Fellow Citizens running like Water thro' King-Street, and the Merchants Exchange the principal Spot of the Military Parade for about 18 Months paſt. Our Blood might alſo be track'd up to the Head of Long-Lane, and through divers other Streets and Paſſages.

At eleven o'clock the inhabitants met at Faneuil-Hall, and after ſome animated ſpeeches becoming the occaſion, they choſe a Committee of 15 reſpectable Gentlemen to wait upon the Lieut. Governor in Council, to requeſt of him to iſſue his Orders for the immediate removal of the troops.

The Meſſage was in theſe Words:

THAT it is the unanimous opinion of this meeting that the inhabitants and ſoldiery can no longer live together in ſafety; that nothing can rationally be expected to reſtore the peace of the town and prevent further blood and carnage, but the immediate removal of the Troops; and that we therefore moſt fervently pray his Honor that his power and influence may be exerted for their inſtant removal.

His Honor's Reply, which was laid before the Town then Adjourn'd to the Old South Meeting-Houſe, was as follows,

Gentlemen,

I AM extremely ſorry for the unhappy differences between the inhabitants and troops, and eſpecially for the action of the laſt evening, and I have exerted myſelf upon that occaſion that a due enquiry may be made, and that the law may have its courſe. I have in council conſulted with the commanding officers of the two regiments who are in the town. They have their orders from the General at New-York. It is not in my power to countermand thoſe orders. The Council have deſired that the two regiments may be removed to the Caſtle. From the particular concern which the 29th regiment has had in your differences, Col. Dalrymple who is the commanding officer of the troops has ſignified that that regiment ſhall without delay be placed in the barracks at the Caſtle until he can ſend to the General and receive his further orders concerning both the regiments, and that the main guard ſhall be removed, and the 14th regiment ſo diſpoſed and laid under ſuch reſtraint that all occaſion of future diſturbances may be prevented.

The foregoing Reply having been read and fully conſidered—the queſtion was put, Whether the Report be ſatisfactory? Paſſed in the Negative, (only 1 diſſentient) out of upwards of [illegible] Voters.

It was then moved & voted that John Hancock, Eſq; Mr. Samuel Adams, Mr. William Molineux, William Phillips, Eſq; Dr. Joſeph Warren, Joſhua Henſhaw, Eſq; and Samuel Pemberton, Eſq; be a Committee to wait on his Honour the Lieut. Governor, and inform him, that it is the unanimous Opinion of this Meeting, that the Reply made to a Vote of the Inhabitants preſented his Honor in the Morning, is by no means ſatisfactory; and that nothing leſs will ſatisfy, than a total and immediate removal of all the Troops.

The Committee having waited upon the Lieut. Governor agreeable to the foregoing Vote; laid before the Inhabitants the following Vote of Council received from his Honor.

His Honor the Lieut. Governor laid before the Board a Vote of the Town of Boſton, paſſed this Afternoon, and then addreſſed the Board as follows.

Gentlemen of the Council,

"I lay before you a Vote of the Town of Boſton, which I have juſt now received from them, and I now aſk your Advice what you judge neceſſary to be done upon it.

The Council thereupon expreſſed themſelves to be *unanimouſly* of opinion, "that it was abſolutely neceſſary for his Majeſty's ſervice, the good order of the Town, and the Peace of the Province, that the Troops ſhould be immediately removed out of the Town of Boſton, and thereupon adviſed his Honor to communicate this Advice of the Council to Col. Dalrymple, and to pray that he would order the Troops down to Caſtle-William." The Committee alſo informed the Town, that Col. Dalrymple, after having ſeen the Vote of Council, ſaid to the Committee, "That he now gave his word of Honor that he would begin his Preparations in the Morning, and that there ſhould be no unneceſſary delay until the whole of the two Regiments were removed to the Caſtle."

Upon the above Report being read, the Inhabitants could not avoid expreſſing the high Satiſfaction it afforded them.

After Meaſures were taken for the Security of the Town in the Night by a ſtrong Military Watch, the Meeting was Diſſolved.

The 29th Regiment have already left us, and the 14th Regiment are following them, ſo that we expect the Town will ſoon be clear of all the Troops. The Wiſdom and true Policy of his Majeſty's Council and Col. Dalrymple the Commander appear in this Meaſure. Two Regiments in the midſt of this populous City; and the Inhabitants juſtly incenſed: Thoſe of the neighbouring Towns actually under Arms upon the firſt Report of the Maſſacre, and the Signal only wanting to bring in a few Hours to the Gates of this City many Thouſands of our brave Brethren in the Country, deeply affected with our Diſtreſſes, and to whom we are greatly obliged on this Occaſion—No one knows where this would have ended, and what important Conſequences even to the whole Britiſh Empire might have followed, which our Moderation and Loyalty upon ſo trying an Occaſion, and our Faith in the Commander's Aſſurances have happily prevented.

Laſt Thurſday, agreeable to a general Requeſt of the Inhabitants, and by the Conſent of Parents and Friends, were carried to their *Grave* in Succeſſion, the Bodies of *Samuel Gray, Samuel Maverick, James Caldwell,* and *Criſpus Attucks,* the unhappy Victims who fell in the bloody Maſſacre of the Monday Evening preceeding!

On this Occaſion moſt of the Shops in Town were ſhut, all the Bells were ordered to toll a ſolemn Peal as were alſo thoſe in the neighboring Towns of Charleſtown, Roxbury, &c. The Proceſſion began to move between the Hours of 4 and 5 in the Afternoon; two of the unfortunate Sufferers, viz. Meſſ. *James Caldwell* and *Criſpus Attucks,* who were Strangers, borne from Faneuil-Hall, attended by a numerous Train of Perſons of all Ranks; and the other two, viz. Mr. *Samuel Gray,* from the Houſe of Benjamin Gray, (his Brother) on the North-ſide the Exchange, and Mr. *Maverick,* from the Houſe of his diſtreſſed Mother Mrs. *Mary Maverick,* in Union-Street, each followed by their reſpective Relations and Friends: The ſeveral Hearſes forming a Junction in King-Street, the Theatre of that inhuman Tragedy, proceeded from thence thro' the Main-Street, lengthened by an immenſe Concourſe of People, ſo numerous as to be obliged to follow in Ranks of ſix, and brought up by a long Train of Carriages belonging to the principal Gentry of the Town. The Bodies were depoſited in one Vault in the middle Burying-ground: The aggravated Circumſtances of their Death, the Diſtreſs and Sorrow viſible in every Countenance, together with the peculiar Solemnity with which the whole Funeral was conducted, ſurpaſs Deſcription.

BOSTON, March 19.

Laſt Wedneſday Night died, *Patrick Carr,* an Inhabitant of this Town, of the Wound he received in King-Street on the bloody and execrable Night of the 5th Inſtant—He had juſt before left his Home, and upon his coming into the Street received the fatal Ball in his Hip which paſſed out at the oppoſite Side; this is the fifth Life that has been ſacrificed by the Rage of the Soldiery, but it is feared it will not be the laſt, as ſeveral others are dangerouſly languiſhing of their Wounds. His Remains were attended on Saturday laſt from Faneuil-Hall by a numerous and reſpectable Train of Mourners, to the *ſame* Grave, in which thoſe who fell by the *ſame* Hands of Violence were interred the laſt Week.

VIOLENCE IN NEW ENGLAND

It is indicative of Washington's state of mind that no mention appears in any of his surviving correspondence about the Boston "Massacre" of March 5, 1770. A year earlier he had drafted a nonimportation agreement that was adopted by his fellow Burgesses, but in 1770 he was still taking his time and maintaining a detached attitude while deciding where he stood on the issues dividing Britain and her colonies. One of the most skillful — and biased — examples of American propaganda appears on the opposite page. Printed in the Boston *Gazette* of March 12, this account included a highly distorted representation of the event by Paul Revere which was cited as "evidence" of British guilt in the unhappy affair. By now, Samuel Adams' "Liberty Boys" had the upper hand in Boston and were subjecting Tories and loyal officials to the kind of treatment depicted in the British cartoon above, where an excise collector has been tarred and feathered and is being forced to drink tea as punishment for attempting to collect the tax required by the Stamp Act. At right is a reproduction of the stamp, which was placed on printed matter, most legal documents, and various other articles, including playing cards.

CONGRESS DECIDES TO ACT

Nearly a quarter of a century after delegates to the First Continental Congress arrived in Philadelphia, Thomas Birch executed a view (left) of the intersection of Second and High Streets, with the spire of Christ Church beyond. That first Congress assembled in Carpenters' Hall, smaller than the State House, but a better choice psychologically, since the meeting place of the master craftsmen bore no signs of royal authority. The following year members of the Second Continental Congress met at the State House, shown below in a wash drawing by Charles Willson Peale done in 1778. Here, in June, 1775, delegates from the thirteen colonies considered the question of how they should aid the New England army that was besieging the British in Boston and decided to establish an "American continental army." Among the names mentioned as possible commanders were those of John Hancock, president of Congress, who wanted the appointment himself; Charles Lee, a former British officer who was actively campaigning for the post; Israel Putnam, an elderly hero of the French and Indian War; Artemas Ward, whom Lee characterized as "a fat old gentleman who had been a popular churchwarden," who commanded the motley army outside Boston; and Washington, whom most delegates regarded as the obvious choice. On June 14, 1775, the "gentleman from Virginia" was nominated for the command by John Adams of Massachusetts, and Congress elected him unanimously. At that moment Washington was the only man actually enrolled in the Continental Army. Not for a year, until independence was declared, would the new nation for which he was fighting exist.

John Hancock

Israel Putnam

Charles Lee

Artemas Ward

COMMANDER IN CHIEF

The appointment of George Washington as commander in chief was Congress' response to the outbreak of hostilities in April, 1775. Amos Doolittle, a Connecticut militiaman who arrived soon after the battle of April 19, engraved the picture above, which shows the Lexington militia dispersing before a volley from the British under Major John Pitcairn, leaving behind eight dead and ten wounded. Shown below is the document, signed by John Hancock, by which Washington was officially named General and Commander in Chief. As a delegate to Congress, Washington customarily wore the uniform in which Charles Willson Peale had first painted his portrait (page 59). In appearance, however, he now resembled the painting on the facing page, a miniature also done by Peale, probably during the winter of 1777–1778.

4

COMMANDER
IN CHIEF

Whether George Washington really believed, as he promised Martha, that he would return home in the fall, no one can say, but in fact it was eight and a half years before he again retired to his beloved Mount Vernon. Eight and a half years is a large slice of a man's life at any time, and especially so in the eighteenth century when the normal span of human longevity was relatively brief. When it is remembered that nearly one-eighth of Washington's sixty-seven years were spent in command of the Revolutionary army it is little wonder that that war and its battles loom so large in an account of his life.

On the other hand, it is astonishing to count how few engagements of any consequence he was actually in during the war. In 1775, the first year of his service, the army under his direct command fought no battles. In 1776 it fought six. During the following year his troops engaged the enemy twice; in 1778, once. In 1779 and 1780 Washington fought no battles of any significance, and in 1781 but one — Yorktown. During 1782 and 1783, when the treaty of peace was finally signed, his army was idle.

What is equally curious — considering his reputation in America and abroad — is that Washington, in all those years as commander of the Continental Army, almost never won an out and out victory. His triumphs were more often those of having eluded or outwitted the enemy, not of vanquishing him in battle. He was criticized frequently, by his countrymen and by men in the army he led, for his failure to win a major victory, and on several occasions there was widespread doubt that he should continue as the commanding general.

So it might be asked, how did Washington achieve military renown when in the course of this long period he fought only nine major engagements — an average of about one a year — and triumphed in so few of them? In part, the answer reflects the nature of eighteenth-century warfare, in which a disproportionate amount of time had to be spent in recruiting, training, and in preparing and maneuvering for the next battle, or in retreating and recuperating from the last one. It was customary for armies to hibernate during the winter season, so that months — perhaps half a year or more — might pass between the conclusion of one campaign and the beginning of the next. Particularly was this true in the vast, unsettled, and forbidding countryside of North America, where roads were poor or nonexistent, where transport facilities were primitive or unavailable, greatly restricting the mobility of large bodies of men.

There was another factor at work, however, and therein lies the real genius of Washington as a commander. During 1776, his first year of combat, he learned through bitter experience that there was no way his army could possibly stand up to the British in head-on combat — no way they could fight and win a pitched battle. They were too few, too inexperienced; they had no cavalry and precious little artillery; they were short of all the necessities — food, clothing, weapons, ammunition; officers and men alike were amateurs — citizen-soldiers who had no business trying to confront an army of professionals who had at their disposal huge resources and the most formidable navy in the world. And, what may have been for Washington the cruelest realization of all, although he and his soldiers were fighting to secure the independence of their fellow countrymen, never at any time did a significant majority of those compatriots give them the all-out support, moral or physical, that might very well have helped to bring victory a little closer to realization.

What Washington discovered was that in order to win he must survive, and the survival of the Continental Army became, after 1776, the guiding star on which all his attention and efforts were fixed. Not that this was easy — in practical terms or from the standpoint of his own temperament — for he was by nature impetuous, eager for action and quick results. Too often, at the beginning, he attempted too much or planned a maneuver that was beyond the capacity of his untaught, unseasoned troops. It was not that his plans would not work, but that the instrument for executing them was wanting. Having served on the frontier before the war, Washington was an improviser, he was daring, and he seems to have believed at times that his men were capable of carrying out tactics that a more conservative or tradition-bound officer would have rejected out of hand. It was in his nature to want to attack, to catch the enemy off guard as he had surprised Jumonville many years before, yet for most of the war he had to content himself with waging a war of defense, fighting small inconclusive actions, relying on attrition or maneuver, since he could never muster enough strength to take on the entire British army. In doing so, the naturally impetuous and aggressive soldier was forced to master the art of the possible, and in the process he became a master of what would later be called guerrilla warfare.

His particular genius was to be able to learn and profit from defeat, and after the hard lessons of 1776 he came to know intuitively that the only way the rebels could win was to hold out long enough for the British to tire of fighting or for some foreign power to intervene.

Lacking trained officers, he made do with and came to rely upon young men of considerable native intelligence — many of whom he trained himself. All youthful, they included Henry Knox, a former bookseller in Boston, who became his artillerist; Alexander Hamilton, in whom Washington found a perfect staff officer; Benedict Arnold, who was — until his traitorous act — the best combat officer in the rebel army; Nathanael Greene, a former ironmonger, whom many regard as the finest field general on the American side; Lafayette, the French nobleman who was to become almost a son to Washington as well as an able fighting man; and many others of the same caliber, each of whom brought to the task courage and daring, plus an ability to benefit from experience. In fact, of all the men who entered the army as general officers, only Washington maintained his reputation intact until the end; the others had been largely supplanted by younger officers.

For George Washington the Revolutionary War was one crisis after another — most frequently the crises of insufficiency, but often enough those of defeat and despair, and it is a measure of his toughness, resiliency, and determination that he never faltered in his objective, never doubted the justice and merit of the cause he had sworn to uphold. Obviously he suffered terrible moments of doubt and uncertainty, periods of dejection and utter discouragement, but for the most part he managed to confide his anguish only to his family. With the civilian leaders of the new nation he conducted an immense correspondence that required the services of several secretaries (in the Fitzpatrick edition of his papers the war years account for ten thousand pages), and the overwhelming burden of his messages to them were appeals for the necessities — foremost among them being soldiers and the money and supplies for their maintenance. Nonetheless, Washington set a pattern of military subservience to the elected civilians that was to have profound significance in the nation's future, and while the war was being waged it was this attitude that proved the foundation for the trust those civilian leaders gave him.

Before selecting a commander in chief for the army, members of Congress had established — in their own minds at least — certain criteria that would govern their choice, and in George Washington they found a man who met nearly all the requirements. As already noted, he was a Virginian, and it was essential in mid-1775 that the army, which then consisted almost entirely of New Englanders, be led by a general from another colony, to give the fighting force some semblance of continental union. Washington was also a native American, which counted for much. But beyond these considerations, he fitted precisely a description contained in the instructions given to New York's congressional delegation — qualifications that were also important in the minds of other representatives. What was wanted, it appeared, was an individual of some eminence and reputation, which Washington possessed. It was also important, as the instructions to the New York delegation indicate, that he would "faithfully perform the duties of his high office, and readily lay down his power when the general weal shall require it." What was manifestly clear to Congress and to the people they served was that Washington was a man of considerable wealth, and that in accepting the command of the army he was committing not only himself and his reputation, but also his property, to the cause. In other words, he had as much or more to lose than anyone, yet he was willing to lay it all on the line, unselfishly. Nor would he accept a salary — only reimbursement for his expenses.

There were other, less tangible factors to be reckoned with. He had the look and manner of a leader of men. No one sat a horse better or rode more gracefully. and on foot he stood six feet two inches tall, in a day when six-footers were rarities. A good head taller than most of his contemporaries, he was a commanding figure who gave people the impression of great strength. He was big-boned, weighed over two hundred pounds, and although he was somewhat heavy in the waist and thighs, he moved with astonishing grace and agility. As a Frenchman serving with the Continental Army once observed, he seemed "intended for a great position — his appearance alone gave confidence to the timid and imposed respect on the bold." Regarded as handsome by some, his face was strong and distinguished. He had a prominent nose, somewhat accentuated by high cheekbones, grey-blue eyes that were set wide apart in deep sockets, and reddish-brown hair. Even a loyalist admitted that he was "a fine figure [with] a most easy and agreeable address"; and a member of Congress admired what he called his "easy, soldierlike air."

At the age of forty-three he was in his physical prime — vigorous and powerful, and a man of mature judgment. He was beyond all doubt incorruptible, a man of character and integrity, of proven courage and audacity, yet nothing in his makeup suggested braggadocio or excessive ambition. As one accustomed by ownership of a plantation and years of military service

to having others defer to his judgment and wishes, he nevertheless appeared to be the kind of individual who would not be overbearing but who would — as events proved — listen to the opinions of others and take them into consideration in making his decisions. (He was, in fact, criticized during the Revolution for relying too heavily on the advice of subordinate officers; yet the council of war was then a common military practice, and Washington was keenly aware of "the limited and contracted knowledge which any of us have in military matters." As a result, he tended to operate on the theory that two or more heads were wiser than one. After all, most of his frontier military experience had been gained in a relatively junior capacity; he had no real knowledge of artillery or cavalry tactics; he had neither commanded nor been responsible for the administration of a large military force; and neither had most of his subordinates. So he heard and accepted what advice he could get.)

Although his wartime correspondence suggests that he was often exasperated, complaining, and impatient (and God knows he had reason to be), outwardly at least he was calm, reserved, even stiff, and normally the soul of courtesy, generosity, and tact. Apparently he exerted considerable charm on those around him. As Abigail Adams wrote, he "has a dignity which forbids familiarity, mixed with an easy affability which creates love and reverence." And a French officer was captivated by his face, which he said was often grave and serious, but "never stern, and, on the contrary, becomes softened by the most gracious and amiable smile. He is affable and converses with his officers familiarly and gaily."

One reason for Congress' selection of Washington was the fact that the Revolution, until July of 1775 at least, had been largely in the hands of radicals, of men like Samuel Adams of Boston and Patrick Henry of Virginia, who could arouse the emotions of ordinary citizens and incite them to behave like an undisciplined mob. Certainly many of the actions taken prior to midsummer of 1775 bore the stamp of these rabble-rousers — the Boston Tea Party, the Boston Massacre, the tarrings and featherings and the harassment of proclaimed loyalists, the destruction of royal and Tory property, and the like. So what was needed was an individual cloaked with respectability, one capable of disciplining an army that might otherwise be no more than a mob, a leader who would convince doubters in America and the intent onlookers in Europe that the struggle was a sincere, honest attempt to preserve or secure certain rights, and not the wanton effort of have-nots to seize power and property from the haves. For a purpose such as this, no man was better suited than George Washington of Mount Vernon.

For all his prior experience on the frontier, for all his youthful efforts to rise in the military profession, the fact was that George Washington, by 1775 — and for the remainder of the war — was a civilian serving half-reluctantly as a soldier. Every week Lund Washington, who was managing the plantation during his absence, sent him a report on Mount Vernon, to which the commander in chief devoted what hours he could spare for a reply. It was the only way he could keep in touch with what he loved most, while dedicating all his energies to the terrible business at hand. Again and again he wrote letters that speak of his devotion to home and family, to the farm that meant so much to him, and almost never is there an expression suggesting affection for war or battle. It was as if the old ardor that prompted his adventures on the frontier had gone, not to be recalled.

What counted with him were not the battles themselves, but the effect those encounters might have on the minds and hearts of his countrymen — which was where the real war had to be waged. If the cause faltered, it would be because people no longer had the stomach to go on, and his constant objective was unity, which would produce support. As he once wrote, "Our actions depending upon ourselves, may be controlled, whilst the powers of thinking, originating in higher causes, cannot always be molded to our wishes."

Washington was by no means certain that he was up to the seemingly insurmountable task Congress had set for him. He informed them frankly that he did "not think myself equal to the command," and he is said to have remarked to his fellow-Virginian, Patrick Henry, speaking with tears in his eyes, "Remember, Mr. Henry, what I now tell you. From the day I enter upon the command of the American armies, I date my fall and the ruin of my reputation." This was the comment of a man innately modest on the one hand, who was intensely concerned about his reputation on the other, and throughout the war his letters reveal that he was haunted by the thought that he might be found wanting in the eyes of others. Pride and ambition were involved in this, but there was genuine humility, too, which accounted for the willingness of Congress to place such faith in Washington and to give him extraordinary powers, confident that he would not betray their trust.

Take, for example, the unusual gesture made in the last days of December, 1776, one of the blackest hours of the Revolution. Congress, fearing the imminent fall of Philadelphia, had adjourned and fled to Baltimore, where they adopted a series of remarkable resolutions. For a period of six months, it was decided, Washington would be given the power of a military dictator — including the authority to raise additional troops, decide on the proper rate of pay for men and officers, appoint officers, and apply to the states for levies of militiamen as long as the emergency lasted. "Wherever he may be," this catalogue of powers continued, he could take "whatever he may want for the use of the army," and if the citizens of any area refused to sell him what he needed, he could arrest them. Granted, this decision was essential because of the exigencies of the moment, but it cannot have been easy for the civilian leaders of government to bestow upon the head of the army such powers unless they were certain the man would not abuse them. "Happy is it for this country," it was observed by Congress, "that the General of their forces can safely be entrusted with the most unlimited power, and neither personal security, liberty or property be in the least degree endangered thereby."

In accepting this handsome tribute, Washington demonstrated that the Congress had not misplaced its belief. "Instead of thinking myself freed from all *civil* obligations by this mark of confidence," he assured the members, "I shall constantly bear in mind that as the sword was the last resort for the preservation of our liberties, so it ought to be the first to be laid aside when those liberties are firmly established." All too often in human history, military men have found immense power suddenly concentrated in their hands and, warming to the taste, have refused to relinquish it. But this idea seems to have been completely alien to Washington, who on this and other occasions might have capitalized on the devotion of his compatriots and used the army under his control to perpetuate his power.

As stated, Congress might have picked another man to command its army — Artemas Ward, Charles Lee, Israel Putnam, possibly even Horatio Gates — but in hindsight it is difficult to see how it could have made a more appropriate or wiser choice. But neither the man riding off toward the sound of the guns in Cambridge nor the men who appointed him to the supreme command could have had any knowledge of this at that moment. Washington would be criticized often enough for his conduct of the war, but not for lack of courage or determination. What frequently appeared to others as personal failings were more often a reflection of the inadequacies of the new nation whose army he led.

Traditionally, the arrival of a new commanding officer is an occasion for much pageantry, with crack units of the army putting on a display calculated to impress the newcomer with their mastery of military drill and discipline. Although the army at Cambridge was a stranger to tradition, having been in existence for little more than two months, someone had decided that the formalities should be observed, and on July 1 — the day George Washington was expected to appear on the scene — some of the rebel troops dutifully paraded, looking as smart as a group of nonuniformed farmers and mechanics could under the circumstances. Unfortunately, Washington did not come.

The next morning the troops lined up again. Then it began to rain, and since there was no certainty that he would arrive on that day either, the men were dismissed. In the afternoon the weather cleared and when the new commander in chief and his escorts unexpectedly rode into the sleepy college town there were only a few idlers to note their coming. Someone was able to direct Washington to the home of Harvard's president, the Reverend Samuel Langdon, where quarters had been procured for him, and soon the New England officers began calling to pay their respects — among them Artemas Ward, a stout, sharp-nosed, slow-moving man whom Washington was to supersede. On July 3 there was a rather unceremonious transfer of authority from Ward to Washington, after which the latter issued his first General Orders and began learning the problems he was to face. They were as difficult as they were numerous.

Boston under siege stuck out into the water like a fat pollywog, bounded on the west by the Charles River and on the east by the harbor, and it was for all the world like an island surrounded by the rebel-held mainland. While it was true that Thomas Gage's redcoats were bottled up in the city, off in the distance ships of the most powerful fleet in the world rode at anchor, their masts looking, one man said, like the trees of a "dry, cedar swamp." So although the rebels might be said to control the land approaches to the town — in a great arc that swept from the Mystic River, northward, around through Cambridge and Roxbury to Dorchester, south of Boston — the city and its harbor were firmly in enemy hands. And how long the British could be penned up would depend entirely on the staying power of Washington's army.

It did not take the general long to realize that the army was in no condition to accomplish much unless a great many changes were made. In the first place,

some of the generals who had held it together since April 19 were angered by the way Congress had treated them (Congress having decided arbitrarily what the order of rank was to be), and three of the men were sufficiently annoyed to decline their appointments. Furthermore, many of the New Englanders were suspicious of the tall, remote Virginian and a staff that included several of his fellow-colonists, and the feeling was reciprocated. The army itself was recovering from the recent battle for Bunker Hill, still counting its dead and wounded and the cost in cannon, gunpowder, entrenching tools, and — perhaps most significant — morale. Although the rebels had held out against two frontal assaults by the cream of the British army, the fact was that they had at last been driven from their redoubt on Breed's Hill in a wild flight from Charlestown peninsula, and the prevailing opinion was that since they had lost the field they had lost the battle. (Not so in London: when news of the British casualties reached England and it was learned that nearly fifty per cent of Gage's men had fallen in the attack, a great many people agreed with the critic who suggested that if there were eight more such "victories" no one would be left to report them. And one immediate effect of the battle was that Washington's old comrade in arms, Thomas Gage, was recalled in disgrace and replaced by General William Howe.)

The amateurs Washington was to lead did not comprise an army; as he remarked later, they were "a mixed multitude of people . . . under very little discipline, order, or government." Command arrangements were sketchy, to say the least; there was little or no money with which to pay the troops; there was no effective means of supplying them. The men were short of tents, sanitary facilities, blankets, and muskets; bayonets were totally lacking; there was only enough gunpowder, Washington was told, for nine rounds per man. Nor was this a real army in the sense that its members had been systematically recruited for service. Originally, these volunteer soldiers had simply appeared on the scene in the chaotic hours following the battle of April 19. Some were members of regular militia companies, in which every man between the ages of sixteen and sixty was expected to serve; some were members of "minute companies," so called because they were to be ready for duty at a minute's warning; but their lack of organization defied description. Men who had left their families on April 19 had come in the clothes they were wearing when they heard the alarm, carrying their own musket, and even those who intended to stay with the army were eager to leave for a while, to see their families and to collect additional clothing and bedding.

Before Washington arrived, Congress had attempted to keep the army in being by authorizing the enlistment for eight months of twenty regiments, each commanded by a colonel and containing ten companies of fifty-six men and three officers. This scheme immediately ran afoul of a hallowed New England tradition, since the idea was that all officers would be appointed by a higher outside authority. For generations, local militia companies had elected their own officers by vote — usually on the basis of popularity, and it quickly became apparent that troops from one town would not willingly serve under an officer from another, and that soldiers from one colony were highly suspicious of those from another. (This spirit of localism that plagued civilian and military leaders throughout the Revolutionary War died hard; it was just as troublesome after the conflict ended, when the new nation was striving to find a workable system of government.) Washington learned to his sorrow that he could almost never count on the unreliable militia companies as an effective fighting force, and from this realization came a strategy he devised during the conduct of the war. He eventually used militia units as roaming bands of guerrillas, to hit the enemy, confuse them, and then to disappear; or they were employed as lookouts and scouts. Small, elite companies of riflemen and light infantry were used to blunt an enemy advance until the main body of the army could move into action, and these units could also strike an important British outpost. But the main army's role, as Washington came to see it, was to remain in reserve, husbanding its strength until the time arrived to mount a major attack on the enemy. At Monmouth, the Continental Army finally came into its own, and although the result was not what Washington had hoped, the battle proved for the first time to the British that Americans were capable of meeting regulars on their own terms. Never again did the British challenge Washington in an all-out confrontation.

What experience Washington could bring to the chaotic situation in Cambridge derived from his days as a frontier soldier and from his activities as owner of a large, complex plantation. He was aided by an inborn sense of order and a logical turn of mind, but what he was up against had no real parallel in his own past or in that of the Congress he was trying to serve. As summer turned to fall, his chief problem was to ensure that he had a body of men ready for duty after

December 31, when the enlistments of the so-called Eight-Months Army would expire. By mid-December only five thousand men had signed up for service in 1776 and it began to look as if the "Grand American Army," as John Adams termed it, would vanish altogether, leaving the British untroubled and untouched in their Boston fortress.

The few veterans who decided to stay on had formed the habit of calling short-term militiamen "Long Faces," and when the latter began departing from camp in droves, Washington unexpectedly ordered that their muskets (which belonged to the individuals) be taken from them in order to arm those who remained. Between measures such as this and the derision they faced from soldiers who had signed on for another hitch, the Long Faces gradually got the word that their departure would mean the end of everything they had fought for thus far, and as some of them returned to camp, shamefaced, to enlist again the ranks began to swell. By mid-January there were eight thousand troops on the rolls, but it was a measure of their condition that only fifty-six hundred were present and fit for duty and that nearly two thousand lacked muskets.

In the meantime, Washington had assigned an important mission to a fat, energetic young officer named Henry Knox, whose knowledge of military matters had come from the volumes he read in his Boston bookstore. Knox left camp in November, traveled to Fort Ticonderoga on Lake Champlain, and before the end of January was back in Cambridge, having collected eighty yoke of oxen to haul some fifty cannon from the fort across three hundred miles of snow-covered mountains, bottomless roads, and icy streams in one of the epic achievements of the war. When the cannon were dragged into place atop Dorchester Heights, where they commanded the harbor and the anchored British fleet, the fate of the Boston garrison was sealed. On March 6, accepting the inevitable, General William Howe and his nine thousand troops left the town, sailing for Halifax with some eleven hundred loyalists who dared not remain when the rebels moved in. On March 17 the Americans walked into the abandoned streets of Boston, whose deliverance was celebrated as the new commander in chief's first victory.

Not that Washington had much time for festivities; he was aware that the British would return, at a time and place of their own choosing, and he realized that the most likely target would be New York. As he observed, that port "secures the free and only communication between the Northern and Southern colonies, which will be entirely cut off by their possessing it, and give them the command of Hudson's River and an easy pass into Canada." With that hunch to guide him, by early April he and the army were on the march, headed for New York.

So the first campaign ended, and despite all the difficulties Washington had encountered, it was a genuine triumph. From the British standpoint, what had occurred in the colonies offered a dismal picture: a year of hostilities had produced a situation inimical to the interests of the empire — the British army now occupied not a square foot of territory in the thirteen colonies; the government had managed to alienate much of neutral opinion in America; and it appeared that the loss of prestige and good will might never be entirely recaptured. From the rebel viewpoint, an army of sorts had been cobbled together, and included in this force were a few units from colonies outside New England, signifying a fragile unity in a common cause. An expedition under Benedict Arnold had even been sent off to invade Canada and seize Quebec, and while it was a costly and tragic failure, its very occurrence proclaimed to Americans and to the rest of the world that Congress meant to prosecute this war to a conclusion. In the long view, however, the rebel army would never become the effective weapon its commander in chief so earnestly desired. Short-term enlistments, a forced reliance on militia companies that might be here today and gone tomorrow, plus all the problems that bedeviled Washington during the siege of Boston, would remain with him throughout the war, never fully resolved, always costly in relation to what he might have achieved, given adequate men and resources.

After arriving in New York, Washington put all available manpower to work building fortifications, meanwhile keeping an eye out for the appearance of British ships on the horizon. On June 29, 1776, they arrived — or began to do so. That day forty-five ships sailed through the Narrows and began to debark men and equipment on Staten Island; the next day eighty-two more vessels came in, carrying nine thousand British regulars. In July another fleet arrived from England, followed by thirty transports and men-of-war which had participated in an attack on Charleston, South Carolina, where they were turned back by the guns of Fort Sullivan. On August 12, twenty-eight transports and more warships appeared. All in all, it was the largest expeditionary force ever sent out from the shores of Great Britain, consisting of thirty-two thousand professional soldiers, well armed and equipped; and the army, led by William Howe, was supported by a flotilla of naval vessels and transports under the command of his brother, Admiral Lord Howe.

To oppose them, Washington had fewer than twenty thousand troops, poorly trained, equipped, and supplied, and on August 22, the rebels watched the awesome British force go into action as boatload after boatload of redcoats and the so-called Hessians — German mercenaries hired by George III to bring the regular army to full strength for the American war — were ferried across the water to Long Island.

From that moment on, the record of the rebel army was a catalogue of disasters. Even when the British flatboats were heading for Long Island, Washington remained convinced that their main attack would be aimed at Manhattan, so he divided his army — sending about eight thousand troops to Long Island while retaining the balance to defend New York. Nathanael Greene, who commanded the Long Island detachment, fell sick, so the command was first turned over to John Sullivan of New Hampshire, who lacked the talent for the job, and on the next day to Israel Putnam, who knew nothing about the terrain and was no man to manage a large body of troops. Howe, who had had enough of frontal assaults after Bunker Hill, sent a diversionary attack against the American right wing, while his main body made a night march that swung around and behind the American left, completely out-flanking the rebels. In the debacle that followed, some rebel units — notably the Delaware and Maryland troops — performed superbly, but the overwhelming attack by British and Hessians was simply too much, the rebels were outmaneuvered and outclassed, and the night of August 28 found the Americans huddled waist-deep in water in flooded trenches on Brooklyn Heights, their ammunition useless, waiting for the British attack. The East River was behind them, a victorious and vastly superior foe was in front of them, they were without food, and Washington and several of his ablest generals were in the trap with the troops.

Washington, who was always at his best when his back was to the wall, had ordered every available boat collected, and after dark on August 29 two Massachusetts regiments, made up of fishermen and sailors, began ferrying the beaten army across the East River. All night the evacuation continued under cover of darkness and fog, and the fact that it went off without a hitch was a near miracle. Between ten and twelve thousand demoralized men had been shuttled across the river in complete secrecy; the only loss was three stragglers who remained behind to plunder and five heavy cannon that were mired in the mud. A day later Washington — who had been one of the last men evacuated — wrote a letter to Congress describing the escape. Apologizing for the delay in informing them, he noted that for six days "I had hardly been off my horse and had never closed my eyes."

Both opposing generals had been at their best and worst during the course of the battle. Howe's attack was brilliantly planned and executed (he was knighted by George III for the victory), but when the battle was won he exhibited the curious failure to follow through that was to prove his undoing; although opportunity lay within his grasp, he failed to destroy the rebel army and perhaps end the war then and there. For his part, Washington had divided his forces, put the men on Long Island under the command of officers who were clearly inadequate to the task, and had been completely fooled by Howe's flank attack. The result was disaster, redeemed only by his masterful evacuation of the troops from Brooklyn Heights.

Although the army had escaped, its morale was at low ebb, and the commanding general had no illusions about the men's capacity for the task ahead: "I am obliged to confess my want of confidence in the generality of the troops," he admitted to Congress. Militiamen were pulling out in droves, heading for home (of eight thousand Connecticut men, only two thousand remained). Greene and other officers were urging that New York be burned to prevent its use by the British as a permanent base, but Congress vetoed the idea and Washington concluded that he would have to abandon the city and withdraw his supplies. (Much of the city went up in flames on September 21 in any event, with both sides accusing the other of having started the fire, and Washington remarked, "Providence, or some good honest fellow, has done more for us than we were disposed to do for ourselves.") The withdrawal from New York was just getting under way when the British attacked again at Kips Bay, where the militiamen who were supposed to oppose their landing took one look at the British landing barges heading toward shore, dropped their muskets, and fled in a panic. Washington galloped to the scene to find his troops running pell mell from the British, leaving muskets, coats, and knapsacks behind in their headlong flight. He and his aides drew their swords and ordered the men to turn around and fight but there was no stopping those terrified soldiers. Washington charged after them, swinging at them in rage with his riding crop, and finally threw his hat to

the ground in disgust, crying out in sheer anguish, "Are these the men with whom I am to defend America?" Meanwhile the British advance was coming on at a run, and there, not eighty yards away, sat Washington, blind with rage and frustration, overcome by the futility of it all. Suddenly an aide rode up, grabbed the bridle of his horse, and led him out of reach of the oncoming redcoats and Hessians. As Nathanael Greene wrote later, "Washington was so vexed at the infamous conduct of his troops that he sought death rather than life." Surely it was one of the most humiliating moments he had ever experienced, and it was one of the rare moments during the course of the war when he completely lost his composure and failed to maintain a grip on his emotions.

Before leaving the island of Manhattan the rebels fought a sharp skirmish at Harlem Heights and had the satisfaction of seeing British regulars retreat in confusion, but despite this heartening little victory, Washington was distraught over the cowardice of his men, who seemed incapable of standing up to the British. To Lund Washington he admitted his despair: "If I were to wish the bitterest curse to an enemy on this side of the grave, I should put him in my stead with my feelings; and yet I do not know what plan of conduct to pursue. I see the impossibility of serving with reputation, or doing any essential service to the cause by continuing in command, and yet I am told that if I quit the command, inevitable ruin will follow from the distraction that will ensue. I tell you that I never was in such an unhappy, divided state since I was born." The discipline of the army seemed to have broken down completely; it was riddled with plunderers and drifters; Washington was now facing the annual problem of those short-term enlistees whose term of service would expire at the end of the year; and as he reported to John Hancock, the president of the Congress, "We are now . . . upon the eve of another dissolution of our Army." If new regiments were not added quickly, he would be forced to rely on what militiamen he could scare up — troops "with whom no man who had any regard for his own reputation can undertake to be answerable for the consequences."

Meanwhile, in one of those small ironies of war, Washington and his staff moved into the house confiscated from loyalist Roger Morris, who had been an officer with the Braddock expedition and who had married Eliza Philipse, whom Washington courted on his first visit to New York at the age of twenty-four. There was talk of reconciliation in the air — a natural result of the disasters that had befallen the rebel army, combined with the efforts of General William Howe and his brother, the admiral, to negotiate a peace settlement — but Washington wanted no part of what he called this "fatal idea." He was well beyond the point of countenancing reunion with Britain.

When the Howes saw no evidence that the rebels sought a peaceful accommodation, the general launched another attack on October 12 — this one an ambitious turning movement which landed a force at Throg's Neck in Westchester, threatening Washington's rear. Leaving about fifteen hundred soldiers to man the isolated stronghold of Fort Washington, overlooking the Hudson River, the American general fell back to White Plains where, after a rough but inconclusive skirmish, his army retreated again. In a matter of ten weeks, Washington's troops had lost Long Island, Manhattan, and much of Westchester, and the only reason it had taken so long was because of Howe's inexplicable delay in following up his victories. About all Washington could claim to have done was to save the little army that was, to all intents and purposes, the Revolution. But worse was to come.

Uncertain where the British would strike next, Washington divided his army again, leaving about seven thousand men with General Charles Lee in North Castle, above White Plains, while he crossed to New Jersey with some two thousand troops. Howe decided to head south toward New York, where on November 16 he invested Fort Washington, the stronghold which the rebel commander in chief — somewhat against his better judgment — had reinforced. This fort and another, Fort Lee, directly across the Hudson, were supposed to bar the passage of British men-of-war up the Hudson River, but that illusion had already been shattered when ships of the Royal Navy sailed past them. Now the defenders put up a game fight, but it was a senseless thing from the beginning and the American commander should have known there was no way a handful of men could hold out against Howe's veterans once the fort was surrounded. To add to his remorse, he had to watch the action in utter frustration from Fort Lee on the New Jersey shore, and the story was told that he saw the final rout of his troops with tears in his eyes.

Four days later the British general Charles Cornwallis led a surprise attack on Fort Lee, and Nathanael Greene, who was in charge there, barely got his men out in time to avoid another crushing defeat, losing most of his stores and equipment in the process. Taken together, the fall of the two forts cost the Americans three thousand men, 150 precious cannon, twelve thousand rounds of artillery ammunition, four hundred thousand cartridges, plus tents, provisions, clothing, and other equipment that were all but irreplaceable. It was one of the most costly defeats of the entire war and an unnecessary one that could be blamed on Washington's willingness to accept the advice of his subordinate officers rather than following his own, more prudent hunches. In any case, the Hudson forts were now abandoned, the rebel flag no longer flew over the island of Manhattan, and the way to New Jersey lay open to the British.

With Cornwallis in pursuit, Washington's "wretched remains of a broken army" ran for its life across the flatlands of New Jersey, barely eluding the British after each halt they made. Washington's rear guard was just leaving New Brunswick as Cornwallis' van marched in and the Virginian reported to Congress, "The Enemy are fast advancing, some of 'em in sight now." In every town the rebel army passed through, loyalists were emerging from hiding, confident that the only force capable of resisting the British was gone, not to return. Men appeared by the hundreds to swear their loyalty to the King and queued up to receive from the British green uniforms that marked them as loyalist troops. Men who had sat on the fence, waiting for the shape of the future to come into focus, now concluded that it did not belong to the insurgents and took an oath of allegiance to George III.

Despite a stream of polite requests from Washington, Charles Lee did not march to join him (the vain, ambitious Lee had concluded that the army would be better off if he were in command, and was doing everything he could to maintain his independence of Washington), and Washington, approaching the Delaware River, admitted in a letter to his brother, John Augustine, "I think the game is pretty near up." On all sides the militiamen were deserting and except for the absence of boats — which Washington had ordered collected and hidden — there was nothing to prevent the British from crossing the Delaware and moving on Philadelphia. Members of Congress, understandably nervous, hastily withdrew from the capital and moved to Baltimore on December 12. The next day Major General Charles Lee — whom some Americans ranked as Washington's equal, if not his superior, in ability — was captured by a British patrol and to a public already sated with bad news it began to appear that the end was truly in sight.

As the weather turned cruelly cold, General Howe decided to call an end to the campaign and returned to New York after establishing a chain of posts between Hackensack and Trenton, but Washington, facing the disappearance of his army when their enlistments expired at year's end, had the luxury of no such options. Characteristically, he settled for action, knowing he must make the most of the waning days of December, and on Christmas night, 1776, led a force of about twenty-four hundred men across the ice-choked Delaware and overwhelmed a Hessian garrison in Trenton. What made the attack even more audacious in hindsight was that the plan had called for two other American parties to cross the river below Washington's position, in a movement reminiscent of the surprise of Jumonville in 1754; but both of those contingents had turned back in the face of the violent storm. Washington had done it on his own, and a week later, after entreating his twelve hundred Continentals to remain with him for another month even though their enlistments had expired, he was on the New Jersey side of the Delaware again.

Stunned by the rebels' surprise victory at Trenton, Howe sent Cornwallis out to "bag the fox," and by nightfall on January 2 he had Washington's army hemmed in against the Delaware and was planning to attack in the morning. But at dawn the entire American army had vanished, having stolen away in the night undetected by the British, and on January 3 they won another battle in Princeton, left town just ahead of the oncoming Cornwallis, and made their way to Morristown, where they could spend the winter in safety.

Those final hours of 1776 and the opening days of 1777 were, in many respects, the finest of George Washington's military career. In the face of all that the weather and the enemy threw against him, he somehow salvaged what remained of his army and accomplished a near miracle by winning two victories that meant, above all else, that the war of the Revolution would go on and the cause endure. For nearly a year he had been seeking one triumph that might rally the country's waning enthusiasm behind the war effort. Because of his achievement in the face of staggering odds the army lived to fight again and the King of France concluded that it might be worth his nation's while to support the Americans against the ancient enemy, Great Britain. There was a marked change for the better in America's morale; new recruits came into camp at Morristown, militia companies in New Jersey and Pennsylvania were arming again; and Washington himself seems to have emerged from the campaign of 1776 with a new confidence, born of the truly momentous achievement.

Not that any of this signified a general improvement in the army — quite the contrary. Washington would never, at any time during the war, have sufficient men or weapons or trained officers or supplies; his soldiers would go hungry, they would freeze in winter and swelter in the summer; the capital would fall to the enemy; there would be attempts to oust him as commander in chief; at least one of his trusted young officers would betray him; and various units of the army would mutiny. But taken all in all, the outlook for the future would never again be quite so bleak as it had been in mid-December of 1776, and it could be said that while the victories at Trenton and Princeton were not conclusive, they signified a turning point and a new beginning.

Yet for all Washington's accomplishment some members of Congress viewed 1777 with dread. The year of the three sevens was also known as the Year of the Hangman, for the last three digits suggesting gibbets that awaited them should the cause fail, and with the coming of spring the British armies were stirring. In the north, General John Burgoyne was moving south from Canada on Lake Champlain toward Fort Ticonderoga and Albany, as part of a plan that called for another British force to strike eastward along the Mohawk and for Howe to move up the Hudson. They were to link up at Albany, thereby severing all connection between the New England states and the rest of the country. But Howe, for reasons of his own, changed his mind and went off with fifteen thousand troops to capture the capital. With his infinite capacity for delay, he did not move from New York until late July and then, instead of marching toward Philadelphia, transported his army by ship and arrived at Head of Elk, in Chesapeake Bay, a month later. For the first time in more than a year, Washington was maneuvered into a battle of positions, and it was the last time he allowed it to happen until Yorktown, when it was he who called the turn. On the banks of Brandywine Creek, Washington's army awaited Howe on September 10 and the battle that commenced the following day was in many respects a repetition of Long Island, with Howe sending a feint against the American center while the main assault fell on the flank. The result resembled Long Island, too: hapless John Sullivan, whose command had been crushed there, saw his raw troops collapse at Brandywine, and Washington — who had insufficient knowledge of the terrain and had been slow to anticipate Howe's intentions — was saved from a shattering defeat only by the fall of darkness. About the only consolation was that the army had not disintegrated in the wake of disaster, and as they retreated toward Philadelphia the commander reported to Congress that the troops were in good spirits, adding, "I hope another time we shall compensate for the losses now sustained."

As Howe moved ponderously on Philadelphia, Congress fled again — first to Lancaster and then to York, Pennsylvania. (In Paris, when Benjamin Franklin was informed that Howe had captured Philadelphia, he replied, "No, Philadelphia has captured Howe" — and so it proved.) An American attempt to make a stand west of the capital was repulsed not by the enemy but by a violent thunderstorm that soaked their powder and made fighting impossible, and on October 4, after the British occupied Philadelphia, the two opposing forces met again at Germantown. Here an overly ambitious, two-pronged attack conceived by Washington failed in part because of a heavy fog that made communications and recognition virtually impossible, and in part because of determined British resistance that delayed one American wing long enough to prevent it from joining the other. The battle ended in murky chaos and a panicky retreat, yet ironically it raised the spirits of the Americans because so many of them believed they had *almost* won.

A week before Christmas, Washington's army went into winter quarters at Valley Forge, selected because it lay between the British in Philadelphia and Congress at York. Little else recommended it. So many refugees from the capital had moved into neighboring settlements that no buildings were available for the army, and until mid-January, when some rudimentary log huts were completed, the army — including Washington — faced the onset of winter camped on the ground and in tents. Barefoot and half-naked, many of them froze to death; hundreds of horses perished of starvation; and before the winter ended nearly one-fourth of the men who had gone to Valley Forge were dead of privation. Actually, the winter was relatively mild, but while the enemy rested warm and serene in Philadelphia, the rebels huddled in makeshift huts and went without food, bitterly cursing the Pennsylvania farmers who were selling produce to the British for cash. Strangely, morale never sank to the low point that preceded the battle of Trenton, even though the ordeal was almost beyond the capacity of men to endure. "God grant we may never be brought to such a wretched condition again." Nathanael Greene wrote Washington. The worst of it, Washington observed, was that the army

suffered far more from the neglect of fellow Americans, who were guilty of graft and speculation or simply of ignoring the troops, than they did at the hands of the enemy.

The remarkable aspect of the winter was that the army emerged from the ordeal an entirely new force, largely as a result of what they had learned from a Prussian officer named Friedrich Wilhelm Augustus von Steuben. Speaking almost no English, the European volunteer somehow managed to inculcate a respect for discipline and the rudiments of drill and the manual of arms into the raw American boys, and the first demonstration of his teachings came on a particularly historic occasion. General Orders for Tuesday, May 5, 1778, called for the brigades to pass in review, after which "the whole Army will *Huzza!* 'Long Live the King of France.'" The men in the ranks at Valley Forge were honoring Louis of France because their commander had been formally notified of an alliance with that country, signed in the wake of Horatio Gates' stunning victory over Burgoyne at Saratoga in October. After learning the news, Washington wrote to Congress, "I believe no event was ever received with more heartfelt joy." As well it might have been, since it meant an increasing flow of the arms, ammunition, uniforms, and financial aid already received from France as well as the services of one of the world's great navies, without which the Americans would always be at the mercy of the British fleet.

In the meantime, an old face had returned to the American camp and the British army had a new commander in chief. Charles Lee had been exchanged after a year and a half of comfortable imprisonment in New York (during which time, it was learned long afterward, he had discussed with Admiral Howe a plan for defeating the rebel army). William Howe had resigned his command and set sail for England and his replacement, Sir Henry Clinton, immediately discovered how the nature of the war was being altered as a consequence of the Franco-American alliance. From London he received orders to send five thousand troops to the West Indies for an attack on the French island of St. Lucia, and another three thousand to St. Augustine in Florida. He was to abandon Philadelphia and take the remainder of his army to New York, which seemed to indicate that operations in North America were about to become of secondary importance in a widening conflict. In any event, Clinton had never taken much stock in Howe's decision to divide the British forces (an opinion reinforced by the defeat at Saratoga), and on June 18, 1778, he abandoned Philadelphia.

The move caught Washington by surprise but he saw at once that an opportunity had been handed him to strike a crippling blow at the British by hitting Clinton's long, strung-out army from the flank with a strong force. On June 28, a day of incredible heat, Washington caught up with Clinton near Monmouth Court House and sent Charles Lee with the vanguard of the army to attack the enemy's line of march. Lee had already voiced opposition to such a plan at a council of war in Valley Forge, saying that it would be "criminal" to bring on a general engagement, and when he approached the enemy it was without much conviction; he was slow to move and Clinton was given time to concentrate his forces, and then to attack. Washington galloped to the front to find Lee's men retreating, demanded an explanation, and when Lee produced none, reputedly swore "till the leaves shook on the trees." Then he took personal charge of the fight, with a result that the young Marquis de Lafayette never forgot: the retreat stopped and "all along the lines" Washington rode "amid the shouts of the soldiers, cheering them by his voice and example and restoring to our standard the fortunes of the fight. I thought then, as now, that never had I beheld so superb a man." But a real counterstroke was impossible; the men, as one officer said, were "beat out with heat and fatigue," and the golden chance to cut up Clinton's army was gone, irretrievably. When day broke the next morning the British had vanished.

What was significant about the affair was not the apparent timidity of Lee (he was found guilty of insubordination, suspended from command, and later dropped from the army), but the behavior of the men Steuben had trained, who, before Lee ordered a retreat, had not only stood up to the regulars but had forced them to give ground. That, and the unshakable courage and aggressiveness of Washington. Against the advice of many of his officers, he had done his utmost to bring on a major battle in the belief that the country badly needed a victory to bolster morale, and only the failure of Lee had frustrated the attempt. Not for three more years would he have a similar opportunity; no one could have foreseen it just then, but Monmouth was the last major battle fought in the North.

The war had changed for good with the French alliance. No longer could the British afford to scatter their forces hither and yon; no longer did they have quite the same opportunity of destroying Washington's army with one sudden blow; no longer could their fleet range American waters so freely, untroubled except by the occasional privateer.

Washington, yearning for peace and quiet, often wrote to Lund to inquire after the state of Mount Vernon. "How many Lambs have you had this spring?" he would ask. Was Lund able to obtain paint and oil for the buildings? Was he planning to repair the piazza? But there was to be no respite yet; the Biblical image of his own vine and fig tree might be in his mind, but at hand was the necessity to prosecute the war. And now the French had arrived.

Through Alexander Hamilton, Washington arranged with the French admiral, Count d'Estaing, for a combined land and sea attack on British-held Newport, Rhode Island, and at the end of July the French fleet closed in on the port while rebel forces under John Sullivan moved overland toward it. Unlucky as ever, Sullivan quarreled with the French, a British fleet under Lord Howe approached, and after a violent storm scattered both French and British ships to the winds, Sullivan's men were pinned down by the British garrison. The first joint American-French operation proved to be, as a Rhode Islander ruefully described it, "the worst concerted and executed of the war."

The long days of summer passed uneventfully for Washington and winter found the troops "better clad and more healthy than they had ever been since the formation of the army," in his opinion. During 1779 the general's only direct involvement in action was at Stony Point, on the Hudson, which he directed Anthony Wayne to attack with the bayonet. It was a minor victory, but it demonstrated something new about the Continental Army — its capability of assaulting British regulars even when they held a well-fortified position.

Morristown, New Jersey, was selected again for winter quarters that year and the experience proved the worst the army had ever suffered. Snowdrifts six feet deep, cold beyond all enduring, and lack of food (at one time, Washington wrote, the soldiers were eating "every kind of horse food but hay") produced a wave of sickness and desertions. "We have never experienced a like extremity at any period of the war," the general informed Congress, and he fully expected that "the Army will infallibly disband in a fortnight." Again the troops survived, but not without rumblings of the most ominous sort: several Connecticut regiments that had not been paid for five months and had gone without meat for ten days mutinied, and although they were finally persuaded to remain in camp there was no telling how long they or others would stay. For Washington, almost the only bright spot of

1780 was the return of young Lafayette from France after a year and a half's absence. Otherwise the news was black indeed.

From the South came word of the worst defeat of the war — the fall of Charleston, with the loss of Benjamin Lincoln's entire command of fifty-five hundred men and enormous quantities of supplies. August saw the rout of Horatio Gates' army at Camden, South Carolina, where, it was reported, Gates had fled the field of battle and had not stopped running for three days. In September Washington accidentally discovered the treason of one of his best officers. He had ridden to Hartford to discuss plans with the French general Rochambeau, and en route from that conference stopped off at West Point to visit Benedict Arnold, who commanded the garrison there. Arnold was absent, Washington subsequently informed Congress, and while he was gone some Westchester militiamen picked up a stranger dressed in civilian clothes, trying to get through to the British lines. The man identified himself as John Anderson, and on his person the militiamen found plans of the West Point defenses, summaries of confidential reports written by Washington, and a pass signed by Benedict Arnold.

The pieces of this ugly business fell quickly into place. Anderson turned out to be John André, Clinton's attractive young adjutant general, and Arnold, when he learned that André had been apprehended, had fled from West Point just before Washington's arrival and was rowed downstream to board a British man-of-war. The man generally regarded as the best combat officer in the Continental Army, embittered by a long series of grievances, real or supposed, had gone over to the enemy.

Although André had been taken in civilian clothes and was therefore clearly operating as a spy, there was considerable sympathy for the charming fellow in the American camp and among Washington's officers, but the general was absolutely unbending in his determination that the Englishman be treated according to the rules of war. A Board of Officers questioned André, found him guilty, and condemned him to die, and the findings were passed to the commander in chief. Although he was expected only to approve or confirm those findings, Washington went further: he *directed* that the sentence be carried out, and despite Clinton's efforts to rescue his aide, André was hanged on October 2. There was widespread admiration of the manner in which André had faced death, but Washington doubted that Arnold would suffer regrets over the affair. "He wants feeling!" he observed. "From some traits of his character which have lately come to my knowledge, he seems to have been so hackneyed in villainy, and so lost to all sense of honor and shame that while his faculties will enable him to continue his sordid pursuits, there will be no time for remorse." Whatever Arnold's reasons for betraying his country, they were incomprehensible to Washington. He had the faults common to most mortals, but lack of integrity was not one of them.

Those signs of discontent that had showed themselves in the mutiny of the Connecticut regiments were growing. In January of 1781 privates and noncoms of the Pennsylvania Line mutinied, fired on the troops who tried to restrain them, and marched from Morristown to Philadelphia with their arms and artillery to demand the redress of their grievances. Pennsylvania authorities negotiated with them and ended by discharging more than half of the men from the army, but there was no blinking the justice of the complaints, which centered on hunger, privation, the lack of pay, and longevity of service. Later in the month, when there was a mutiny of New Jersey troops, it began to look as if the army would fall apart completely, despite all of Washington's efforts. That winter, out of necessity, he was making little effort to hold onto his troops; he let them leave camp when their enlistments expired so that those who remained would have enough to eat. "At what point this defection will stop, or how extensive it may prove, God only knows," he wrote the New England governors, but he was not relying on Providence. After the shattering experience with the Pennsylvania mutiny he took a hard line with the New Jersey soldiers and ordered a detachment at West Point to "compel the Mutineers to unconditional submission, and . . . to grant no terms while they are with Arms in their hands in a state of resistance." In a situation that demanded harsh measures he was no man to hang back: the New Jersey troops were rounded up, two ringleaders executed, and order was restored.

With spring came signs of hope. After five years of intermittent debate and equivocation, the states at last ratified the Articles of Confederation originally proposed by Richard Henry Lee at the time he offered his resolution for independence in 1776. The Second Continental Congress ceased to exist as such and became, instead, The United States in Congress Assembled, suggesting that there might be some permanence to the notion of unity after all. In the South, which had become the scene of most of the fighting, Nathanael Greene was now in command, and although he was outnumbered by the British and unable to win a major victory, he handled his little army so effectively, playing at hare and hounds with the pursuing Cornwallis, that the enemy was eventually forced out of Georgia and the Carolinas, except for bases at Savannah and Charleston. In the spring of 1781, after suffering a stinging defeat at Cowpens and losing a fourth of his army at Guilford Court House, Cornwallis resolved to carry the war into Virginia, and with that decision the long-awaited denouement approached. Cornwallis sent a strong detachment into the state under the renegade Benedict Arnold, who was now a British brigadier, and Washington, sensing an opportunity to inflict a blow on the British and capture Arnold — which he described as "an event particularly agreeable to this country" — dispatched Lafayette to the South in February with about twelve hundred men. The movement was to be part of a combined operation, with the French fleet convoying a similar number of French soldiers to Virginia by sea.

By May the British were pouring into Virginia. Major General William Phillips had arrived by sea; Cornwallis, after resting his troops, marched into the state; and a contingent from Clinton's New York garrison arrived, bringing the total to about seventy-two hundred men. Vastly outnumbered, Lafayette retired to the interior of Virginia, from where he commented wryly to Washington, "Were I anyways equal to the enemy, I should be extremely happy in my present command, but I am not strong enough even to get beaten." By June, help was on the way. Anthony Wayne and three Pennsylvania regiments joined Lafayette; Virginia militia and Continentals arrived; and Cornwallis, concluding that he should establish closer communications with Clinton in New York, seized Yorktown and Gloucester, two little towns facing each other on the York River, and fortified them.

On May 21, in Wethersfield, Connecticut, Washington and Rochambeau had met and the French admiral reluctantly consented to a joint attack on New York, to be launched in concert with the West Indian fleet under De Grasse. By June the army of Louis XVI was on the march at last, swinging down the roads from Newport, across Connecticut, and on to a rendezvous with Washington's Continentals at North Castle, near the Hudson. Some skirmishing near New York indicated that the proposed attack on that city would not be easy and then word came that De Grasse had decided to sail for the Chesapeake area instead of New York. He would remain there, he

informed Washington, until October — no later. The alternative was inaction, and after Washington replied that "It has been judged expedient to turn our attention towards the South," the allied armies of France and America were ferried across to the west bank of the Hudson during the third week of August and began marching southward.

In advance went the Americans — men from New England, New York, and New Jersey, men who had fought at Bunker Hill, Trenton, Princeton, Germantown, and Monmouth; and behind them came the French — Soissonnais in white coats with rose-colored facings; Bourbonnais in white and black; Saintonge in white and green; and the Royal Deux-Ponts in blue coats with yellow facings and cuffs. Through Trenton they marched, crossed the Delaware, and went on to Philadelphia and Head of Elk, where they boarded transports furnished by De Grasse for the last leg of the trip to Williamsburg, Virginia.

Clinton, assuming that the armies intended to strike Staten Island to cover the entrance of a French fleet into New York harbor, had not moved, and by the time the French and Americans crossed the Delaware it was too late for him to stop them. Tight security had controlled the operation; Washington had not even trusted the Congress to know his plans until the last moment, and not until August 27 did he inform the members that "a very considerable Detachment of the American Army and the whole of the French Troops" were on the march for Virginia. Two weeks later, on September 10, he spent a few days at Mount Vernon — his first visit there since he became commander in chief six years earlier. He was introduced to three step-granddaughters and a step-grandson, accepted his stepson Jack Custis' offer to become a member of his staff, and after writing Lafayette, telling him to "keep Lord Cornwallis safe, without Provisions or Forage untill we arrive," rode off toward Yorktown. Between September 14 and 24 the French and American contingents arrived, joining Lafayette and some French troops already landed by De Grasse, and eventually there were sixteen thousand of them — Americans camped on the right and French on the left — forming a huge semicircle around Cornwallis' defenses.

What had made this possible was a crucial sea battle won by De Grasse earlier in September. A British fleet under Admirals Graves and Hood had left New York on the first, intending to head off De Grasse, but the French had won the race to the Chesapeake, took up position in the James River to prevent Cornwallis from escaping to the south, and plugged up the mouth of the York River. When the British ships arrived they were outnumbered and, in the Battle of the Capes, badly outmaneuvered by the French. Finally Graves abandoned the attempt to rescue Cornwallis and sailed off to New York, leaving the general to his fate. "We cannot succour him, nor venture to keep the sea any longer," Graves admitted, and from then on the end was predictable.

On October 9 George Washington touched off the first shot in a cannon barrage that continued through the night and for five successive days while American and French infantrymen pushed parallel siege lines forward inexorably. On the night of October 14 two British redoubts were stormed by bayonet and taken and the next day Cornwallis informed Clinton that his situation was critical. There was an abortive British effort to escape by way of Gloucester, and when that failed Cornwallis concluded that it would be "wanton and inhuman to the last degree to sacrifice the lives of this small body of gallant soldiers" and he wrote Clinton to tell him that he would have to capitulate.

On the morning of October 17, 1781, a lone figure in scarlet and white appeared on a parapet facing the French army and began beating out the request for a parley on his drum. One Pennsylvania officer remembered that he had "never heard a drum equal to it — the most delightful music to us all." It was a message the American commander in chief had been awaiting for six years. In reply to Cornwallis' request for a twenty-four hour cessation of hostilities, Washington responded that he would "listen to such terms for the surrender . . . as are admissible," and on October 19 the capitulation agreement was signed. On the following day eight thousand British and German troops, their flags cased, marched out of the Yorktown fortifications between two half-mile-long lines of French and American soldiers whose colors waved above them in the breeze. In dirge time the British band played a popular tune of the day, called "The World Turn'd Upside Down," while Cornwallis' veterans moved slowly forward to stack their arms in a field.

If Washington had hoped to enjoy a moment of personal triumph by receiving Cornwallis' sword, he was disappointed. Not surprisingly, the British general refused to participate in the last rites and, pleading indisposition, sent a deputy, General Charles O'Hara, to handle the mortifying business. Courteously, Washington indicated that deputy should deal with deputy, and he nominated General Benjamin Lincoln, who had been humiliated by the British at Charleston, to act for him. At the end of the day Washington gave a dinner for O'Hara, a military nicety characteristic of eighteenth-century warfare, and afterward worked with his two secretaries on a brief, matter-of-fact report to Congress. Enclosing with it copies of his correspondence with Cornwallis and what he called the "Definitive Capitulation," he revealed his emotions only to the extent of saying that the important event had occurred "at an earlier period than my most sanguine Hopes had induced me to expect," and expressed his satisfaction at the performance of the army, which had filled his "Mind with the highest pleasure & Satisfaction."

What is so often forgotten is the long, drawn-out aftermath of Yorktown — the two years that separated Cornwallis' surrender and the signing of a peace treaty — a frustrating period during which Washington had to keep watch over Clinton's army in New York, expecting at any moment that hostilities might commence again, wondering how he could hold his own army together when he lacked money to pay them or clothing to keep them warm. Fighting continued on the western frontier; there was a potentially dangerous British force in Charleston, South Carolina; and there was no positive indication of when the war would end.

In the wake of the triumph at Yorktown, Washington had suffered the loss of his stepson, Jack Custis, who contracted "camp fever" during the siege and died shortly afterward. Washington stopped at Mount Vernon for a few days after the funeral, then made his way northward in November with Martha, traveling by way of Annapolis and Philadelphia, where he was embarrassed by the acclaim he received on all sides, and finally rode to Newburgh on the Hudson, where the army was going into winter quarters, and where he would face once again the problem of raising money and recruiting men. Rumors of peace came to his ears again and again, but he was skeptical. In his opinion the talk of a settlement was a trick on the part of the British "calculated to quiet the Minds of their own people, & to lull the exertions of ours." Even when he learned that George III's war minister, Lord North, had resigned and that Clinton had been replaced by Sir Guy Carleton as commander in America, he continued to argue that the talk of peace was only talk and would be followed by a reopening of hostilities once the British had dealt with the French. Time wore on and gradually Washington's pessimism waned, but not until April of 1783, when he was informed that a treaty of peace had brought an end to the conflict that had gone on for eight years, did he entirely relax his vigilance and his concern for the welfare of the army.

On two separate occasions during this period, Washington made decisions that profoundly affected the future of the nation. In May, 1782, he received from a colonel named Lewis Nicola a letter summarizing the grievances of the army — largely having to do with the back pay owed the men — and blaming the situation on the inadequacy of Congress and the weakness of republics in general. It was plain, Nicola argued, that the military man who had led the army to victory in war must also lead the nation in peace, and he proposed that Washington be designated king and take charge of the chaotic situation. (The title of king troubled Nicola, since monarchy and tyranny were so interrelated in people's minds, and he confessed that a more suitable title should be found; but the crux of his suggestion was that George Washington become George I of America.)

It was apparent to everyone that the Congress in Philadelphia was virtually helpless: there was no money in the treasury to pay off foreign loans or to meet current expenses of government, much less pay the army, and Nicola's proposal was by no means an isolated one. There was talk in the capital that efforts should be made to force a crown on Washington, and the talk had even turned to suggestions of alternative leaders, should Washington decline. In Newburgh, Washington responded immediately to Nicola, stating that "no occurrence in the course of the war has given me more painful sensations than your information of there being such ideas existing in the army." Nor could Nicola have found a person "to whom your schemes are more disagreeable." Washington was fully aware of the injustices suffered by the troops and would do his utmost to remedy them, but in the meantime Nicola should "banish these thoughts from your Mind" and never again communicate them to anyone. That, Washington may have thought, would be the end of it.

Suddenly, the victory at Yorktown had given the people and the army a vision of peace, but the vision was clouded by questions concerning the nature of the government that must be established for the future. Would it be some sort of union of the states, held together by the now feeble, bankrupt Congress? Or would it take the form of an alliance of separate, sovereign states? Whatever happened, it seemed increasingly likely that Congress, discredited and weak, was unlikely to provide the cement needed to bind the nation together, and when certain people

discussed these matters it occurred to them that the army was the only institution possessing sufficient strength to accomplish anything.

In March of 1783 Washington received a copy of an anonymous summons to all officers announcing a mass meeting where methods of settling grievances would be aired. Although it was not known at the time that the Newburgh Address, as it was called, had been written by an aide to General Horatio Gates, the identity of the author was far less important than the burden of his message. Addressing his fellow soldiers, he described the ingratitude of a nation that "tramples upon your rights, disdains your cries, and insults your distresses," and proposed boldly that the army had two alternatives. One was to "Go starve and be forgotten." The other was to take matters into its own hands and refuse to disband until justice had been obtained, the inference being that the army, freed from civilian interference and responsible to no higher authority than its own, could act in such a manner as to achieve almost any political end it desired. Implicit in all this was that the army might take over the country. Washington had already received strong indications from Philadelphia that such a movement was afoot, but his first impression was that it originated not with the military but with a group in the capital. Alexander Hamilton had written him to say that the army should push its claims on the legislators "with moderation but with firmness" and that Washington himself should lead this effort, which would unquestionably be supported by "creditors of the United States." So when the general received the anonymous call for a mass meeting, he had had time to consider "the predicament in which I stand as Citizen and Soldier" and issued an order stating his "disapprobation of such disorderly proceedings." Asserting his authority, he called a meeting of his own for March 15, 1783.

When Washington entered the hall to address his officers he seemed to one of them to be "sensibly agitated," as well he might be. It was not difficult to see that the old wartime camaraderie and respect had been replaced by resentment and anger, and these unfamiliar attitudes were not dispelled as he read his prepared speech. He reminded the men of his own constancy and friendship for them throughout the war; he asked if the author of the Address was not "an insidious foe" of the country, plotting its ruin "by sowing the seeds of discord and separation between the civil and military powers of the continent"; and he urged them to ignore this attempt to overturn the liberties of the country and to behave in such a way that posterity might say, "had this day been wanting, the world had never seen the last stage of perfection to which human nature is capable of attaining."

There was no perceptible change in the mood of his listeners as he concluded his speech; the air of hostility and resentment still hung in the room. For a moment there was an uncomfortable silence, then a rustling as Washington reached into a pocket and pulled out a scrap of paper, remarking that he had a letter from a member of Congress listing the efforts the members were willing to make in behalf of the army. The audience, waiting for him to go on, was stunned to see that the general seemed unable to read the letter. There was a long, embarrassing pause during which Washington appeared to be confused, uncertain what to do, and then he reached into his pocket again and drew out an object that only a few close associates had seen him wear — a pair of spectacles. As he put them on he looked out at the faces of the men he knew and loved so well and remarked quietly, "Gentlemen, you will permit me to put on my spectacles, for I have not only grown grey but almost blind in the service of my country."

It was all that was needed to break the spell — that simple, moving statement to remind them of his absolute devotion to a cause that was theirs as well as his. Many officers were in tears as he read the letter; then he finished, and without a word walked out of the hall, mounted his horse, and rode away. As he had done so often during the war, he fashioned a victory from what seemed an impossible situation, and in a manner thoroughly characteristic — by going direct to the heart of the matter. None of his lengthy, reasoned arguments had won them over; it was his example that counted.

Before the meeting broke up the officers drew up a new address to Congress stating that they "view with abhorrence and reject with disdain the infamous propositions" contained in the anonymous letter. The incipient plot was laid to rest, the danger of armed insurrection ended, and what might have been a tragic aftermath to the years of hardship and suffering averted.

Finally, the war appeared to be ended. An armistice had been agreed to, England having acknowledged the independence of the United States, and it only remained for a definitive peace treaty to be signed. On April 18, 1783, Washington published formal congratulations to the army for having "assisted in protecting the rights of human nature and establishing an asylum for the poor and oppressed of all nations and religions." Congress voted to act on the back pay due each soldier, awarded the officers certificates for five years' additional pay plus six per cent interest on the face amount, and the army was sent home on a furlough that was to last until a peace treaty was signed. (No cash for the men was forthcoming, despite Washington's appeal to Congress that they not send his men home paupers. There simply was no money in the treasury.)

Washington's sense of duty made him remain with the tiny force guarding the lower Hudson until the British finally left New York, and for seven tedious months he was there, taking some time off to wander through the Highlands and the New York frontier, visiting unfamiliar battlefields like Saratoga, and even making some unsuccessful offers for land in the region. There was a good deal of accounting to be done: he had insisted during the war that Congress should pay him nothing beyond his out-of-pocket expenses, and the infinitely detailed reckoning of eight years' service had to be sorted out. As he calculated it, his expenses had amounted to £8,422 16s. 4d. (£1,982 10s. of it for "secret intelligence" he had paid for) and Congress still owed him £1,972 9s. for expenses not previously reimbursed.

He journeyed to Princeton, where Congress was sitting, to discuss arrangements for a peacetime military establishment, and in November he received notice that the British would depart from New York on the twenty-fifth of that month. The peace treaty had been signed in Paris at last.

When Washington and the handful of men who constituted the remnants of the Continental Army rode into the scarred, nearly deserted city, British sailors were rowing out toward the waiting ships in the harbor, and thirteen cannon shots signaled the hoisting of an American flag over the final outpost of George III's empire on the eastern seaboard of the United States. There was a triumphal procession, followed by several days of celebrations — fireworks, official dinners, speeches — and on December 4, at Fraunces Tavern, Washington met with his officers for the last time. Visibly upset, he was unable to eat, and he poured a glass of wine, sent the bottle around the table, and when all the glasses were filled raised his own to say, "With a heart full of love and gratitude, I now take leave of you. I most devoutly wish that your latter days may be as prosperous and happy as your former ones have been glorious and honorable."

In what one eyewitness described as "almost breathless silence," the officers drank; then Washington, his voice choked with emotion, spoke again. "I cannot come to each of you," he said, "but shall feel obliged if each of you will come and take me by the hand." The 280-pound Henry Knox was nearest him; they clasped hands, embraced, and the tears rolled down Washington's cheeks. Every other officer in the room came to bid him farewell in the same manner and Major Benjamin Tallmadge wrote afterward that it was "Such a scene of sorrow and weeping I had never before witnessed." The thought that none of them would see their commander again seemed to him "utterly insupportable."

When it was over Washington left the room, walked past several thin lines of infantrymen to the waterfront, and climbed into a waiting boat while civilians cheered and his officers stood by silent and grief-stricken, watching as he was rowed out into the harbor and across the water to New Jersey on the first leg of his journey home.

At every stop along the way he was detained by people who wanted to shake his hand or speak to him, and on December 23, 1783, he was ushered into the hall in Annapolis, Maryland, where Congress was now sitting. He had come to deliver his resignation to the body that had appointed him commander in chief of the army on a June day eight years before. It was quite apparent that the makeup of Congress had altered substantially since the days of 1775. Virtually all the giants of yesteryear were gone — John Adams and Benjamin Franklin were still in Europe as members of the peace commission; Thomas Jefferson was in Virginia; Samuel Adams, John Hancock, Patrick Henry, and the other fire-eaters had vanished. What was equally evident was that one figure now dominated the American scene — had, indeed, since his appointment as commander in chief in 1775. George Washington was in fact, if not in title, the chief executive of the new nation, having survived the long conflict with reputation not only intact but vastly enhanced, while that of the Congress that appointed him had steadily declined.

Now, as at Fraunces Tavern, Washington's emotions almost got the better of him. He bowed to the delegates, steadied with his left hand a trembling right hand in which he held his speech, and began to read. He congratulated Congress on the achievement of independence, commended his loyal staff to their attention, gave thanks for the support of his countrymen during the war, and then, agitated beyond measure, faltered noticeably before recovering himself and commending "our dearest country to the protection of Almighty God."

"Having now finished the work assigned me, I retire from the great theater of action," he went on, "and, bidding an affectionate farewell to this august body under whose orders I have so long acted, I here offer my commission, and take my leave of all the employments of public life." With that he drew the document from inside his coat and handed it to the president, Thomas Mifflin, as the roomful of legislators dissolved in tears.

It was Christmas Eve of 1783 when George Washington rode up the drive to Mount Vernon past the rows of trees he had planted long ago and found Martha waiting for him in the doorway. Almost nine years had passed since he left her there, promising that he would return in the fall. In the days that followed he tried to sort out his thoughts in letters to friends, among them the young Lafayette, who had been like a son to him in the war. He was free at last, he wrote the Frenchman, "under the shadow of my own vine and my own fig tree," and he had a sense of utmost relief and satisfaction. Ahead stretched a vision of peace and quiet, a time spent "in cultivating the affections of good men and in the practice of the domestic virtues," as he traveled "gently down the stream of life until I sleep with my fathers."

A REBEL RING AROUND BOSTON

The new commander in chief of the army had been at Mount Vernon when the battles of Lexington and Concord were fought; he was in New York, en route to Boston, when he received news of the fighting for Bunker Hill; and not until he arrived in Cambridge was he able to assess the situation at first hand. Strategically, it appeared promising. The map on the facing page, drawn by John Montresor, a British engineer, shows the predicament in which General Thomas Gage found himself. Protruding into the bay, the town of Boston was surrounded on three sides by land held by the rebels — from Charlestown peninsula, where the battle for Bunker Hill was fought, to Dorchester Heights, south of Boston. Of necessity, Gage's lifeline was the British fleet, which commanded the sea approaches to the city. The series of watercolor drawings below, made by a British officer, shows the outlook from Beacon Hill. Dorchester Heights is visible in the first frame; the large house in the second section is John Hancock's; Bunker and Breed's Hills are to the right of the steeple in the last panel; and the entire horizon, bristling with entrenchments, was in rebel hands. Despite the appearances that the British were in a tight spot, Washington soon learned that the army under his command was in near-desperate straits — short of food, clothing, qualified officers, and all the necessities of war. There was also a question of how many men would remain in the ranks when their enlistments expired, and to this trying business Washington gave his first and longest attention. "Such a dirty, Mercenary spirit" pervaded the army, he wrote, "that I should not be at all surprizd at any disaster that may happen. . . . Could I have foreseen what I have, & am like to experience, no consideration upon Earth should have induced me to accept this Command." Instead of the twenty thousand men he considered essential, he had, on January 9, 1776, only 8,200, of whom only 5,600 were present and fit for duty, and two thousand of those lacked muskets. Despite all the disappointments, however, he was laying plans to oust the British from Boston.

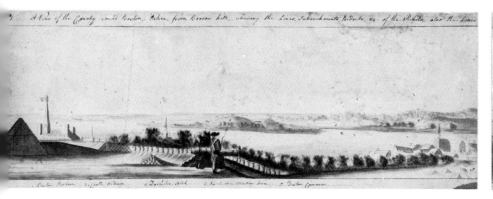

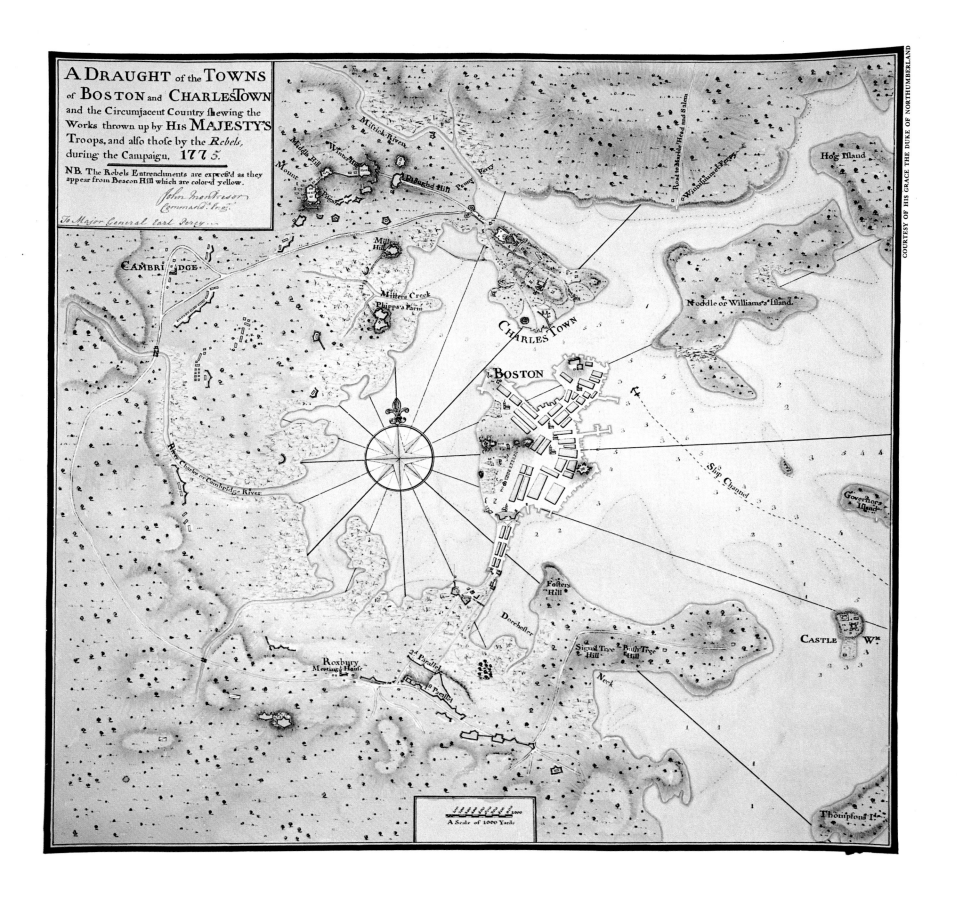

A DRAUGHT of the TOWNS of BOSTON and CHARLESTOWN and the Circumjacent Country shewing the Works thrown up by HIS MAJESTY'S Troops, and also those by the *Rebels*, during the Campaign, 1775.

NB. The Rebels Entrenchments are expres'd as they appear from Beacon Hill which are color'd yellow.

John Montresor
Command'd Troops.

To Major General Earl Percy.

A Scale of 1000 Yards

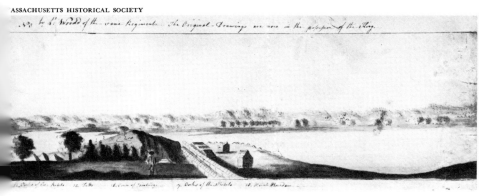

121

THE SIEGE IS BROKEN

In Henry Knox, the portly young Bostonian portrayed in the painting above by Charles Willson Peale, Washington found the aggressive, energetic kind of aide he liked. A former bookseller, Knox had some limited experience in an artillery company, and Washington sent him off to Fort Ticonderoga to collect the fort's heavy guns. Knox hired teamsters and oxen, rented or built sleds, and in the dead of winter, through heavy snows and sudden thaws, brought the cannon eastward across the mountains in what was truly an epic accomplishment. When he delivered fifty-nine pieces of ordnance of all calibers — a "noble train of artillery," as he called it — to the commander in chief, the fate of British-held Boston was settled. On March 4, in a prodigious night's work, the cannon were placed in position on Dorchester Heights, commanding the town and much of the anchorage, and William Howe, who had replaced Thomas Gage, chose to abandon the city and sail to Halifax with his army and some twelve hundred loyalists. On March 17, 1776, Washington's men entered the city.

As the note at right suggests, authorities at Harvard were not happy about the manner in which Washington's troops "greatly defaced & Damaged" the college buildings where they were quartered during the siege of Boston. One of the many skirmishes that occurred during this period was sketched by Archibald Robertson, an officer in the Royal Engineers. His drawing (above) shows the action on January 14, 1776, when about eight hundred British regulars crossed the ice to Dorchester Neck, took a few prisoners, and burned some empty houses. Six weeks later, on the heels of what Robertson called "a most astonishing nights work," rebel guns positioned on the same heights cannoned the British, forcing them to evacuate Boston on St. Patrick's Day. The enemy's departure was commemorated in a special medal commissioned by Congress (below), executed in Paris in 1786. One of the medals was struck in gold and presented to Washington.

Memorial to the Gen.l Court for Repairing the College

Votd 3. That the following Memorial be presented to the General Court of this Colony:—

To the Hon.ble Council & House of Representatives of the Colony of the Massachusetts Bay in New England in General Court assembled.

The Memorial of the President & Fellows of Harvard College in Cambridge humbly sheweth

That immediately after the Commencement of the present War, in defense of American Liberties, on the 19th of April 1775, all the Buildings & Appurtenances of the S.d College were entered, & ever since have been occupied by the Army, then suddenly assembled & formed, as Barracks, & for other necessary Purposes.

That S.d Buildings, with their Appurtenances, are greatly defaced & Damaged by the Army, so that the Repairs must amount to a considerable Sum, if put into the same good Order as when occupied by the Students.

123

A SOLEMN
DECLARATION

On June 7, 1776, Washington's fellow-Virginian
Richard Henry Lee introduced a resolution to
Congress "That these United Colonies are,
and of right ought to be, free and independent
states, that they are absolved from all
allegiance to the British Crown, and that all
political connection between them and the State
of Great Britain is, and ought to be, totally
dissolved." There was opposition to the
proposal, mainly from conservative members
from Pennsylvania, New York, and South
Carolina, and debate was postponed until
July 1. Meanwhile, a committee to draft
a declaration, consisting of Thomas Jefferson,
John Adams, Benjamin Franklin, Roger Sherman,
and Robert Livingston, was appointed and
on June 28 their draft — largely the work
of Jefferson — was completed and presented
to Benjamin Harrison, the president pro tem.
The moment was depicted (right) by Edward Savage
and Edward Pine. On July 2 the great decision
was taken; on the night of July 4 the document
was printed; and early in August it was finally
signed by the members, who used the inkstand
illustrated above. Washington and his army
were in New York on July 9 when he received
a resolution proclaiming that the "UNITED
STATES OF AMERICA" were "free and independent,"
and he ordered that the Declaration be read "with
an audible voice" to the troops and expressed
the hope that "this important event will
serve as a fresh incentive to every officer
and soldier to act with fidelity and courage."

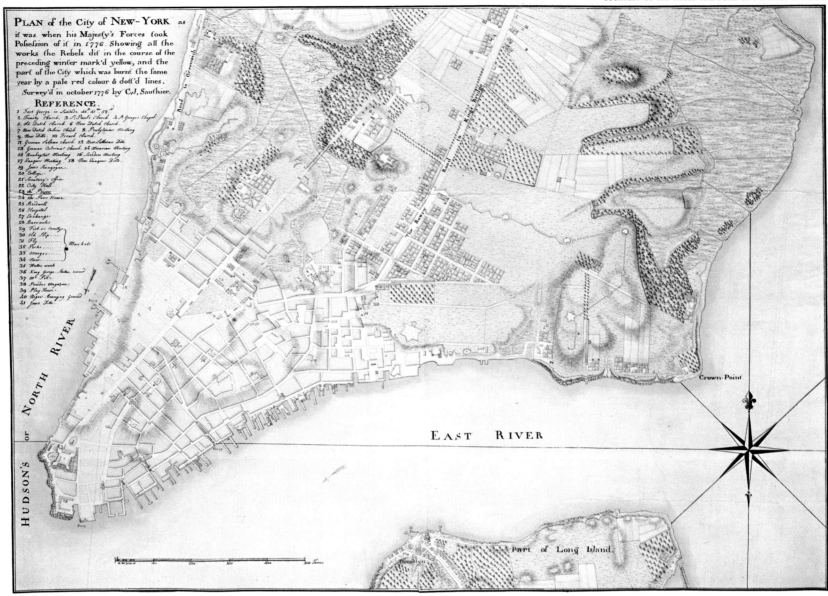

THE BRITISH RETURN

So certain was Washington that New York would be the next British objective that he headed there immediately after turning command of the Boston area over to Artemas Ward, and by April he was writing, "I have brought the whole Army which I had in the New England Governments . . . to this place." At once the troops were set to work building fortifications — many of which are indicated on the British map reproduced above. The settled area of the city is at the tip of Manhattan Island; beyond are farms and a handful of houses. At the bottom of the map is a spur of Long Island, the village and outskirts of Brooklyn. When the British appeared at last on June 29, 1776, they came with a vengeance; by August 12 ten ships of the line, twenty frigates, hundreds of transport vessels, and some 32,000 professional soldiers had arrived, comprising the greatest expeditionary force ever sent out from Britain's shores. On July 12, Captain Archibald Robertson, a British engineer and deputy quartermaster general, sketched the fleet at anchor off Staten Island, where the troops were disembarked (right). In the foreground are the farmlands of Staten Island; off to the left is Long Island; and in the distance are the Narrows. The vessel under sail is the flagship of Admiral Howe, whose brother, General William Howe, commanded the army. The bay where the ships ride at anchor was the staging area of the August 22 amphibious assault on Long Island.

On July 9, 1776, the Declaration of Independence was read to the soldiers in Washington's army in New York and that evening, local Sons of Liberty climbed the statue of George III that dominated Bowling Green, attached ropes to the gilded horse and rider, and pulled it to the ground. Although Washington deplored this "appearance of riot," the statue was to serve him well. Most of the lead was taken to Connecticut, where it was melted and molded into 42,088 bullets. The king's head fared somewhat better: it was retrieved by New York loyalists, hidden, and later shipped to England, where it reposed in the home of Lord Townshend, who liked to show it to friends as an "instance of American loyalty." The engraving at right is one of a series made in Germany to illustrate the British occupation of New York in 1776.

LONG ISLAND
DISASTER

Washington's first pitched battle with William Howe resulted in disaster. When British troops waded ashore on the western end of Long Island they were unopposed — Washington having thought until the last moment that the main attack would fall on New York. The battle was decided before it began: Howe learned that the rebel left was unprotected and led ten thousand men through unguarded Jamaica Pass in a brilliant flank attack that caught the Americans by surprise. The map opposite depicts the engagement of the British and American forces on August 27. The only effective rebel resistance was made by Maryland and Delaware regiments, who held off the British and Germans near Gowanus Creek and a mill pond long enough for the rest of the army to escape into the Brooklyn lines. Inexplicably, Howe did not move against the trapped foe; he contented himself with digging approaches to their lines, permitting the entire American force to escape by boat to Manhattan on the night of August 29. Despite his failure to destroy the rebel army, George III was grateful for the victory and conferred on Howe the red ribbon of the Bath, which he wears in the contemporary engraving at left. Below, the ships of Howe's fleet are seen at anchor off Long Island, in a painting by one of Howe's officers.

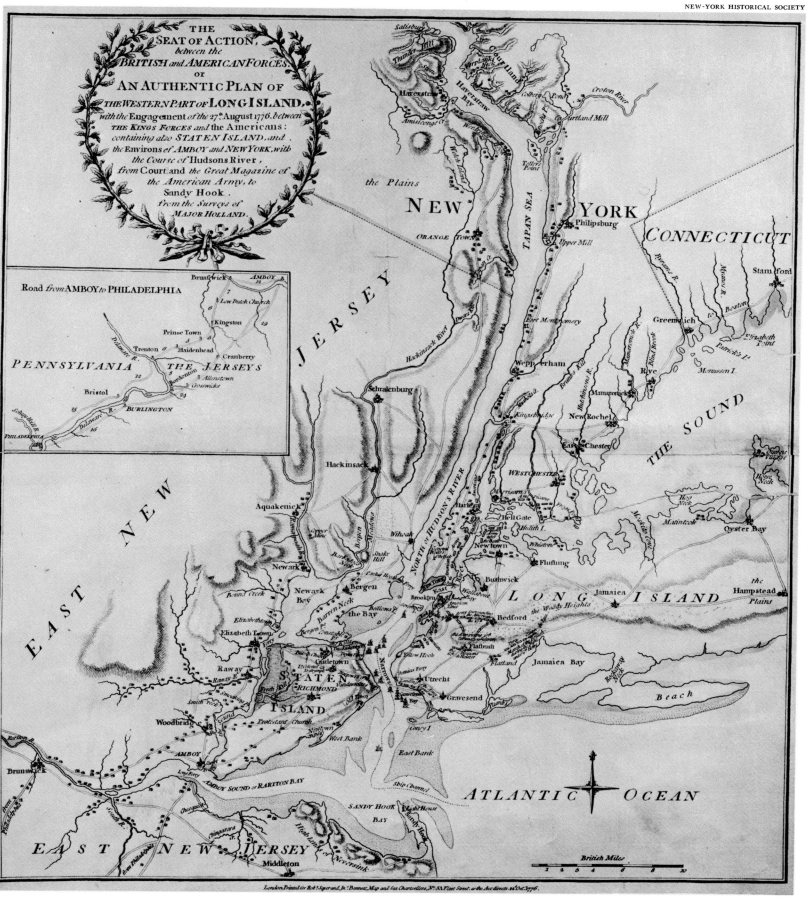

THE
SEAT OF ACTION,
between the
BRITISH and AMERICAN FORCES
or
AN AUTHENTIC PLAN OF
THE WESTERN PART OF LONG ISLAND,
with the Engagement of the 27th August 1776, between
THE KINGS FORCES and the Americans:
containing also STATEN ISLAND, and
the Environs of AMBOY and NEW YORK, with
the Course of Hudsons River,
from Court and the Great Magazine of
the American Army, to
Sandy Hook.
from the Surveys of
MAJOR HOLLAND.

Road from AMBOY to PHILADELPHIA

PENNSYLVANIA   THE JERSEYS

London, Printed for Robt Sayer and Jno Bennett, Map and Sea Chart sellers, No 53 Fleet Street, as the Act directs 15 Oct. 1776.

MANHATTAN IS LOST

On September 15 Howe was on the move again, this time making another unopposed landing at Kips Bay on the East River above New York. Archibald Robertson sketched the movement (above), which was preceded by such a withering cannonade from the British frigates that the rebel militia fled "with the utmost precipitation." Opposite, top, by the same artist, is a view of the Hollow Way, where rebels on Harlem Heights, at right center, won a minor victory but lost an able officer, Colonel Thomas Knowlton (shown here in a sketch by John Trumbull). In the distance in Robertson's drawing is Fort Washington, overlooking the Hudson River. Built by the rebels during the summer of 1776, this bastion and Fort Lee on the New Jersey bank of the river were supposed to prevent the British from sailing up the Hudson. But it proved a vain hope: on October 9, six ships ran the gantlet successfully, as depicted in Dominic Serres' painting opposite (bottom). The view is to the north and shows the vessels abreast a chevaux-de-frise, or chain of obstructions that had been stretched from Fort Lee, at the left, across the river to Fort Washington (top right).

THE HUDSON FORTS

Following an inconclusive engagement at White Plains, in Westchester, Howe moved against Fort Washington. Thomas Davies' watercolor above shows British flatboats, filled with troops, under way down the Harlem River to attack the fort (barely visible on the heights) while the frigate *Pearl*, at extreme right, fires from the Hudson. Surrounded, the defenders had no chance, and when the fort fell three thousand men and their equipment were lost. A few days later a British force under General Cornwallis crossed the Hudson (below, in another picture by Davies), climbed the Palisades over an unguarded path, and seized Fort Lee. The loss of the two forts was one of the costliest of the war and resulted in part from the overconfidence of their commander, Nathanael Greene, who developed into the best field general in the rebel army. This portrait of him was painted from life by Charles Willson Peale.

133

*NEW YORK
OCCUPIED*

While the rebels still held New York some of Washington's officers urged that the city be burned to keep the enemy from using it as a base, but horrified Congressmen vetoed the proposal. Then the British marched in, as suggested in the German engraving at left, and during the night of September 20, 1776, a disastrous fire (above) broke out in the Whitehall section and destroyed five hundred buildings, including the 180-foot spire of Trinity Church which crashed to the ground in flames. Although both sides accused the other of starting the conflagration, Washington said privately that "Providence, or some good honest fellow, has done more for us than we were disposed to do for ourselves." The drawing by John Trumbull at right reveals something of the dreadful conditions aboard the British prison ship *Jersey,* a rotting hulk anchored off Brooklyn, where captured rebels were interned. This was one of the prisons to which the captives from Fort Washington were taken, and it is indicative of their treatment that of 2,800 men who marched out of the fort when it fell, only eight hundred survivors remained when they were exchanged eighteen months later.

The *American* CRISIS.

NUMBER I.

By the Author of COMMON SENSE.

THESE are the times that try men's souls: The summer soldier and the sunshine patriot will, in this crisis, shrink from the service of his country; but he that stands it NOW, deserves the love and thanks of man and woman. Tyranny, like hell, is not easily conquered; yet we have this consolation with us, that the harder the conflict, the more glorious the triumph. What we obtain too cheap, we esteem too lightly:---'Tis dearness only that gives every thing its value. Heaven knows how to set a proper price upon its goods; and it would be strange indeed, if so celestial an article as FREEDOM should not be highly rated. Britain, with an army to enforce her tyranny, has declared, that she has a right (*not only to* TAX, but) "*to* " BIND *us in* ALL CASES WHATSOEVER," and if being *bound in that manner* is not slavery, then is there not such a thing as slavery upon earth. Even the expression is impious, for so unlimited a power can belong only to GOD.

WHETHER the Independence of the Continent was declared too soon, or delayed too long, I will not now enter into as an argument; my own simple opinion is, that had it been eight months earlier, it would have been much better. We did not make a proper use of last winter, neither could we, while we were in a dependent state. However, the fault, if it were one, was all our own; we have none to blame but ourselves*. But no great deal is lost yet; all that Howe has been doing for this month past is rather a ravage than a conquest, which the spirit of the Jersies a year ago would have quickly repulsed, and which time and a little resolution will soon recover.

I have as little superstition in me as any man living, but my

* " The present winter " (meaning the last) " is worth an " age, if rightly employed, but if lost, or neglected, the whole " Continent will partake of the evil; and there is no punish- " ment that man does not deserve, be he who, or what, or " where he will, that may be the means of sacrificing a season " so precious and useful." COMMON SENSE.

THE TIMES THAT TRIED MEN'S SOULS

An inspired message that rallied the faltering American cause after Washington's flight through New Jersey was written by a transplanted Englishman, Thomas Paine, who was with the army during its humiliating retreat. Paine's earlier pamphlet, *Common Sense,* published in January of 1776, had called Americans to action, urging them to fight for liberty, and had much to do with the groundswell for independence. *The American Crisis,* the first and most popular pamphlet in a series published under that title, was partially written in or near Newark, during a pause in the retreat, and completed in Philadelphia, where Paine went to have it printed. Published on December 19, it was read to Washington's troops on the west bank of the Delaware River, while they waited for boats to take them across toward Trenton on Christmas night. The portrait of Paine was painted by John Trumbull in 1788. The desperate plight of the army described so vividly by Paine is suggested by the broadside on the opposite page, in which men were offered bounties to enlist until year's end.

IN ASSEMBLY, DECEMBER 12, 1776.

WHEREAS there is a Necessity of calling upon the Associators of Pennsylvania, at this inclement Season, to assist in defending their Country threatened with instant Invasion,

Resolved, That over and above all Encouragement heretofore offered, the following Bounties be given to all Volunteers who shall join General WASHINGTON by the several Days hereunder mentioned:

On or before the 20th of this Month —— 10 Dollars.
Between the 20th and 25th —— 7 Dollars.
Between the 25th and 30th —— 5 Dollars.

The Volunteers to be well armed, and with each of them a Blanket, and to remain in the service six Weeks, unless sooner discharged; the Bounty to be paid immediately on their Arrival at Camp; and, that no Time may be lost, the Volunteers are exhorted not to wait at home to be collected into Companies, but that they march off with the utmost Speed, to be formed on their Arrival.

But it is not meant or intended to discourage the Associators from coming, with their Officers, in Battalions or Companies, in the Whole, or in Part, which will be most agreeable,

Resolved, That the first mentioned Bounty of ten Dollars be extended to the Inhabitants of the City and Liberties of Philadelphia not possessed of real Estates, and to all other Volunteers, without Limitation of Property, who have already joined General Washington, and shall serve the above Time.

Extracts from the Minutes.

JOSIAH CRAWFORD, Clerk Pro. Tem.

AMERICA LOSES A GENERAL

When he learned that the British had captured
General Charles Lee on December 13, 1776,
Washington worried lest this "melancholy
intelligence" prove one blow too many for
a public already sated with bad news. Yet it may
have been a blessing in disguise. Lee had been
chafing for months about his subordinate
role; he had ignored Washington's requests to
join him in New Jersey; in correspondence with
Joseph Reed, Washington's aide, he had criticized
the commander in chief's "fatal indecision of mind
which in war is a much greater disqualification
than stupidity"; and after the loss of the Hudson
River forts rumors were rife that the former
British officer would supersede the man who had
presided over so many defeats. Lee's capture
removed from the scene a man who was lining up
allies for a final power struggle with Washington.
Taken to New York, he was held in gentlemanly
confinement and was exchanged in the spring of
1778, before the battle of Monmouth. The
profane, eccentric Lee, who always traveled with
"a troop of dogs," was caricatured (below) by a
contemporary. The engraving at right is a romanticized
conception of his surrender to British dragoons, one
of whom was Banastre Tarleton, shown on the
facing page in a portrait by Sir Joshua Reynolds.

GEORGE III'S GERMAN MERCENARIES

Nothing outraged Americans more than George III's decision to hire troops from a number of petty principalities in Germany for service in America. Actually, the King had to do something of the sort: recruiting was going badly in England and the regular army was spread thin, manning the garrisons of empire around the world. Since many of the mercenaries came from Hesse-Cassel and Hesse-Hanau, they were erroneously called "Hessians," even though substantial numbers were from Brunswick, Waldeck, Anspach-Bayreuth, and Anhalt-Zerbst. By treaty, a prince who furnished subjects to fight for George III received "head money" of more than £7 for each soldier, plus a similar amount for each man killed. In all, nearly thirty thousand Germans came to America during the Revolution, of whom twelve thousand never returned home (at least five thousand deserted, preferring to remain in the New World). These 1784 drawings show, at left, men of the Prinz Carl Regiment; at right, in blue and white, troops of the Knyphausen regiment; and, far right, in green, two jägers, former foresters who were often employed as scouts. The regimental flags include one, at top, that was captured by Washington at Trenton. The caricature is of General Knyphausen, conquerer of Fort Washington, who had a penchant for buttering bread with his thumb. Arriving in America with a fearsome reputation, the Germans were accused of numerous atrocities, as typified by the account on the opposite page. Even the British admitted that they were "Outrageously Licentious and Cruel," but in fairness to the accused, the wonder was that the unfortunate men — most of whom were poverty-stricken peasants, taken from their homes by a press gang, brutalized by officers and noncoms, and sent to fight in a strange land for a king and cause they cared nothing about — were not more barbarous than the Americans made them out to be.

Bucks County, December 14, 1776.

THE PROGRESS of the *British* and *Heffian* Troops through NEW JERSEY, has been attended with fuch fcenes of Defolation and Outrage, as would difgrace the moft barbarous Nations. Among innumerable other inftances the following are authenticated in fuch a manner, as leaves no doubt of their truth.

WILLIAM SMITH, of *Smith's* Farm, near *Woodbridge*, hearing the cries of his daughter, rufhed into the room, and found a *Heffian* Officer attempting to ravifh her, in an agony of rage and refentment, he inftantly killed him ; but the Officer's party foon came upon him, and he now lays mortally wounded at his ruined, plundered dwelling.

On Monday Morning they entered the houfe of SAMUEL STOUT, Efq; in *Hopewell*, where they deftroyed his deeds, papers, furniture and effects of every kind except what they plundered ; they took every horfe away, left his houfe and farm in ruin, injuring him to the value of £2000. in lefs than three hours.

Old Mr. PHILIPS, his Neighbour, they pillaged in the fame manner, and then cruelly beat him.

On Wednefday laft three women came down to the Jerfey fhore in great diftrefs, a party of the American Army went and brought them off, when it appeared that they had been all very much abufed, and the youngeft of them a girl about fifteen, had been ravifhed that morning by a *Britifh* Officer.

A number of young women in *Hopewell*, to the amount of 16, flying from this ravaging and cruel enemy, took refuge on the mountain near Ralph Harts, but information being given of their retreat, they were foon brought down into the *Britifh* Camp, where they have been kept ever fince.

The fine fettlements of *Maidenhead* and *Hopewell* are intirely broke up ; no age, nor fex has been fpared ; the houfes are ftripped of every article of furniture, and what is not portable, is entirely deftroyed ; the ftock of Cattle and Sheep are drove off ; every article of cloathing and houfe linnen feized and carried away ; fcarce a foldier in the army but what has a horfe loaded with plunder ; hundreds of families are reduced from comfort and affluence, to poverty and ruin, left at this inclement feafon to wander through the woods without houfe or cloathing.---- If thefe fcenes of defolation, ruin and diftrefs, do not roufe and animate every man of fpirit to revenge their much injured countrymen and countrywomen, all Virtue, Honour and Courage muft have left this Country, and we deferve all that we fhall meet with, as there can be no doubt the fame fcene will be acted in this Province upon our own Property, and our beloved **Wives** and **Daughters.**

141

A GAMBLE BORN OF DESPERATION

In COUNCIL of SAFETY,

PHILADELPHIA, *December* 8, 1776.

SIR,

THERE is certain intelligence of General Howe's army being yesterday on its march from Brunswick to Princetown, which puts it beyond a doubt that he intends for this city.—This glorious opportunity of signalizing himself in defence of our country, and securing the Rights of America forever, will be seized by every man who has a spark of patriotic fire in his bosom. We entreat you to march the Militia under your command with all possible expedition to this city, and bring with you as many waggons as you can possibly procure, which you are hereby authorized to impress, if they cannot be had otherwise—Delay not a moment, it may be fatal and subject you and all you hold most dear to the ruffian hands of the enemy, whose cruelties are without distinction and unequalled.

By Order of the Council,

DAVID RITTENHOUSE, Vice-President.

To the COLONELS *or* COMMANDING OFFICERS *of the respective Battalions of this* STATE.

TWO O'CLOCK, P. M.

THE Enemy are at Trenton, and all the City Militia are marched to meet them.

The approach of the British toward Philadelphia was cause for considerable alarm in the capital, as the broadside above suggests. On December 12, 1776, Congress adjourned and fled to Baltimore, where they would meet until the danger passed. Meantime, they delegated dictatorial powers to the commander in chief of the army, on whom rested the nation's fleeting hopes. On Christmas night he made an audacious move; embarking the remnants of his army in Durham boats, he crossed the ice-choked Delaware River and surprised the German garrison in Trenton, killing and wounding about thirty, and capturing nearly a thousand. The accomplishment was made possible in part by Colonel John Glover (shown below in a life drawing by Trumbull), whose regiment of Marblehead seamen had evacuated Washington's army from Long Island and who ferried them across the river for the attack on Trenton; but in the main it was a personal triumph for Washington, who had fashioned a victory at the moment when the cause seemed irretrievably lost. John Trumbull's heroic canvas, at left, is far from an accurate depiction of the event, but it captures the drama of the German surrender as Washington offers a hand to the mortally wounded enemy commander, Johann Rall.

TRIUMPH AT PRINCETON

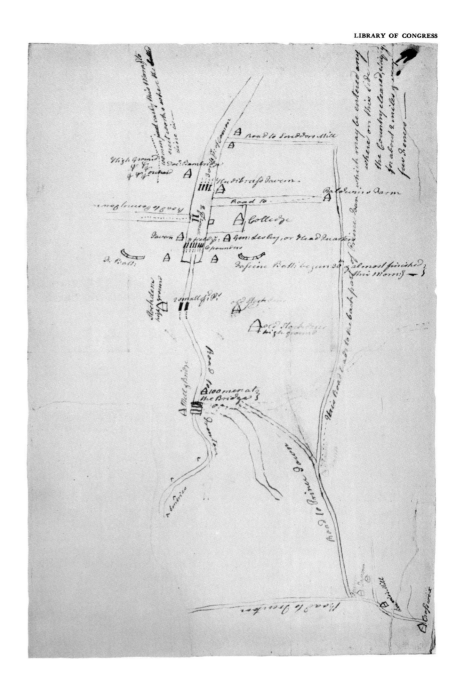

A map received from a spy gave Washington the opportunity to outwit the British again. Thoroughly alarmed by events at Trenton, Howe had sent Cornwallis from Princeton to attack the rebels, whom Washington had led across the Delaware again on December 30. A delaying action fought by several rebel units held off Cornwallis until nightfall on January 2, and he decided to wait until morning to attack. But during the night the Americans vanished; they were marching to Princeton over back roads in a daring move. With his genius for improvisation, Washington had spotted a little-known route (at right, on the spy's map above) that would enable him to slip undetected around the British defenses in the town. Unfortunately, the British sighted a detachment that took the left fork of the road, and the battle began before Washington was ready. It was a near thing: the Americans were almost routed before Washington took personal command, rode out between the two battle lines, and led his men to victory. At left is a painting by William Mercer, the deaf-mute son of an American general mortally wounded in the engagement. His wounded father lies beside his prone white horse in the center of the picture. The calm, mounted officer with drawn sword is undoubtedly meant to be Washington.

COMMANDER'S KIT

OBJECTS: MOUNT VERNON LADIES' ASSOCIATION OF THE UNION

For a man who had been a part of no military unit for seventeen years, the assembling of proper military equipage could not have been easy; but certain essentials Washington had to have, and he began acquiring them in 1775. Among the earliest was a "Ribbon to distinguish myself" as commander in chief — a wide blue band worn diagonally across the right shoulder and left hip. At night what repose he found came in the walnut bedstead shown at left, which collapsed into more manageable size (below). His mess kit (bottom) was a wooden chest covered with leather and lined with green wool, containing tin plates and platters, cooking pots, knives, forks, and bottles of various sizes. Among the several trunks included in the General's baggage was the one on the opposite page, at bottom. The camp towel to the right of it, of homespun linen with a cross-stitched monogram, was made for him by Martha. Above it is a powder bag and puff used to dress his hair. The artist John Trumbull, who served for a time as one of Washington's aides, made a scrupulously accurate portrait of the General at Trenton (right), noting that "every minute article of dress down to the buttons and spurs . . . were carefully painted from the . . . objects" themselves, including the "reconnoitring glass [below] with which he is supposed to have been examining the strength of the hostile army." One of Washington's silver spurs is shown opposite.

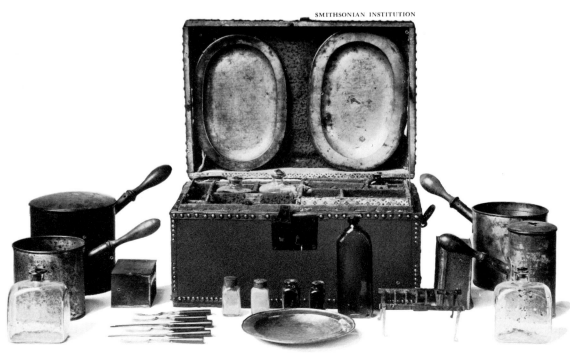

SMITHSONIAN INSTITUTION

146

AIDES · DE · CAMP

Jonathan Trumbull, shown in a miniature by his son John, "painter of the Revolution," became an aide to the General in 1781. Before then he had held the almost impossible jobs of paymaster in the army and first comptroller of the treasury under Congress. After the war he became a member of Congress and was governor of his native Connecticut.

Thomas Mifflin was, with Joseph Reed, one of the General's first ADC's. Then he became quartermaster general, in which post his negligence was largely responsible for the army's suffering at Valley Forge. He and Washington had a falling out and Mifflin was a leader of the Conway Cabal, which sought to replace the General with Horatio Gates.

John Laurens, portrayed here by Charles Willson Peale, was the son of the president of the Continental Congress. Educated in England, in 1777 he returned to America and served as a volunteer aide to Washington before being appointed in 1779. He helped negotiate Cornwallis' surrender and was killed in action in South Carolina a year later.

Alexander Hamilton was by all odds the most brilliant of Washington's young assistants. Portrayed here by Charles Willson Peale, Hamilton became a staff officer in the winter of 1777 while the army was at Morristown, having already distinguished himself in action with the New York Artillery. He was secretary to Washington for over four years.

Samuel Blatchley Webb of Connecticut was the stepson of America's first foreign diplomat, Silas Deane. Webb was wounded at the battle of Bunker Hill and was appointed aide and private secretary to Washington in 1776. Wounded again at White Plains and Trenton, he was captured by the British in 1777 and was exchanged a year later.

Joseph Reed, a cosmopolitan, intelligent man, was an enigma to many of his contemporaries. He was not radical enough to suit the radicals and was too reluctant a soldier for many Continental officers. Named an aide in 1775, he became Washington's most trusted adviser, yet he was unfairly accused of treason and of disloyalty to his chief.

During the Revolution thirty-two men served as aides-de-camp to General Washington and of these, six acted as his secretary, assisting him with the voluminous correspondence he was obliged to carry on. At least one visitor to headquarters pronounced them "all polite, sociable gentlemen," and they were undoubtedly that; but in several of these young men the General found exceptionally able and talented assistants. Best of the lot was Alexander Hamilton, seen at the far left on the bottom of the facing page. Above, in a detail of a painting by James Peale, brother of Charles Willson Peale, Washington is shown standing with his generals. To his right is the Marquis de Lafayette, who became one of the General's most valued friends. Standing behind Washington is Benjamin Lincoln. To Washington's left is Jean Baptiste de Rochambeau, commander of the French forces dispatched to aid the Americans. Behind Rochambeau is the Marquis de Chastellux, who served under the French commander. At the far right stands staff officer Tench Tilghman, aide-de-camp and military secretary to General Washington.

THE WAR COMES TO PENNSYLVANIA

In the spring of 1777 a British army under John Burgoyne moved south toward Albany from Canada as part of a plan calling for William Howe to join him there. But Howe had other ideas: apparently assuming that Burgoyne could cope without him, he loaded fifteen thousand troops aboard a huge fleet and set to sea, taking a full month to reach the northern edge of Chesapeake Bay. As Howe marched toward Philadelphia, Washington met him at Brandywine Creek on September 11, where the rebels were defeated. Ten days later Howe surprised Anthony Wayne's division in a night attack at Paoli (on the facing page) inflicting over 150 casualties, and on October 4 Washington retaliated in what was his first major assault on the British army in three years of war. At Germantown he sent several separate columns against the enemy, but when one of them was delayed by a stout British defense at the Chew residence (above) the attack lost its momentum, American units fired at each other in the fog, and a near-victory became another defeat. Even so, Washington was proud of his men, who "behaved with a degree of gallantry that did them the highest honor." Both of these paintings were made by Xavier Della Gatta for a British officer who saw the engagements.

You will have heard Dr Sir I doubt not long before this can have reached you that Sir W. Howe is gone from hence. The Rebels imagine that he is gone to the Eastward, by this time however he has filled Cheasapeak bay with surprize and terror Washington marched the greatest part of the Rebels to Philadelphia in order to oppose Sir Wm army. I hear he is now returned upon finding none of our troops landed but am not sure of this, great part of his troops are returned for certain I am sure this must be ruin to them I am left to Command here, half my force may I am sure defend every thing here with as much safety I shall therefore send Sir W. 4 or 5 Batn I have to small a force to invade the New England provinces, they are too weak to make any effectual efforts against me and you do not want any diversion in your favor I can therefore very well spare him 1500 men I shall try some thing certainly towards the close of the year not till then at any rate. It may be of use to inform you that report says all yields to you. I own to you I think the business will quickly be over now. Sr W's move just at this time has been Capital Washingtons have been the worst he could take in every respect I sincerely give you much joy on your success and am with great Sincerity   your hbl obt st

H C

When Burgoyne, trapped near Saratoga by Horatio Gates, wrote Henry Clinton asking for reinforcements, the latter replied in a letter that appeared innocuous until Burgoyne's staff fitted a prearranged dumbbell-shaped mask over it. This revealed the disheartening news that Howe and "the greatest part of the army" had departed for another destination.

AID FROM ABROAD

In December of 1775 Congress began investigating means of finding able foreign officers for the Continental Army, and when Silas Deane was sent to Paris in the spring of 1776 he was given authority to make contracts with foreigners desiring commissions. Unfortunately Deane was unable to distinguish the good ones from the opportunists; as Henry Laurens wrote, he "would not say nay to any Frenchman who called himself Count or Chevalier." By 1777 the general feeling in the army was that most of the adventurers who had arrived had been given rank far beyond their merits; as Washington remarked, "our officers think it exceedingly hard, after they have toiled in this service and probably sustained many losses, to have strangers put over them, whose merit, perhaps, is not equal to their own but whose effrontery will take no denial." Happily, some extremely capable recruits came to fight, among them the Marquis de Lafayette (on the facing page), an idealistic French nobleman to whom Washington took an instant liking, treating him almost as a son. Thaddeus Kosciusko, shown above right recuperating from wounds suffered in action against the Russians in 1794, was a Pole who served brilliantly at Saratoga and later designed the fortifications at West Point. Below right is Baron von Steuben, a former Prussian captain who, although he spoke no English, managed to teach Washington's soldiers the fundamentals of drill and maneuver during the winter at Valley Forge. Below is Casimir Pulaski, another Pole, whose career in America as a cavalryman was one of embittered disappointment. He died in a forlorn cavalry charge at Savannah in 1779 and was remembered largely for his gallantry.

By His Excellency

GEORGE WASHINGTON, Esquire,

GENERAL and COMMANDER in CHIEF of the Forces
of the United States of America.

BY Virtue of the Power and Direction to Me especially given, I hereby enjoin and require all Persons residing within seventy Miles of my Head Quarters to thresh one Half of their Grain by the 1st Day of February, and the other Half by the 1st Day of March next ensuing, on Pain, in Case of Failure, of having all that shall remain in Sheaves after the Period above mentioned, seized by the Commissaries and Quarter-Masters of the Army, and paid for as Straw.

GIVEN under my Hand, at Head Quarters, near the Valley Forge, in Philadelphia County, this 20th Day of December, 1777.

G. WASHINGTON.

By His Excellency's Command,
ROBERT H. HARRISON, Sec'y.

LANCASTER; Printed by JOHN DUNLAP.

A TEST
OF WILLS

After the close of the Philadelphia campaign the Continental Army took up quarters on the Schuylkill River, twenty miles from the capital, on terrain that favored defense. A supply of wood and water was close at hand, but until mid-January no huts were built at Valley Forge, and the winter was one of terrible privation — much of it caused by the mismanagement of Thomas Mifflin as quartermaster general, and more by the indifference and greed of neighboring farmers, who sold their produce to the British for cash rather than let the troops have it. The map here, drawn by the French engineer Duportail, shows the encampment, with Washington's headquarters at the junction of the river and "Vallee Crique." Washington's announcement above, designed as a threat to recalcitrant farmers, had little effect, and the ominous chant, "no pay, no clothes, no provisions, no rum," was heard on more than one occasion. Actually, the winter was relatively mild; it was neglect by their countrymen that caused the army's suffering.

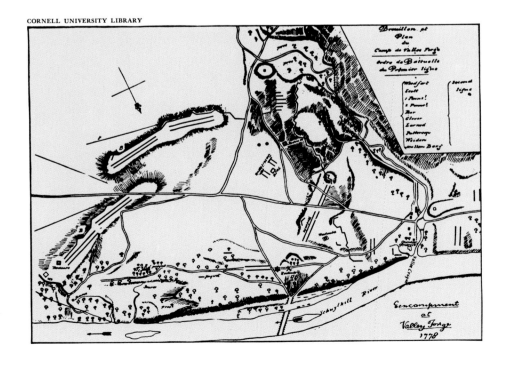

Not all historians agree that there was a genuine plot, known as the Conway Cabal, to unseat Washington from command of the army, but the evidence suggests that the general himself believed there was. The complex sequence of events began when Lord Stirling, one of Washington's trusted officers, sent the latter a message quoting Thomas Conway — an Irish-French officer of small capabilities and large ambition — as telling General Gates that "Heaven has been determined to save your country; or a weak General and bad Counsellors would have ruined it." There developed a trial of strength between Washington, with his record of defeats, and Gates, the victor at Saratoga, and certain members of Congress took sides. In a protracted correspondence that occupied much of his time during the winter at Valley Forge, Washington's sarcasm and logic forced Gates to abandon one position after another, and when it was over, Washington was in undisputed control of the army; Gates' reputation was considerably dimmed; and Conway's career was at an end. At right is an excerpt from one of Washington's letters to Gates. Below is an engraving of Du Simitière's life portrait of Horatio Gates.

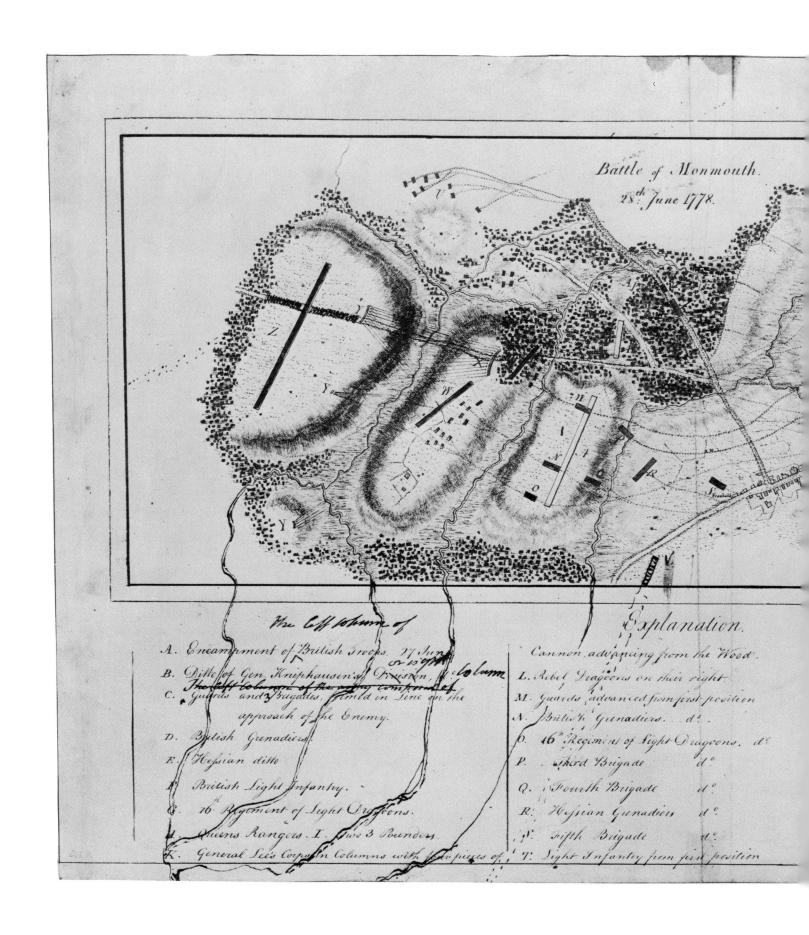

Battle of Monmouth.
28th June 1778.

The *Left Column* of   Explanation.

A. Encampment of British Troops. 27 June   Cannon, advancing from the Wood.
B. Ditto of Gen. Kniphausen's Division,   L. Rebel Dragoons on their right.
C. Guards and Brigades, formed in Line on the   M. Guards advanced from first position.
   approach of the Enemy.   N. British Grenadiers.   do.
D. British Grenadiers.   O. 16th Regiment of Light Dragoons. do.
E. Hessian ditto.   P. Third Brigade   do.
F. British Light Infantry.   Q. Fourth Brigade   do.
G. 16th Regiment of Light Dragoons.   R. Hessian Grenadiers   do.
H. Queens Rangers. I. Two 3 Pounders.   S. Fifth Brigade   do.
K. General Lee's Corps, in Columns with two pieces of T. Light Infantry from first position.

LAST BATTLE IN THE NORTH

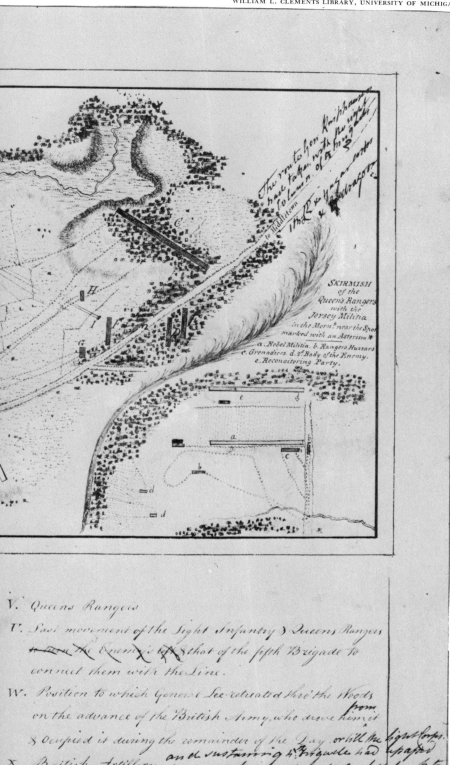

The battle of Monmouth marked the end of the line for ambitious, cantankerous Charles Lee. He accused Washington of "cruel injustice" and requested a court martial, which found him guilty of disobeying orders, by calling for a "shameful retreat," and disrespect to the commander in chief. He was suspended from command — a sentence that inspired the cartoon above, by Kosciusko, titled "A Suspended General." Below is a portrait of Sir Henry Clinton.

One of the least understood battles of the Revolution is annotated above, in a map drawn for Sir Henry Clinton, the British general who replaced Howe. At first, Lafayette commanded the American force sent to attack the British rearguard. Then he was superseded by Charles Lee, who had already opposed such an engagement in a council of war. Lee ordered the Americans to retreat, and as Clinton counterattacked, Washington came up with the main force (extreme left on the map), dismissed Lee, and stood off a succession of British attacks. The killing heat, the fatigue of the men, and approaching darkness put an end to the battle, and that night Clinton slipped away and by July 5 was in New York. Monmouth was the last important engagement in the North.

157

STRONGHOLD OF THE HUDSON

This splendid watercolor of the place Washington called the "key to America" was done in 1777 by Pierre Charles L'Enfant, a Frenchman who was given a commission as a lieutenant of engineers by Silas Deane and who later designed the nation's capital. The significance of West Point (right, center) was that it effectively neutralized British-held New York, by preventing the enemy fleet from coming up the Hudson. Its high cliffs were beyond reach of ships' cannon, and a vessel negotiating the bend of the river that lay at its feet was obliged to lose headway by changing course directly under the fort's batteries. Near the sailboat at left a huge chain had been stretched across the Hudson to stop navigation.

After a conference at Hartford with his new French allies,
Washington decided to visit Benedict Arnold and his wife Peggy
and inspect the fort at West Point, which Arnold commanded.
Arriving on September 25, he found Arnold mysteriously gone,
and in the course of a harrowing day learned that the man who had
been an audacious, gifted battlefield commander had sold out to
the British. Obsessed by the desire to make a quick fortune, nagged
by a belief that he had not received the recognition due him,
Arnold had offered to turn over the fort at West Point, with its
3,000-man garrison, its artillery and stores, to Sir Henry Clinton
for £20,000. What led to the discovery of his treason was the
accidental capture, behind the American lines in Westchester, of a
man who called himself John Anderson, who was found to be carrying
an official pass from Arnold along with a transcript, in Arnold's
handwriting, of secret information Washington had given a council
of war, as well as other incriminating documents. "Anderson"
admitted that he was Major John André, Adjutant General of the
British army, and while Arnold escaped to a British ship on the
Hudson, André was interrogated by a board of American officers and,
despite appeals from Clinton, hanged as a spy on October 2, 1780.

THE GREAT BETRAYAL

Arnold, a former druggist's apprentice and
successful merchant, is shown above in an
engraving after Du Simitière's life portrait.
His second wife was 19-year-old Peggy Shippen, a
prominent Philadelphia beauty. The portrait at
right, painted in London some years after Arnold's
treason, shows her with one of her five children
by him. Washington was convinced of Peggy's
innocence. Not for a century and a half did it become
known that she was involved in the duplicity.

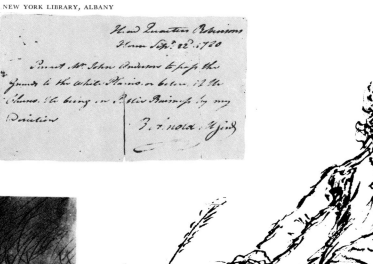

André, a talented artist, sketched this self-portrait while awaiting execution, and on the day before he was hanged made the drawing of the boat in which he had been rowed to a rendezvous with Arnold. At top is the pass signed by Arnold which André was carrying when he was stopped. The German engraving below, left, shows the capture of André; the illustration of his death is taken from a contemporary English book.

FINANCING THE REBELLION

New Windsor. Jan 15. 1781

Sir,

[handwritten letter, partially legible]

Lack of pay for his soldiers was the bane of George Washington's existence and nearly proved the army's undoing. At times his only ally seemed to be Robert Morris, a successful merchant and financier who ran the Secret Committee of Congress, which controlled all foreign trade and imported munitions and supplies. It was Morris who found the money to make good Washington's promise of a ten-dollar bounty for those soldiers who stayed with the army for six weeks after the battle of Trenton — without which the battle of Princeton could not have been fought. In January, 1781, Washington received a dispatch from Anthony Wayne, reporting that noncoms and privates of the Pennsylvania Line had mutinied, killing one officer and wounding others before marching on Philadelphia to demand that the authorities give them back pay and food, and adjust the terms of their enlistment and bounties. Washington advised Congress of this ominous development on January 15, 1781, writing from New Windsor, New York (a portion of the letter appears at left). Encouraged by the Pennsylvanians' success, New Jersey troops mutinied on January 20, but Washington acted immediately to quell the uprising. In the wake of these events Morris was appointed Superintendent of Finances and given the task of salvaging the chaotic fiscal situation.

Robert Morris, painted by Charles Willson Peale, was criticized during the war for insisting that he be allowed to carry on his profitable private business ventures while serving the government, but Congress agreed because no one else seemed capable of handling trade and finance on the scale required. On the facing page is an iron chest in which Morris kept what little hard money he could lay his hands on. At left is an example of Continental paper currency. In June, 1775, Congress decided to finance the war by issuing paper money, backed by the Spanish milled dollar, which was minted in the New World and was the most common coin in the colonies. By January, 1777, the value of Continental currency was a third that of specie; by 1779, it was 90 per cent lower; by 1781, when the phrase "not worth a Continental" became widespread, it had collapsed. It was then that Morris was made Superintendent of Finances; the next year he was helped immeasurably by the arrival of a French fleet carrying over $200,000 in specie.

FRUITS OF ALLIANCE

"We are at the end of our tether," Washington wrote in the spring of 1781, "and now or never our deliverance must come." The only hope lay with the French, and after making plans with Rochambeau to attack New York, Washington received on August 14 the news that forced him to cancel that operation and employ the strategy that brought about the end of the war. The Comte De Grasse, whose portrait appears at left, with twenty-nine ships and three thousand troops, was sailing for Chesapeake Bay, where Cornwallis' army now was, and by August 20 the combined armies of Washington and Rochambeau were marching to join him. A British fleet under Samuel Hood looked in on Chesapeake Bay on August 25 and, finding no French ships, sailed for New York to join Admiral Thomas Graves. Meanwhile, De Grasse slipped in to the Chesapeake, and when Graves and Hood returned the Frenchman stood out to sea, to fight the battle depicted above. The English battle line was badly mauled and while the two fleets maneuvered another French fleet under Admiral Barras arrived from Newport, giving the French a two-to-one superiority. When Graves asked Hood for suggestions the latter replied, "Sir Samuel would be very glad to send an opinion, but he really knows not what to say in the truly lamentable state we have brought ourselves." So off they sailed to New York, leaving Cornwallis without support or hope of escape.

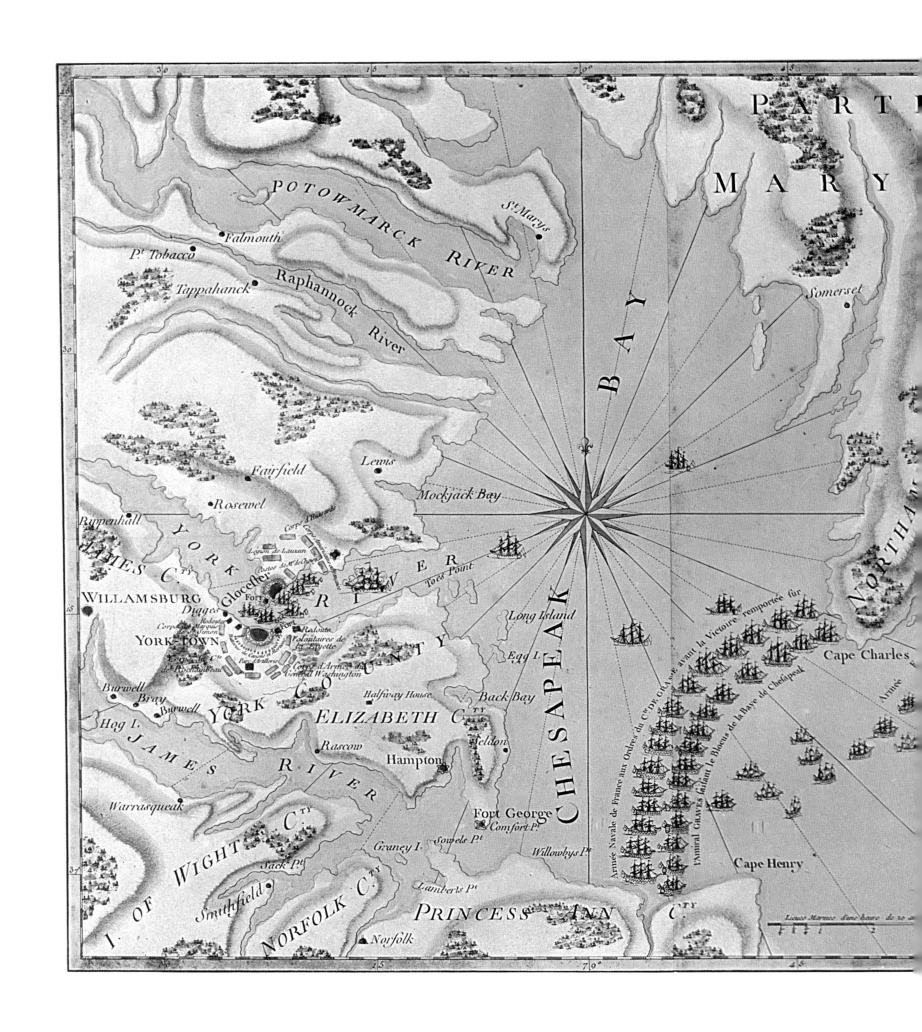

THE CRUCIAL BATTLE OF THE CAPES

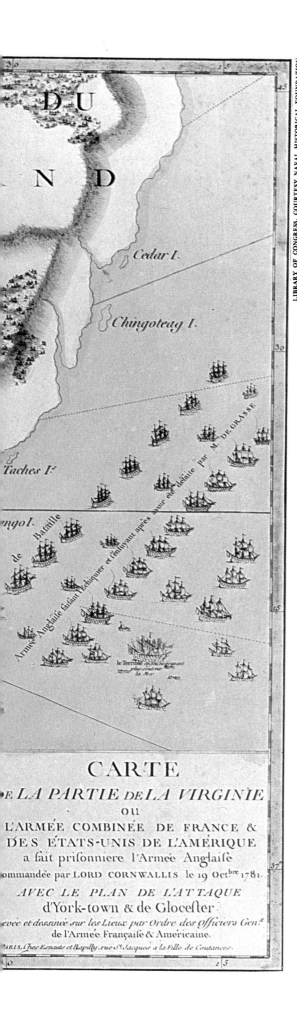

On September 2, 1781, troops of the Continental Army marched into Philadelphia, pausing long enough to inform Congress that they wanted a month's pay in hard money before heading south, and obliging Robert Morris to borrow $20,000 in cash from Rochambeau's war chest. Then came the French, dazzling the city's residents with the precision of their marching, their brilliant uniforms, and their accomplished bands. Afterward, Washington stopped off at Mount Vernon for four days — his first visit there in six years — and on September 14 he and Rochambeau arrived on the peninsula between the James and York Rivers where Cornwallis' army was entrenched. Most of the allies' heavy equipment was brought down the Chesapeake by ship from Head of Elk, while the troops marched to Baltimore and Annapolis, where they boarded transports for the remainder of the journey. The powderhorn above belonged to a Revolutionary soldier, who carved on it a rare depiction of a Continental artillery unit on the march. The French map at left shows the allied siege that began as the combined armies marched in to ring Yorktown on the south bank of the York River, and the town of Gloucester on the opposite shore. De Grasse's fleet is shown blockading the entrance to the bay, and then fighting the action with Graves that made possible the siege and ultimate victory.

INTO THE LINES

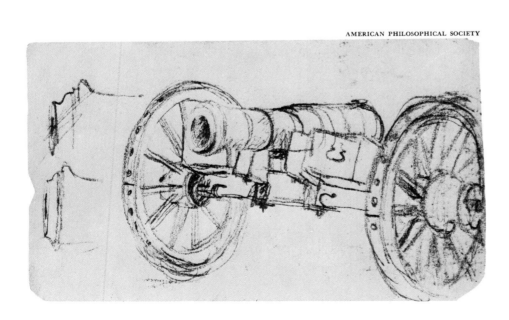

The white-uniformed divisions of Louis XVI of France marched from Williamsburg to the outskirts of Yorktown on September 28 and headed into the siege lines with flags flying, as shown in the painting above by Louis Van Blarenberghe, an eyewitness. Between the allied armies and the town was a sandy plain from which all vegetation had been removed; beyond were the enemy redoubts, with the main defensive works farther back. The town itself had only one main street and four cross streets, where some five or six thousand British regulars were dug in, but the Americans and the French outnumbered them almost three to one and were backed by De Grasse's fleet. Rochambeau discovered that the Americans were "totally ignorant of the operations of a siege," but as engineers laid out parallels, trenches were dug by day and each night cannon were hauled forward toward the enemy works. On October 9 the artillerists were ready and Washington stepped forward, gave the sign to open fire, and watched with delight as the cannonballs struck the British fortifications. At left, in a sketch from Charles Willson Peale's diary, is one of the allies' powerful cannon.

168

...T YORKTOWN

The big guns rode on carriages, designed by Henry Knox, that enabled shot to be fired almost horizontally at the target, thereby devastating the enemy's walls. Stragglers from the besieged town reported that Cornwallis had "built a kind of grotto . . . where he lives underground," to avoid the incessant fire from the French and American cannon. He was still expecting relief from Henry Clinton's troops in New York and hoped to buy time until reinforcements arrived by concentrating his limited forces in a small defense perimeter. On October 14 the allies captured two important British redoubts. Two nights later Cornwallis, having learned that he could expect no help from Clinton, attempted to ferry his troops across the York River, to fight his way out through Gloucester, but a severe storm put a stop to the embarkation and on October 17 the heaviest allied barrage to date began. By then the town was a shambles, no hope remained for the British, and between 9 and 10 A.M. a drummer boy like the one at right appeared on a parapet and began beating the parley. A British officer stepped out in front of the lines with a white handkerchief and slowly the guns ceased firing.

CORNWALLIS' ARMY SURRENDERS

York, Virginia 17th Octr. 1781

Sir

I propose a Cessation of Hostilities for Twenty four hours, and that two Officers may be appointed by each side to meet at Mr. Moore's house to settle terms for the surrender of the posts of York & Gloucester. I have the honour to be

Sir

Your most obedient & most humble Servant

Cornwallis

His Excellency General Washington &c. &c. &c.

The effects of the incessant pounding on Yorktown can be seen in the watercolor above by Benjamin Latrobe. The worked-over building in the foreground is the Nelson house, which had served as Cornwallis' headquarters during the siege. Thomas Gainsborough's portrait of Charles, first Marquis and second Earl Cornwallis (opposite), was painted two years after his surrender at Yorktown. Ironically, although it was his decision to move his army into Virginia, when he returned to England he was treated more as a hero than a defeated general; Clinton received most of the blame. The brief note at left was carried to Washington along with the white flag. In it, Cornwallis proposed a truce to work out capitulation terms, and the next morning Lafayette's brother-in-law, Viscount De Noailles, and John Laurens met the British half a mile downriver from Yorktown to settle details. Haste was essential: Washington had heard a rumor that Clinton and five thousand troops were leaving New York, bound for Chesapeake Bay.

CHARLES EARL CORNWALLIS. 1783.

"IT IS ALL OVER!"

Above, Van Blarenberghe's painting of the climactic moment of the Revolution shows the troops of Cornwallis' command marching out of their works between long lines of French and American troops, to stack arms in the field at the extreme left. Cornwallis did not accompany them; he claimed to be indisposed and remained at headquarters, sending a deputy to attend to the humiliating business. His British and German troops — many in new uniforms, but with their flags cased — marched out to the melancholy strains of a tune called "The World Turn'd Upside Down," played by British

bands and pipers. After watching the proceedings toward which all his
energies had been dedicated for six years, Washington wrote a letter to
Congress describing the occurrence only as an "Important Event" and voicing
his concern lest this success produce "a relaxation in the prosecution of the
war." In England those in authority knew better. When news of Cornwallis'
surrender reached George III's war minister, Lord North, an observer said
he received it "as he would have taken a ball through his breast" and agitatedly
paced the room, repeating, "Oh God! It is all over!" As indeed it was.

TRIUMPH
AT
LAST

Even in victory, Washington was denied the satisfaction of receiving the sword of a defeated British general. As the officer leading the vanquished troops out of Yorktown approached, Washington could see that he wore the insignia of a brigadier, and when he reached the awaiting American and French commanders the man turned to the French and asked which one was Rochambeau. An aide replied, "You are mistaken. The Commander in Chief of our army is on the right," and the English officer was forced to turn toward Washington. Explaining that Cornwallis was ill, he introduced himself as Brigadier Charles O'Hara and offered the American commander his sword. With a gesture, Washington refused it and directed O'Hara to give it to Benjamin Lincoln, a brigadier general who had been humiliated in defeat at Charleston, South Carolina. The version of the scene below is an oil sketch done by John Trumbull for his painting of the British surrender at Yorktown. In it, Lincoln, his head bared, waits while O'Hara walks over to hand him the sword; in the right background is Washington, surrounded by his officers. The glorious news of the surrender spread like wildfire across the country, through accounts like the one reprinted at far right. The "Illumination" notice at right was published on October 24, six days after the victory. In the cartoon (below right) from a British magazine, America — represented by Mrs. General Washington — is bestowing thirteen stripes on Britannia's back, urged on by figures representing the European allies of the United States.

Illumination.

COLONEL TILGHMAN, Aid de Camp to his Excellency General WASHINGTON, having brought official acounts of the SURRENDER of Lord Cornwallis, and the Garrisons of York and Gloucester, those Citizens who chuse to ILLUMINATE on the GLORIOUS OCCASION, will do it this evening at Six, and extinguish their lights at Nine o'clock.

Decorum and harmony are earnestly recommended to every Citizen, and a general discountenance to the least appearance of riot.

October 24, 1781.

Glorious Intelligence!

NORWICH, OCTOBER 26, 1781.
Friday Evening, Six o'Clock.

By a Gentleman this Moment from New-London we are favoured with the following Hand-Bill.

NEWPORT, OCTOBER 25.

YESTERDAY afternoon arrived in this harbour, Capt. Lovat, of the schooner Adventure, from York-River, in Chesapeake-Bay, (which he left the 20th inst.) and brought us the glorious news of the surrender of Lord Cornwallis and his army prisoners of war to the allied army under the command of our illustrious General, and the French fleet under the command of his Excellency the Count de Grasse.

A cessation of arms took place on Thursday the 18th inst. in consequence of proposals from Lord Cornwallis for a capitulation.----His Lordship proposed a cessation of twenty-four hours, but two only were granted by his Excellency Gen. Washington. The articles were compleated the same day, and the next day the allied army took possession of York-Town.

By this glorious conquest Nine Thousand of the enemy, including seamen, fell into our hands, with an immense quantity of warlike stores, a forty gun ship, a frigate, an armed vessel, and about One Hundred Sail of Transports.

NORWICH:
PRINTED AT JOHN TRUMBULL.

Two years after Cornwallis' surrender, a group of Continental Army officers met near Fishkill, New York, and, largely at the urging of Henry Knox, formed America's first veterans' organization — the Society of the Cincinnati. Certificates of membership (left) were printed and a medal, or badge, was designed by Major Pierre Charles L'Enfant. Limited to Army officers (the Navy was included later), membership passed, on an officer's death, to his eldest son. Actually, the Society — which took its name from the fifth-century-B.C. farmer who left his plow to lead fellow Romans against an invader — was regarded by its founders as a means of perpetuating wartime camaraderie and of helping brother officers in need; but it was attacked almost immediately by one Aedanus Burke, who wrote the pamphlet illustrated at right, signing himself "Cassius." Raging against a hereditary peerage that would destroy democratic ideals for which the war had been fought, Burke described the organization as "planted in a fiery, hot ambition, and thirst for power," and predicted that it would "end in tyranny." Washington, having reluctantly accepted the title of president general of the Cincinnati (in recognition of which he was given the dazzling, jewel-studded version of the Society's badge below), was embarrassed by the public outcry. When Thomas Jefferson wrote him that the Cincinnati's principles ran contrary to "the equality of man," he moved quickly to persuade the Society to abolish all rules that suggested "a political tendency" and to discontinue the hereditary qualification for membership, threatening to resign as president general unless members agreed to do so.

THE SOCIETY OF THE CINCINNATI

CONSIDERATIONS

ON THE

SOCIETY OR ORDER

OF

CINCINNATI;

LATELY INSTITUTED

By the Major-Generals, Brigadier-Generals, and other Officers of the AMERICAN ARMY.

PROVING THAT IT CREATES

A RACE OF HEREDITARY PATRICIANS,

OR

NOBILITY.

INTERSPERSED WITH REMARKS

On its CONSEQUENCES to the FREEDOM and HAPPINESS of the Republic.

Addressed to the PEOPLE of SOUTH-CAROLINA, and their REPRESENTATIVES.

BY CASSIUS. *Burke*

Supposed to be written by ÆDANUS BURKE, Esquire, one of the Chief Justices of the State of South-Carolina.

Blow ye the Trumpet in Zion.   The BIBLE.

PHILADELPHIA:

Printed and Sold by ROBERT BELL, in *Third-Street.*

Price, one-sixth of a Dollar. M,DCC,LXXXIII.

FIRST IN WAR

On November 30, 1782, a treaty of peace was signed by representatives of the United States and Great Britain, but not until March 12, 1783, did Congress receive the official text — brought by Captain Joshua Barney aboard a ship fittingly named *Washington*. Even then, the war was not officially at an end, since the pact stated that the treaty was not effective until terms were agreed to between Great Britain and France. Nonetheless, the long period of waiting appeared to be over when King George III issued a proclamation (below) calling for a cessation of hostilities on February 14, 1783. At last, Washington heard the news he had been waiting for: at the end of March a servant sent across the Atlantic by Lafayette brought word that France, Spain, and Britain had signed a treaty in Paris. "The news," Washington wrote, "has filled my mind with inexpressible satisfaction." Yet he was already thinking ahead to what must follow. "We have a national character to establish," he observed to Alexander Hamilton, and he was concerned lest "local or state politics will interfere too much with that liberal and extensive plan of government which wisdom and foresight, freed from the mist of prejudice, would dictate. . . ." The General, as he appeared in uniform in the middle of the war, is seen in Charles Willson Peale's full-length portrait on the facing page. The painting shows Washington in triumph at Trenton, the German flags captured by his men at his feet — a stark contrast with what Peale himself had witnessed only three weeks before the battle. Watching Washington's sick, exhausted, nearly naked men scramble up the bank of the Delaware River as they retreated into Pennsylvania, the painter described it as "the most hellish scene I ever beheld."

By the KING.

A PROCLAMATION,

Declaring the Cessation of Arms, as well by Sea as Land, agreed upon between His Majesty, the Most Christian King, the King of *Spain*, the States General of the *United Provinces*, and the United States of *America*, and enjoining the Observance thereof.

GEORGE R.

HEREAS Provisional Articles were signed at *Paris*, on the Thirtieth Day of *November* last, between Our Commissioner for treating of Peace with the Commissioners of the United States of *America* and the Commissioners of the said States, to be inserted in and to constitute the Treaty of Peace proposed to be concluded between Us and the said United States, when Terms of Peace should be agreed upon between Us and His Most Christian Majesty: And whereas Preliminaries for restoring Peace between Us and His Most Christian Majesty were signed at *Versailles* on the Twentieth Day of *January* last, by the Ministers of Us and the Most Christian King: And whereas Preliminaries for restoring Peace between Us and the King of *Spain*

179

5

FIRST PRESIDENT

Everything pointed to Washington's determination to retire within himself, as he put it. He resigned as a vestryman of Truro Parish and made no effort to take part in Virginia politics, resolving to occupy his time entirely with those pursuits he had dreamed of during the war years. The only office he now held was an honorary one: president-general of the Society of the Cincinnati, an organization of former officers of the Continental Army (which had come in for a good deal of criticism on grounds that it was antithetical to the spirit of republicanism and smacked of militarism).

As it turned out, he had three favorite enthusiasms in mind. As might be expected, there was his beloved Mount Vernon, to which Lund had added a north wing in 1776 balancing the south wing built in 1774. The new addition was still unfinished; Washington also wanted the new "banquet hall" suitably decorated and furnished, the piazza paved, the chimneys repaired, and soon the place was humming with activity—joiners and bricklayers moving in and out, a greenhouse under construction, roads and walks being laid, lawns and shrubbery being planted, a fruit garden set out, fences being built, and amid it all Washington busy selecting wallpapers and Venetian blinds.

Then there was the plantation itself—a huge establishment worked by some two hundred slaves, its acreage extending ten miles along the Potomac River and inland for as much as four miles. This complex, self-contained community included a mill, carpentry and blacksmith shops, a ferry, a fishery, and weaving rooms, along with herds of cattle and horses, sheep, and hogs, and fields that must be cultivated and sowed and harvested. By inclination and necessity Washington was a farmer, and he plunged into his work with a vengeance, seeking advice from agriculturists in America and Europe, experimenting with new crops and systems of rotation, breeding new strains of livestock, all in the pursuit of what he considered "the most delectable" of occupations.

And thirdly there was the old will o' the wisp, the dream of western lands. Early in September of 1784 he journeyed forth once again over the Alleghenies, following the route he had come to know so well, accompanied by his nephew Bushrod Washington, Dr. James Craik, and Craik's son. Washington was eager to visit his lands on the Kanawha River, but en route he learned that it would be a risky trip: the Indians were on the warpath. So he contented himself with another project that lay in the back of his mind—locating a practical route that would connect the waters of the Potomac with those of the Ohio, linking

Virginia with the West, for Washington envisioned a water system that would eventually carry commerce between East and West and past his own front door. He was also aware that something of the sort must be done before long lest the settlements beyond the Alleghenies turn their backs on the Atlantic seaboard and hitch their future to the rivers that flowed westward to the Mississippi, linking them to New Orleans or Detroit, to the Spanish or the British. As he knew, the headwaters of the Potomac and Ohio Rivers were separated in the mountains by a relatively short portage, and although this was deep wilderness country, Washington's 1784 trip convinced him that the fur trade of the Northwest could ultimately be brought over a network of streams and portages to Virginia. And for the upriver travel, he believed that a curious craft he had been shown by its inventor, James Rumsey, at Berkeley Springs (now renamed Bath) on his way west, was the answer. This was a rival to Fitch's steamboat, and consisted of two hulls with a paddle wheel between them, which was set in motion by the current of the stream and which, in turn, drove poles that pushed against the bottom and moved the boat against the current.

Filled with enthusiasm, Washington returned from his expedition and obtained the approval of the Virginia and Maryland legislatures to form a Potomac River Company, which he somewhat reluctantly agreed to serve as president, and in the summer of 1785 he went on an inspection trip as far as Harpers Ferry, discovering that there were numerous difficulties in store for the ambitious project. Although it remained a constant enthusiasm of his, nothing came of the idea during his lifetime, because the little company had insufficient resources and Rumsey's self-propelling boat turned out to be impractical. Washington had set his sights on a canal, but out of his efforts came, ultimately, something entirely different and far more wondrous. The states of Maryland and Virginia, having seen these tentative steps toward cooperation blossom into the Potomac River Company, decided that it would be a good idea to send representatives to an annual meeting to discuss other mutual problems. The idea caught on and in January of 1786 the Virginia legislature invited men from all the states of the new Union to meet with its representatives to discuss common problems of commerce and trade. From *that* proposal came the Annapolis convention of 1786, attended by only five states. Alexander Hamilton recommended at Annapolis that still another convention be held in Philadelphia in May of 1787, and the delegates to the Philadelphia meeting produced a document known as the Constitution of the United States.

Between 1783 and 1787 one of Washington's most trying and time-consuming tasks was the drudgery of putting his affairs in order. Faithful as Lund's stewardship of Mount Vernon had been, he was neither businessman nor accountant, and the plantation's books and records were in a sad state of disarray. Not only must Washington attend to these, discover who owed him money and what his own debts were, while coping with the day-to-day exigencies of the place, but he found that although he might wish to retire within himself, his countrymen were not about to let him do so. He was besieged with letters and callers—neighbors asking for advice or loans, strangers requesting information, as he put it, about "Dick, Tom, and Harry who *may have been* in some part, or at *sometime,* in the Continental service. Letters, or certificates of service for those who want to go out of their own State. Introductions; applications for copies of Papers; references of a thousand old matters with which I *ought* not to be troubled, more than the Great Mogul; but which must receive answer of some kind, deprive me of my usual exercise; and without relief, may be injurious to me as I already begin to feel the weight, and oppression of it in my head." And for all he valued his privacy, Mount Vernon might have been a public house, a mecca for friends and strangers alike, curious visitors from abroad included.

The French sculptor Houdon arrived one night in 1785 after Washington, his family, and other guests had retired. Houdon had come to do a portrait bust of Washington, and somehow or other room was found for him and three assistants. All this at a time when a family wedding was uniting Washington's nephew and Martha's niece, and part of the roof was being shingled. Hardly a day passed when visitors did not arrive out of the blue, expecting to be entertained and wined and fed while rubbing shoulders with the great man. Along with the guests came gifts: a jackass from the King of Spain (which Washington named "Royal Gift"); a marble fireplace from an English admirer; a pack of hounds from France. So public a man had he become that in June of 1785 he recorded a singular fact in his diary: "Dined with only Mrs. Washington, which I believe is the first instance of it since my retirement from public life."

To rescue him from the mounting pile of papers came Tobias Lear, a New Hampshire man who joined his household in 1786 as his secretary and served from that time through his first term as President. (Lear returned during the last year of Washington's life in the same role.) Lear began by putting his papers in order and as he worked came to the conclusion that Washington was out of pocket some ten thousand pounds sterling as a result of the war; many of the debts owed him were so old as to be uncollectible; others had been paid off in nearly worthless paper.

To spare himself from the constant demands of visitors on his time, Washington established a routine that included long rides around the farm and, in winter, fox hunting. It was his nature to be busy, always, to fill his mind with details and his body with exercise, for he had come to realize that idleness only accentuated what Thomas Jefferson once called his "gloomy apprehensions," a dark and moody outlook that intensified with inactivity. So he busied himself as much as possible by keeping "agreeably amused." In a very real sense, he now possessed what he had always wanted: Mount Vernon and the love and respect of his countrymen, and it was not in him to turn visitors away from his door when they came to demonstrate their affection for the hero of the Revolution. He invited them for meals or for the night, he put up their servants and their horses, until Mount Vernon might be "compared to a well-resorted tavern, as scarcely any strangers who are going from north to south or from south to north do not spend a day or two at it," as he wrote. To his former aide David Humphreys he explained that the hospitality of the house was always available to visitors: "My manner of living is plain. I do not mean to be put out of it. A glass of wine and a bit of mutton are always ready, and such as will be content to partake of them are welcome. Those who expect more will be disappointed, but no change will be affected by it."

But the plain living, if one could call it that, and the daily enjoyment of Mount Vernon were about to end. The country had discovered that it needed George Washington again.

In what manner it required his services, or if he would or should serve if asked, were large questions. From the standpoint of men like John Jay and James Madison and others, who had gradually become committed to advocacy of a new form of government to replace the weak, ineffective Articles of Confederation, it was Washington's reputation, his enormous prestige, that was wanted. Quite simply, they felt that if he were on their side they would win; that if he were not, their efforts might well be in vain. Apart from his desire to live out his days at Mount Vernon, untroubled by public problems, Washington had not made up his mind as to where he stood on the subject of a new government. After all, Congress *was* the

legitimate government of the new nation, and who was to say that it should be supplanted by a new structure designed by a group of reformers? By temperament and by experience in the Revolutionary War, Washington was drawn to a strong, centralized authority; after all, the lack of one had been a chief cause of his frustration throughout the war. Yet, for personal reasons, he wanted no part of the movement about which Jay had written him, saying that "An opinion begins to prevail, that a General Convention for revising the articles of Confederation would be expedient." While Washington could agree that the "fabrick" of the present government was "tottering," he neither had a specific proposal of his own to put forward, nor was he attracted to participate in a new government on grounds of ambition. On the contrary, he was fifty-five years old now, he suffered from rheumatism, he worried about his personal finances, and he had collected all the rewards and honors he might have sought. Furthermore, he was concerned that the proposed convention in Philadelphia might, like its predecessor at Annapolis, fail to attract delegates from all the states, and that it might prove no more than a threat to the existing government.

Two considerations ultimately seem to have swayed him in the direction of support for the Philadelphia meeting. The first was an echo of his own sensitivity to criticism from others: it troubled him deeply that the new nation, in whose behalf he had labored so long and hard, presented a spectacle of disunity and weakness to foreign countries. It was a source of humiliation that the British, for example, blithely refused to leave their posts in the West despite their treaty obligations to do so. The second reason was more compelling by far, since it was a clear demonstration of the urgent need for a strong central government.

In the fall of 1786 armed insurrection erupted in Massachusetts. The postwar depression had produced a large debtor class, mostly farmers and small property owners whose grievances centered on unfairly high property taxes, exorbitant legal fees, and what they regarded as inequitable salaries paid to public officials. Alarmed and angered by the rising incidence of foreclosures and imprisonment for debt, they gathered under a former captain in the Revolution, Daniel Shays, seized arms from an arsenal, and marched on Springfield to intimidate the state's Supreme Court. The situation became more ominous when Shays' followers seized a quantity of arms from the Springfield arsenal. To his friend Henry Lee, Washington wrote, "Precedents are dangerous things — let the reins of government then be braced & held with a steady hand, & every violation of the Constitution be reprehended: if defective, let it be amended, but not suffered to be trampled upon whilst it has an existence."

Eventually the insurgents were put down by militiamen under Benjamin Lincoln, who had taken the sword of General O'Hara at Yorktown, but in the spring of 1787 the Massachusetts legislature backed down and enacted numerous reforms advocated by Shays' men, leading conservatives to suspect that a republican form of government might be unworkable after all. Washington, who had viewed the episode with profound misgivings, decided at last that it was his duty to attend the convention in Philadelphia, and he left Mount Vernon on May 9, 1787.

In Philadelphia he accepted lodgings at Robert Morris' mansion, where he remained until mid-September, when the Constitutional Convention had completed its business. By May 25 a quorum of the states had assembled and Washington was elected president by unanimous vote. It was a role entirely to his liking, leaving him free from the debates; only when an issue was put to a vote was he required to step down from the chair and make known his choice; otherwise he could appear to be impartial or neutral. Despite his attitude of aloofness, there was no doubt that his commanding presence was a major factor in the writing of a new Constitution, and afterward, James Madison, one of the leading framers of the document, wrote to Thomas Jefferson, "Be assured, his influence carried the government."

The magnitude of the questions confronting the delegates, whose only charge was to revise the Articles of Confederation but who went far beyond it, drafting an entirely new form of government, was and is staggering. There were no precedents for what they were attempting to do, no sure guidelines they could follow. What form of government was it to be? they had to ask themselves, and they settled on a plan brought forth by the Virginia delegates, which called for three separate branches — executive, legislative, and judicial. Small state men argued interminably with those from the large, determined that they should obtain the equality of representation granted them by the Articles of Confederation; the large states feared that their power and influence would be broken by the federal government itself, if not by the smaller states. Gradually the proponents of a strong national government and a powerful executive — of whom Washington was one — carried the day, and although the resulting document was a compromise between many shades of opinion, all but three of the delegates present were willing to sign it at last.

It had been an exhausting four months of tedious debate with the delegates often sitting seven hours a day, but at the end a majority of them agreed with their president, who called it a "momentous work." What no doubt pleased him as much as anything else was that the form of government recommended was so close to the one he knew best — Virginia's. The duties of its executive were analogous to those of Virginia's governor; its Senate resembled the Governor's Council; and its House of Representatives was little different from his own state's General Assembly. Equally important, Virginia as the most populous state in the new nation would have the lion's share of representatives in the House. And finally, it appeared to be a workable entity — a government whose carefully defined powers would be able to deal with foreign nations, collect revenues, regulate finances, and function under a system of laws, providing certain rights to each of its citizens.

To Washington's mounting dismay, however, a large number of his countrymen saw the matter differently, and the arguments that erupted in the aftermath of the convention revealed dissatisfaction over the Constitution as often as the support of it. By January of the following year only five states had ratified, and when Massachusetts joined the ranks by a narrow vote, it was only on condition that certain amendments would be made to the document to meet the objections of those in that state who had opposed it. Time wore on, the debate continued, then two more states ratified, making eight. Early in June, 1788, it was Virginia's turn to decide, and on the twenty-ninth of the month Washington wrote his old friend Benjamin Lincoln that his state had ratified, to stand with all those who would "preserve the Union, establish good order and government — and to render the Nation happy at home and respectable abroad."

New Hampshire had done likewise, making ten, and in July, New York ratified (in November of 1789 North Carolina finally acted, leaving only Rhode Island — which had not even called a convention yet). Meanwhile, the old Congress had decided that a new government should be installed on March 4, 1789, and after much discussion it was agreed that its seat should be in New York. Before that event occurred, it was almost universally conceded that there was only one man who could hold the office of Chief Executive; there seemed no question in anyone's mind that it should be George Washington of Virginia.

For the man himself, there were nothing but questions. How could he bring himself to leave his beloved plantation again to devote four more years to the public service? How could he possibly prepare himself for the unknown difficulties involved in the task? And beyond these doubts concerning his fitness for the job, how could he properly discuss his acceptance or rejection of the office until such time as someone offered it to him?

Whatever his own reservations, events were pushing toward a climax. During the fall of 1788 letters came to him from acquaintances, unanimous in their assurance that it was his duty to serve. The old Congress, charged with settling the numerous bits of business relating to the establishment of a new government, selected New York as the provisional capital and established the first Wednesday in January as a date for the election of presidential electors, fixed the first Wednesday in February for their meeting, and the first Wednesday in March for the commencement of the new government. Reluctant Washington may have been at first, but as the moment of decision approached he seems to have accepted the inevitable and begun planning for the future with a certain exhilaration. In years past his mind had been filled with doubts about the course on which he was embarking: no one in 1775, for example, could foresee what the future held for the First Continental Congress; no one in 1776 could say what the outcome of the Revolution would be; no one in 1787 could predict success for the Constitutional Convention. But this was an undertaking Washington knew to be right for the country, and there was a grandeur about it that appealed to him.

As he wrote the Irishman Sir Edward Newenham, "A greater drama is now acting on this theater than has heretofore been brought on the American stage, or any other in the world. We exhibit at present the novel and astonishing spectacle of a whole people deliberating calmly on what form of government will be most conducive to their happiness." Even before the Electoral College met, the Virginia planter had drawn up instructions for the management of his farms while he was away and was writing his old friend Lafayette to say that he could now perceive a "path as clear and as direct as a ray of light" for the new nation.

He even composed, with the assistance of David Humphreys, a seventy-three-page inaugural address which, although it was never delivered, gives a good many insights into his thoughts for the Presidency. What was of utmost importance, he had concluded, was to win over the anti-Federalists—that is, those who had opposed adoption of the Constitution—to the new government by adopting certain amendments that would constitute a Bill of Rights. He had no wish to alter the remainder of the Constitution, but realized that adoption of a Bill of Rights would enable the government to begin on a note of harmony, for above all he wanted the government to function in a spirit of unanimity, without philosophical or sectional differences to mar it. He envisioned a strong and healthy economy, the encouragement of American manufactures, regulation by Congress of coinage and currency and a system of weights and measures, and support by that body of improved "education and manners of a people" as well as the arts, science, invention, and "institutions favorable to humanity." As for the nation's defense, he saw the oceans as a natural bulwark against foreign aggression and believed that an active merchant marine, supported by government arsenals and shipyards, would provide adequate protection. And, amazingly for a man who had suffered so long during the Revolution from the lack of a strong military arm, he advocated a reliance on militia, saying that he would be happy, when Congress was not in session, to review local companies in an effort to preserve "the ancient military spirit." In those who would serve the new government as officials, he desired "rectitude" above all else.

Although this undelivered address was later suppressed and partially destroyed by the overzealous historian Jared Sparks, who edited the first edition of Washington's papers and may have burned certain pages that did not conform to his image of the first President, one passage survives to indicate Washington's feelings about the role of the Chief Executive. The two Houses of Congress, as he put it, would be "the pivot on which turns the first wheel of the government, a wheel which communicates motion to all the rest." There was no doubt in his mind that the President should be the moving force in public affairs.

After months of waiting, the word finally came to Mount Vernon: Washington had received the unanimous vote of the Electoral College and John Adams of Massachusetts, who obtained thirty-four of the sixty-nine votes, would be Vice-President. But if Washington had supposed that the wheels of government would commence turning at once, he was badly disappointed. The frustrations that beset prior Congresses emerged: bad weather, muddy roads, long distances to be traveled, a seeming lack of interest on the part of newly elected legislators, the press of other matters — all conspiring to delay the business at hand. Since Washington could not be declared President until a president pro tem of the Senate, elected for the purpose, officially opened the ballots in the presence of both Houses and pronounced him the winner, the moment had to wait a quorum. By March 5, a day after the date set for the convening of Congress, only eight senators and seventeen representatives had shown up. While Washington fumed over "the stupor or listlessness" of the incoming representatives, his mood darkened and he wrote his former comrade in arms Henry Knox to say, "My movements to the chair of government will be accompanied by feelings not unlike those of a culprit who is going to the place of his execution, so unwilling am I, in the evening of a life nearly consumed in public cares, to quit a peaceful abode for an ocean of difficulties, without that competency of political skill, abilities and inclination which is necessary to manage the helm. . . . Integrity and firmness is all I can promise; these, be the voyage long or short, never shall forsake me although I may be deserted by all men. For of the consolations which are to be derived from these (under any circumstances) the world cannot deprive me."

Finally, enough senators and representatives reached New York, the votes were officially counted, and on April 14 Charles Thomson, secretary of Congress, appeared at Mount Vernon and delivered a brief speech to the Virginian, informing him of his election. Washington replied by reading his speech of acceptance, and two days later he and Thomson, accompanied by David Humphreys, left Mount Vernon in Washington's coach. It was an emotional moment for Washington, as his diary reveals: "About ten o'clock I bade adieu to Mount Vernon, to private life, and to domestic felicity; and, with a mind oppressed with more anxious sensations than I have words to express, set out for New York . . . with the best disposition to render service to my country in obedience to its call, but with less hope of answering its expectations."

After stopping in Alexandria for a poignant farewell to old friends and neighbors, the journey began, taking on almost at once the attributes of a triumphant march. Along his route bridges were decked in laurel and other greenery, the new Chief Executive was escorted from one town to the next by companies of horsemen, to be greeted by the pealing of churchbells, the roar of cannon, wildly cheering crowds, and the inevitable speeches and presentations. The bridge over the Assunpink at Trenton, where he had once stood off Cornwallis' redcoats, was a virtual tunnel of boughs, and here a chorus of young ladies met him with a welcoming song while children strewed baskets of flowers in his path; from Elizabeth Town he was rowed in a barge across the bay to New York, where the first tumultuous reception was followed by a week's festivities. Not until April 30, when Congress finally completed its arrangements for the inauguration, did the great occasion take place at the corner of Wall and Broad Streets, where Congress met. Washington, in a suit of brown cloth woven for him in Connecticut (it was his first public gesture toward encouraging American manufactures), white silk stockings and silver-buckled shoes, with a dress sword at his side, was driven to Federal Hall in a huge state coach provided by Congress, mounted the stairs, and entered the Senate chamber where he was escorted by John Adams to the central chair of three that sat on a dais. Adams announced that the oath of office would be administered by Robert R. Livingston, Chancellor of the State of New York, and led the way to a balcony overlooking the spectators.

Standing above a crowd that filled the streets as far as the eye could see, Washington faced Livingston, placed his hand on the Bible, and swore that he would "faithfully execute the office of President of the United States" and would, to the best of his ability, "preserve, protect, and defend the Constitution of the United States." He bowed to kiss the Bible and Livingston announced, "It is done," and then shouted, loud and clear, "Long live George Washington, President of the United States!" Cheers echoed through the city, church bells pealed out their song, and from the harbor came the boom of cannon from all the ships at anchor. Washington bowed again and again and finally retreated from the crowd to make his way into the Senate chamber to deliver his speech. Nervously shifting his manuscript from one hand to the other, he read in a voice so "deep and a little tremulous," one listener said, that the audience had to lean forward to hear him. For about twenty minutes he spoke and then sat down, looking weary and old beyond his years. ("Time," one Senator observed, "had made havoc upon his face.")

Reading the speech, it is quite clear that it was neither stirring, eloquent, nor profound; in fact, it was somewhat ponderous, as so many of Washington's official writings were. But to all those who heard it —

most of whom were reduced to tears by the experience — there was something intensely moving about the plain, straightforward address, delivered rather awkwardly by a plain, straightforward, unpretentious man who made no claim to expertise in the arts of government, politics, or diplomacy. He was, they knew, a man of honor and probity, who had nothing to gain from the office (he even proposed that he receive no salary but be reimbursed for his expenses, as he had insisted during the Revolution, and although Congress later fixed his salary at $25,000 a year he drew only his expenses, which, in four years, about equaled what his salary would have been). As events would show, he was honest and methodical rather than brilliant in reaching decisions and in administering the government, and possessed of abundant good sense. And these qualities — coupled with the immense prestige and standing he had — were about all the new republic would need as it got off to a start in life.

How uncertain most of the leading participants in that government were about the role they were to play and the functions they were to perform is illustrated by an incident that immediately followed Washington's address. After leaving Federal Hall he made his way through the crowds to Saint Paul's Chapel for a service, and when he returned home for dinner, prior to the fireworks and illuminations scheduled for the evening, the Senate convened and immediately fell into acrimonious debate over the question of how to reply to Washington's speech. What prompted the wrangle was the suggestion, probably made in all innocence, that reference should be made to his "most gracious speech," but this phrase reminded too many members of the way the British Parliament addressed the King and it was decided at last to eliminate the words. Americans, it was thought, might consider them "the first step of the ladder in the ascent to royalty."

Nor was Washington himself any more confident of himself. As he wrote a friend in Virginia, "So much is expected [of me] in such a new and critical situation, that I feel an insuperable diffidence in my own abilities."

So the ship of state was launched at last, its course to be determined in large part by two new institutions of American life — the President and the Constitution. The Virginian whose public utterances and conduct would be studied as carefully by future generations as by his own was fully conscious of the fact of being first and realized the significance that would be attributed to precedents he set, rules he followed. Washington wrote in May to Vice-President Adams, John Jay, and Alexander Hamilton in a memorandum seeking advice on what he should do about social functions, "Many things which appear of little importance in themselves and at the beginning, may have great and durable consequences from their having been established at the commencement of a new general government."

Happily for all concerned, the summer of 1789 brought no problems to the new general government more serious than matters of protocol, and as Washington moved to establish his own pattern of social life, around which the activities of the capital would center, his decisions were based upon the need to preserve his independence from the throngs of visitors who might call on him at all hours, while making himself sufficiently visible to the public as the figurehead of government. Although Adams and Hamilton advised him to remain aloof from the public, Washington compromised, characteristically: he decided to hold a weekly dinner for government officials; he established a system of weekly "levees," at which any citizen might call and meet the President; but he accepted no private invitations. He also proposed to travel, whenever he could, to various parts of the country — not only to see those sections that were unfamiliar to him, but to be seen by his countrymen.

There was some question as to what his form of address should be, and the Senate proposed that he be called "His Highness, the President of the United States of America, and Protector of their Liberties." Happily, the House would have none of that, preferring simply "President of the United States," and as time went on Washington became generally known as "Mr. President." Ludicrous as it sounds to a twentieth-century ear, the senatorial title had its roots in the mood of the moment. Virtually all members of government were so conscious of precedents to be set, so jealous of their privileges and perquisites, that the tone of the first administration was stiff and formal, with everyone a little uncomfortable about it, but determined to preserve the dignity of public affairs at all costs. For better or worse, the pattern of government that had been foreseen by some architects of the Constitution, in which the Senate would serve as a select, privy council to the President, never did evolve. Perhaps its was Washington's fault, perhaps the Senate's — no matter; what happened was that the Chief Executive and the senators maintained their distance from each other (on only one occasion did he visit the Senate, to confer on a matter of foreign policy, and he never repeated the unsuccessful experiment), and what advice the President sought was from personal friends — Virginians, most of them — and from the men he appointed to head executive departments. Nothing in the Constitution, of course, had suggested anything like a "cabinet" of advisers, but by usage that is what evolved in Washington's first term.

Most of what came to be called cabinet offices had existed in one form or another under the previous government, and when Washington appointed men to fill certain posts he was merely following tradition, for the most part. As Secretary of the Treasury he named the brilliant young Alexander Hamilton, who had served under him in the Revolution; another veteran, Henry Knox, became his Secretary of War; Edmund Randolph of Virginia was appointed Attorney General; and another Virginian, Thomas Jefferson, was the Secretary of State. John Jay of New York was appointed Chief Justice of the Supreme Court.

After a somewhat uneventful summer Congress adjourned on September 29, 1789, and on October 15 the President departed for a month's tour of New England that was to take him through Westchester and Connecticut on to Springfield and Boston. From there he journeyed to Portsmouth, New Hampshire, and to Kittery (later part of Maine, but then a province of Massachusetts), and on November 13 he was back in New York, having completed a tour that gave him more knowledge of New England manufactories and commerce than he had ever known. He had also resolved a small contretemps involving states' rights. In Boston, Governor John Hancock had invited him to dine, but when Washington arrived in the city the governor was not among those who called upon him; he sent his regrets, saying that an attack of gout kept him housebound. The President was not about to be upstaged by Hancock; realizing immediately that the Massachusetts man was trying to establish the precedent that the President visited a state only as a guest of its governor, he canceled the dinner engagement and, the next day, received a contrite Hancock at his own lodgings.

When Congress reconvened in January, the mood of the capital changed almost immediately from one of unity and harmony to that of rancor and faction. Despite Washington's hopes that opposition political parties could be avoided, certain issues confronting the government were so fundamental that it was inevitable that strongminded men would have opposing and sometimes irreconcilable views on them. The first such issue was to split Washington's advisers irrevocably, polarizing them in rival camps from which a permanent two-party system evolved in the United States. As James Madison concluded ruefully, "the spirit of party and faction" was a natural state of affairs in any civilized nation, but to Washington it was a painful experience. The one thing he had wanted to avoid at all costs — dissension — proved to be the dominant theme of his administration.

Washington had always attracted talented young assistants to his side, and in Alexander Hamilton, his Secretary of the Treasury, and Thomas Jefferson, Secretary of Foreign Affairs, he had two of the most brilliant men the nation would ever produce. Hamilton, not yet thirty-five years old, had served as Washington's secretary and aide in the Revolution, had made the first proposal for a constitutional convention, and in collaboration with James Madison had written *The Federalist* papers, leading the fight for adoption of the Constitution. A restless, ambitious, supremely confident young man, he was Washington's closest confidant in the early months of the administration and as such was thought to dominate the Chief Executive's thinking on matters of public policy. Jefferson, the political philosopher, lacked Hamilton's ambition, had little of his love for a fight, but was just as stubborn in defense of his ideas, and the brilliance of the two men, their different temperaments and ideologies, made it virtually certain that they would clash on the basic questions facing the new republic. What brought matters to a head was Hamilton's plan — presented to Congress a week after Washington's first annual message — for strengthening public credit and reducing the national debt.

During the Revolution, both Congress and the individual states had gone deeply in debt — to the extent of about eighty million dollars, of which the states still owed about twenty-five million. Hamilton was convinced that national honor and confidence in the new government demanded that this entire debt be refunded at par, and he proposed to accomplish this by assuming the state debts as a national liability. To do so, he would call in the old certificates, replacing them with new notes at full face value, and establish a sinking fund for repayment of principal and interest. Unfortunately, the securities representing the obligations were not only greatly depreciated, but a large number of the original certificates, which had been held by farmers and soldiers, had by this time passed into the hands of speculators at enormous discounts. Hamilton's plan, which was supported by conservative northern business and mercantile groups, was violently opposed by Jefferson, who championed the interests of agrarian and libertarian elements, as well as the southern states, all of which — except South Carolina — had already paid off their war debts.

As spring turned to summer no resolution was in sight, and Hamilton cast about for a compromise to break the impasse. Since the sectional partisans had failed to resolve the question of where the permanent capital would be located, Hamilton proposed to Jefferson that the latter should support his plan for funding the debt in return for Hamilton's backing location of the capital in the South. And so it was done, Hamilton and his northern friends acceding to the placement of the capital on the banks of the Potomac (at a site to be selected by Washington), Jefferson and the Southerners going along with the funding scheme. As a compromise within the compromise, both factions appeased the powerful Pennsylvania bloc by agreeing to move the capital from New York to Philadelphia until the new Potomac site was ready.

Jefferson thought he had been gulled, as perhaps he had, and Hamilton's next scheme found him firmly aligned against it, to Washington's despair. Hamilton put before the Congress in December, 1790, a brilliantly conceived plan for the establishment of a national bank, and in the hue and cry that followed this proposal the President asked his cabinet members for their opinion on its constitutionality. What he received from Hamilton and Jefferson were two masterful arguments — each diametrically opposed to the other — and when Congress passed the bill, Washington had to decide whether or not to veto it, and in so doing, to decide between his two advisers. He chose to support Hamilton's view. Similarly on the question of an excise tax recommended by Hamilton — to the point where it seemed to Jefferson and his supporters that the evil genius Hamilton was in effect the President's prime minister, threatening to destroy the government with his policies and to ruin all they had worked so hard to bring about. To make the situation worse, Hamilton was not only getting his way on financial matters, he was also meddling, secretly or openly, in other departments of government.

Adding to the controversy was the feud between two rival newspapers — John Fenno's *Gazette of the United States*, which supported Hamilton; and the *National Gazette*, edited by the poet Philip Freneau, who was a friend of Madison and Jefferson. The papers were little more than propaganda sheets, but they gave public utterance to the ugly and fundamental quarrel that had split Washington's official family. By this time, the terms Federalist and Anti-Federalist, which had originally denoted those favoring or opposing adoption of the Constitution, had

largely lost their meaning. "Federalist" was now attached to partisans of Hamilton, the label suggesting one who favored a vigorous and powerful central government that supported industry, finance, and commerce. Those who once thought of themselves as Anti-Federalists gradually adopted a new label, Democratic-Republican, which was eventually shortened to Republican, and these were the followers of Jefferson, who believed that the best government was a decentralized one and that the nation's future lay in the hands of the small farmer and artisan, who were fully capable of governing themselves without undue interference.

One effect of this factionalism was a changing public attitude toward Washington. The resentment against Hamilton's "Federalist tendencies" had inspired charges that the Treasury Secretary, and perhaps the President himself, were preparing the way for a change from the republican form of government to that of a monarchy. Washington's habitual unbending nature, his reserve, his punctilio, the formality of his public appearances — all seemed to give credibility to the rumor that he was secretly yearning to adopt the manners, if not the title, of a king.

The struggle between Hamilton and Jefferson tended to overshadow most other events of Washington's term of office, yet the business of government went on, and reasonably well, all things considered. By May of 1790 Rhode Island finally ratified the Constitution — the last original state to do so; the first ten amendments, which had been shepherded through Congress by James Madison, were presented to the states for ratification and by mid-December of 1791 were incorporated into the Constitution; and in the fall of 1790 the President and members of the Congress were preparing to move to the new but still temporary capital in Philadelphia. In May of that year Washington had come down with a severe case of pneumonia and for a time was so ill the doctors thought he might not pull through it, but in June he was fit again and on August 30 left for Philadelphia to inspect the house of Robert Morris, which was to be placed at his disposal.

It was, he informed his secretary Tobias Lear, "the best they could get" and was certainly "the best *single House* in the City; yet, without additions it is inadequate to the *commodious* accommodation of my family." And the man who was accustomed to the capaciousness of Mount Vernon went on to tell Lear what ought to be done to make the Morris house more to his liking. Afterward he left for Mount Vernon, where he stayed for several months, and returned to Philadelphia in November to deliver his second annual address to the Congress. Summarizing the situation as he saw it, he could report steady and encouraging progress: trade and agriculture were prospering and the nation's credit, thanks to Hamilton's efforts, was showing marked improvement, as evidenced by a loan recently obtained from Holland. On the western frontier, however, the struggle between white settlers and Indians, which had gone on almost unabated for more than a quarter of a century, showed no sign of cessation; in fact, the situation was worsening if anything. The problem was enough to have tried the patience of Job. On the one hand, the administration had signed certain treaties with various Indian tribes, establishing boundaries of sorts and agreeing to respect them; but on the other, there was no stopping restless Americans from moving into these territories and settling wherever their fancy took them. The situation was exacerbated by the activities of the British in Detroit and the Spanish in Florida and Louisiana, who found it advantageous to encourage Indian tribes to resist American encroachment and were stirring up trouble wherever they could find it. Most worrisome was the state of affairs in the Northwest Territory, which ordinances of 1785 and 1787 had divided into townships for settlement, providing the governmental framework through which local autonomy and statehood would eventually come about. In 1787 the Territory still had a population of some forty-five thousand Indians and about two thousand French and before American settlers could occupy it a great deal of bloody fighting would have to take place. At the time he delivered his message to the Congress Washington had learned that an expedition led by General Josiah Harmar had been roundly defeated. The Indian problem, as Washington of all men might have foreseen, would not be settled for a long time to come.

In March, 1791, after Congress adjourned, Washington set off on a tour of the South, duplicating his successful inspection trip to New England a year and a half earlier. His little caravan consisted, as he wrote in his diary, of an aide, Major Jackson, five servants— his valet, two footmen, a coachman and postilion— and his "Chariet" drawn by four horses, a baggage wagon, and five extra horses. After crossing Chesapeake Bay—where he was nearly lost in a sudden storm—he visited Annapolis and then went on to Georgetown, which was contiguous to the site of the new permanent capital city. There he saw sketches made by the Frenchman Pierre Charles L'Enfant,

whom he had engaged to design the place, and discussed plans with the commissioners appointed by Congress to carry out the work. Then he was off across Virginia, traveling south to New Bern and Wilmington, North Carolina, and on to Charleston, to be royally greeted by the citizens of that city, who took him to see the ruins of Fort Moultrie on Sullivans Island. He visited most of the important Revolutionary battlefields in the area, which he had never seen, and, after a stopover in Savannah, made his way to Philadelphia via Mount Vernon, having journeyed nearly two thousand miles in a springless carriage over roads which must have made the trip hideously uncomfortable. But he had shown himself to the people of the South and had seen with his own eyes the general state of that region, finding it on the whole poorer and far less populated than New England, with little industry but with a hospitality that could scarcely be matched elsewhere in the land.

Upon his return he learned, as has each of his successors in office, that the most pressing problems never vanish of their own accord. Before the year was out he would receive word that the expedition sent out against the Indians in the wake of Harmar's defeat had been disastrously defeated, at a cost of six hundred casualties. The Spanish, in control of the mouth of the Mississippi, still bottled up the flow of commerce from the western settlements; the British still refused to yield their northern outposts on grounds that the United States had not honored the terms of the 1783 peace treaty. And from Europe came ominous news— word that Louis XVI and Marie Antoinette of France, attempting to flee the country, had been captured and brought back to Paris on Lafayette's orders, to be placed in virtual imprisonment. Jefferson, who brought Washington the tidings, recalled that he had never seen the latter "so dejected by any event." When the Bastille had fallen in 1789 Washington remarked that the events that produced a constitutional government in France seemed to him as distant as if they had occurred on "another planet." Yet with remarkable prescience he described the beginning of the French Revolution as but "the first paroxysm." The uprising, he believed, "is of too great magnitude to be effected in so short a space and with the loss of so little blood," and he foresaw the inevitable "licentiousness of the people" that would ultimately lead to disastrous consequences for the idealists who had begun the business. After receiving from Lafayette the "main key" to the Bastille and a picture of the ruined prison, Washington sent thanks to his former protégé, who was then in nominal control of the government, expressing hope that he might travel safely "through the quicksands and rocks which threatened instant destruction on every side." But it was not to be, and the news Washington received in August of 1791 meant that all Europe might soon be embroiled in the upheaval. Luckily, he could not foresee then how his own administration would be torn asunder when the opposing factions led by Hamilton and Jefferson took sides on the issues created by the Revolution in France.

In the spring of 1792, Washington was thinking toward retirement the following year, trying to decide how and when to announce his intentions. The years and illness had taken their toll (in addition to the bout of pneumonia in 1790 he had suffered a tumor on his thigh the year before) and his memory had begun to fail. Beyond that, of course, he longed for Mount Vernon and tranquillity, a respite from his responsibilities and relief from the divisive arguments that troubled his days and nights. He had discussed his feelings with James Madison and on May 20 wrote him from Mount Vernon, requesting that Madison put his mind "to a Valedictory address from me to the public; expressing in plain & modest terms . . . that having arrived at a period of life when the private Walks of it, in the shade of retirement, becomes necessary, and will be most pleasing to me . . . that I take my leave of them as a public man. . . ." Having unburdened himself of that, he also confided to Madison that only one circumstance would cause him to change his mind—that was, if his yielding of office "would involve the Country in serious disputes respecting the chief Magistrate." He was all too conscious of the "floating, & divided opinions which seem to prevail at present." It was not ego that prompted him to imagine that only he was capable of holding the highest office in the nation; it was, as he and Madison realized, the simple fact that no other individual possessed the confidence of the public at a time when the government was still a rather shaky affair, new and largely untested. Certainly neither Jefferson nor Hamilton was capable of inspiring or maintaining unity; John Adams was too strongly Federalist, and was distrusted as a New Englander and a snob to boot; Jay was another staunch Federalist; Knox was, too, and was no man for the task in any case. That left Madison, who was well known as a Republican. Or Washington. And no sooner had the latter given voice to his fears than the quarrel between Hamilton and Jefferson turned more vituperative, changing from an argument over opposing political philosophies into a violent and open personal vendetta that was "harrowing & tearing our vitals," as Washington perceived.

Although it may have occurred to him that one of the two antagonists would have to go, in an effort to achieve harmony, he had no wish to lose the services of either. Not only were they men of uncommon ability whose counsel was invaluable; their presence in his "cabinet" gave it a balance he might otherwise have been unable to achieve, and he probably assumed that it was better to have them at his side, where he could watch over them, than elsewhere, stirring up trouble.

Then came a long letter from Jefferson enumerating twenty-one charges against Hamilton and his followers, most damning of which was their putative objective of changing "the present republican form of Government, to that of a monarchy; of which the British Constitution is to be the model." Determined to put an end to the controversy, Washington wrote Hamilton, listing Jefferson's complaints against him without revealing the source, saying only that they were charges he had heard from various parties. As might have been expected, Hamilton responded angrily, eloquently, and at length, categorically denying each criticism in turn and labeling the lot "malignant and false."

With the second presidential election in the offing, other troubles were brewing in the fall of 1792. From western Pennsylvania came reports that opposition to Hamilton's new excise tax on whiskey was increasing daily. The Indians in the North, spurred on by the British, had murdered two officers sent to treat with them; in the South the Spanish were not only arousing the Creeks to resist a recent treaty with the United States but were also assembling troops, ordnance, and stores in New Orleans for some unknown but threatening purpose. From France the news continued bad, and although Washington remained convinced that a war there would not affect the United States, he feared for the safety of his friends—chiefly Lafayette—as much as for the peace of the Old World. In the face of all these troubles, domestic and foreign, the long-suffering President wrote letters to both Hamilton and Jefferson, appealing to them to end the dispute that was so disruptive lest it ruin "the goodly fabric we have been erecting."

Their replies were hardly reassuring. Jefferson, who had informed Washington he wished to retire, was truculent, laying all the blame on Hamilton; the latter placed the onus on Jefferson and stated flatly that he refused to discontinue his attacks on the Republicans as long as they disparaged his own reputation and endangered the nation's well-being. Meanwhile, the election approached and the newspaper war between the two factions increased in intensity and bitterness, to a point where Washington wondered if "any living man [could] manage the helm or . . . keep the machine together." By now his dilemma was acute. If he decided to retire from office at this critical juncture he risked the possibility, as his Philadelphia friend Mrs. Eliza Powel wrote him, "that a great deal of the well-earned popularity you are now in possession of will be torn from you by the envious and malignant should you follow the bent of your inclinations." Not only that, she went on, it might be said that when his reputation was threatened he "would take no further risks" for the people. From his secretary Tobias Lear, Washington heard that "the universal desire" in Philadelphia was that he accept a second term; from Jefferson came word that in the South "there was but one voice . . . which was for his continuance." Although the President himself may have doubted the wisdom of remaining in office, the country at large did not, and on February 13, 1793, the Electoral College echoed the balloting held the previous November by choosing him unanimously. John Adams, the incumbent, received seventy-seven votes as Vice-President; George Clinton of New York had five; Jefferson four; and Aaron Burr one.

Despite the gratification he felt at being re-elected unanimously (he admitted that he would have experienced "chagreen" had he not received "a pretty respectable vote"), he faced a second term reluctantly. It had been his "fixed determination," he wrote Governor Henry Lee of Virginia, "to return to the walks of private life." For one thing, the affairs of Mount Vernon seemed more pressing and time-consuming than ever before; his nephew George Augustine Washington, who had managed the plantation since 1787, died in 1793, to be replaced by one Anthony Whiting, and there was no surcease from the lengthy correspondence that traveled back and forth between him and the President — involving the planting of crops, the health of the help, supplies of nails, bricks, and other materials for repair and construction work. On and on it went, distracting Washington from his official duties, which became more onerous almost as soon as he had taken the oath of office for the second time.

The ceremony was a brief one. On March 4, 1793, Washington appeared at the Senate chamber; John Adams announced that a Supreme Court justice was prepared to administer the oath; Washington delivered the shortest inaugural address in U. S. history; and after repeating the oath, returned to his office to work. A crisis of major dimensions was brewing, brought on by events in Europe. Lafayette had been imprisoned by a new radical French government; France was at war with Austria and Prussia, and, after sending Louis XVI and his queen to the guillotine, declared war on England, Spain, and Holland. The question was, where would America stand? Would she side with her former ally which had made possible the success of the Revolution? Or would she align herself with Britain, lately the enemy, but still America's most important customer? To complicate matters further, there existed two treaties with France, signed in 1778 during the war. One called for mutually advantageous trade relations; the other was a pact stipulating that France would guarantee American independence and territorial boundaries while the United States would guarantee France's possession of her West Indies islands. On the face of it, there was a strong risk that the United States might be honor-bound to enter the European war on the side of France, and Jefferson's Republicans were emphatically arguing that the treaty of alliance was binding. Federalists denied that this was so, maintaining that the original treaty had been made with a monarchy and was null and void now that a revolutionary government had seized power.

In April, Washington gave the members of his cabinet a list of thirteen questions covering the subject of involvement in France's war. Although he carefully avoided using the word "neutrality," that was what he and his cabinet finally agreed to proclaim, and on April 22 the President signed a document calling upon citizens of the United States to "adopt and pursue a conduct friendly and impartial towards the belligerent powers." Officially, therefore, the U.S. was to be neutral; but unofficially Americans in all walks of life began making their views known, and the arrival of a new minister from France polarized public opinion.

Edmond Genêt, soon to be widely known as "Citizen Genêt," landed in Charleston, where he commissioned four privateers to attack British shipping before journeying to Philadelphia to present his credentials to President Washington. Along the way he was wildly acclaimed by "Gallomen" and bitterly denounced by "Anglomen," and in Philadelphia he met with a decidedly cool reception from Washington. Three weeks later the President ordered Secretary of State Thomas Jefferson to inform Genêt that his activities in Charleston were a violation of U.S. sovereignty and that the privateers he had commissioned would have to depart from American waters.

Although Genêt agreed to comply with Washington's wishes, his mischief-making was by no means over. Shortly it was discovered that he was arming a British ship, the *Little Sarah*, which had been captured by the French, and when Jefferson — reluctantly, and tardily — ordered him to send her to sea, Genêt threatened to take his case to the people of America. Furious, Washington asked Jefferson, "Is the Minister of the French Republic to set the Acts of this Government at defiance, *with impunity?* and then threaten the Executive with an appeal to the people? What must the world think of such conduct & of the Government of the U. States in submitting to it?" Genêt had behaved reprehensibly and even Jefferson was forced to admit, at last, that the French minister was *persona non grata*. Following the *Little Sarah* incident (the ship was belatedly sent to sea after Washington's outburst), Genêt was installed as president of the radical "Friends of Liberty and Equality" in Philadelphia, Jacobin clubs were founded in other cities, and Washington came under increasing attack for what seemed an ungrateful and unsympathetic attitude toward the French. His fear, of course, was that the United States might be pulled unwittingly into France's orbit, and despite his emotional ties to the former ally, he foresaw correctly that France was in less danger from enemies beyond its borders than from those in power, who "are ready to tear each other to pieces, and will, more than probably, prove the worst foes the country has." His aim was to avoid at all costs that the United States enter the bear pit of European power politics: hence his Neutrality Proclamation and hence his decision, in January of 1794, that Genêt must be recalled. The next month a new French minister arrived with a request for the arrest of Genêt and his return to Paris where, presumably, he would be put to death by a government more radical than the one that had sent him to America in the first place. Rather than see Genêt sent to the guillotine, Washington permitted him to remain in the United States, where he happily retired to obscurity.

Jefferson's Republicans regarded Washington's actions in the Genêt affair as those of a man who had been transformed from the war hero into a partisan schemer, a man who had turned his back on the old ally and was selling the nation out to the British, and their suspicions were confirmed by the next imbroglio in foreign affairs. In 1794 Washington dispatched Chief Justice John Jay to London to negotiate the outstanding differences be-

tween Britain and America — chief among them the continued presence of British troops in the Northwest. To the Republicans, Jay was not only a Federalist but an Anglophile, and when the results of the treaty he had signed became known in America they reacted with predictable outrage — burning Jay in effigy, denouncing Washington as a "political hypocrite" and the "Step-Father" of his country.

In sending Jay to England, Washington had not expected his emissary to work miracles. What he desired, above all, was that Jay preserve existing commercial relations, or improve them if that were possible, since the financial well-being of the new nation depended so heavily on the continuation of revenues from the British trade. He wanted, in addition, to remove the King's troops from those forts in the Northwest. In asking for a little, he was in truth playing for time, hoping against hope that the nation might be granted a respite from foreign involvements while consolidating its strength within its own borders. It was quite possible, had the Republicans had their way, that the United States would have found itself at war again with Britain, and that was a prospect too disastrous to contemplate. So while Washington was somewhat disappointed by the meager results of Jay's treaty he was reluctantly prepared to go along with it, and its terms were kept secret until an angrily divided Senate commenced debate behind closed doors. It was then that the Republican press got wind of the terms, then that the floodgates of criticism were opened, then that Hamilton, who was regarded as the arch-Federalist, was stoned in New York when he spoke in favor of the treaty. (Perhaps Hamilton had it coming. He had been so intent on maintaining the status quo with Britain in order to solidify his fiscal policies that he had — unknown to Jay — informed the British negotiators in advance of Jay's bargaining position.) The attacks continued long after the treaty was signed, but Washington stuck to his policy with the same dogged determination that had characterized his actions during the Revolution.

Meanwhile, the faces of his official family were changing as his second term wore on. In 1793 Tobias Lear, his secretary, departed, to enter business in the new Federal City on the Potomac. At the end of the year Jefferson resigned as Secretary of State, to be replaced by Edmund Randolph. Despite their differences, it was a loss to the President as well as to the nation. Washington had always regarded Jefferson as a balance wheel, a corrective voice to the dominant views of Hamilton, and indeed had often sided with

Jefferson at cabinet meetings. Now, if anything, he needed him more than ever before, and for a reason that Jefferson himself had noticed: "The firm tone of [Washington's] mind," Jefferson said, "for which he had been remarkable, was beginning to relax; its energy was abated; a listlessness of labor, a desire for tranquillity had crept on him, and a willingness to let others act, or even think, for him." Torn as always between official responsibilities and the business of his plantation, Washington found no competent substitute for Lear, with the result that his letters to the manager at Mount Vernon now began appearing in his own handwriting, to the detriment of official correspondence. Even the manager there was new; Anthony Whiting died at the same time Lear left, and all the instructions had to be communicated to a man unfamiliar with his duties.

After Jefferson's departure, the President leaned ever more heavily on Hamilton's advice and counsel, and in 1794 the two men were confronted with an ominous threat to the nation's security resulting from Hamilton's controversial financial plan. The plan had included, among other means to pay for the assumption of state debts, an excise tax on whiskey, and this aspect of it had been bitterly contested since 1791 by farmers in the West. There was simply no way a frontier farmer could take his grain to market and make a profit on it unless he first reduced it in bulk, and the best means he had of accomplishing that was to distill it into whiskey. Besides which, jugs of whiskey were an accepted form of currency on the cash-poor frontier, and the man who traded a gallon of liquor for a pig received no money with which to pay a tax to the revenue official. Not only that: since the closest federal court was in Philadelphia, distillers charged with violation of the law had to make a difficult journey that was as costly in time as it was in money in order to stand trial. By mid-summer of 1794 angry backwoodsmen were taking matters into their own hands: a federal marshal who tried to serve papers on a western Pennsylvania distiller was attacked, the home of John Neville, an excise inspector, was put to the torch, and soldiers arriving to stop the violence were compelled to surrender by armed farmers. There followed tarrings and featherings of officials, further destruction of property, and rifling of the U.S. mails — indications that government authority was collapsing, as it had in Shays' rebellion in 1786. It was the first real test of the new republic's ability to govern.

Washington attempted to persuade the state of Pennsylvania to handle its own problem, but Governor Thomas Mifflin refused to send out the militia, saying it was a matter for the courts to resolve. Calling on his cabinet for advice, Washington was urged by Hamilton to put down the insurrection by force, but he elected to send three commissioners to offer amnesty to the rebels in return for their agreement to obey the laws. In Washington's opinion, the trouble had been stirred up by "the Democratic Societies" — those groups that had been formed in support of Genêt — and he was convinced that unless something were done to put an end to them, the country would see "the most diabolical attempts to destroy the best fabric of human government & happiness that has ever been presented for the acceptance of mankind." So while he awaited a report from the commissioners, he called thirteen thousand militiamen into federal service and warned the rebels to disperse by September 1.

The insurgents had not thought it possible for Washington to raise an army against them and they defied the commissioners, only to learn that the President's supporters and foes alike rallied to his side in a gesture of extraordinary loyalty to the man and the Constitution he had sworn to uphold. (More volunteers turned out than Washington had been able to assemble during most of the Revolutionary War.) In the temporary absence of Henry Knox, the Secretary of War, Alexander Hamilton became Acting Secretary, and thus it happened that Washington made one of the worst blunders of his political career.

Hamilton had argued that he, as the man who had proposed the excise tax in the first place, ought to be the one to enforce it, so on the last day of September, 1794, when Washington rode off in command of the army, Alexander Hamilton was at his side. For several years now, Republicans had been accusing Hamilton of trying to establish an elitist, authoritarian form of government, and a good many of them considered that he had deliberately created the crisis in western Pennsylvania as a means of advocating a military dictatorship. So when he and the man whom many Republicans considered his cat's paw marched off at the head of an army to put down a group of plain citizens, their worst suspicions seemed to be confirmed. As it turned out, the campaign itself was uneventful; the arrival of the army was enough to take the starch out of the insurgents. Washington discovered that he was now too old to sit in the saddle all day; he rode part of the way with the troops in a phaeton to rest his aching bones, and by the time they reached Bedford and he impressed on the commanders his desire for conciliation of the rebels, he decided to go no further and to return to Philadelphia. In bidding farewell to the soldiers, he gave them his views on the principles of a free government. They were, he said, to "combat and subdue all who may be found in arms in opposition to the national will and authority," and to "aid and support the civil magistrate in bringing offenders to justice." But he wanted no reprisals, no terrorism — only justice. After his departure, a few rebels were arrested and two condemned to death (Washington subsequently pardoned them), but the army behaved in such a way as to quiet the fears of many of Washington's detractors. Even so, Jefferson condemned the campaign as "an armament against people at their ploughs," and Madison believed that if it had come to fighting, a permanent standing army would have resulted, which was certainly what Hamilton wanted. The President would have none of that, however: he recommended that Congress maintain a small force in western Pennsylvania until the trouble had entirely subsided, and contented himself with suggesting that the militia laws be revised to make it easier to assemble a force to deal with future uprisings.

He had not forgotten those Democratic Societies, however, and when he delivered his annual address to Congress on November 15, he abandoned all pretense of impartiality and called upon his countrymen "to root out internal sedition." So immense was his prestige that the Democratic Societies began to disappear, one by one, but Jefferson and others saw Washington's attack on these organizations as an assault on popular participation in government, on "the freedom of discussion, the freedom of writing, printing, and publishing." Madison regarded Washington's speech as "perhaps the greatest error of his political life" — one that put him "ostentatiously at the head of the other party," making him the head of a faction rather than the head of state, and there is reason to suspect that Washington himself regretted what he had done. Although he admitted to no mistake, never again as President did he single out what he regarded as the opposition for censure.

Early in 1795 Washington's cabinet underwent another upheaval. Henry Knox, pleading the press of personal financial problems, resigned as Secretary of War and retired to his home in Maine. And Alexander Hamilton, concluding that he could accomplish little more in office, resigned. As he told his sister, "Public office in this country has few attractions. . . . The opportunity of doing good, from the jealousy of power and the spirit of faction, is too small to warrant a long continuance of private sacrifices." Besides, he went on, there was not even much prospect of "gratifying in future the love of fame." Hamilton would continue to exert a dominant influence on national affairs (he remained an éminence grise, a shadow cabinet figure, partially at Washington's request, while practicing law in New York), but his departure meant that the President's stalwarts — men on whom he had relied constantly — had deserted him at a time when he most needed their help. Nowadays, when Washington wrote letters to Jefferson and Madison, they dealt with such matters as crops or education — not national policy, on which he had so often come to them for counsel. His cabinet was composed of four avowed Federalists whose political attitudes were his own, but these were lesser men. Timothy Pickering of Massachusetts was a rather surprising choice to replace Knox as Secretary of War, since Pickering had been implicated in the Conway Cabal during the Revolution; Oliver Wolcott, former Comptroller of the Treasury, succeeded Hamilton; and William Bradford was Attorney General. The only holdover from the original cabinet was Edmund Randolph, a Virginian and a friend for twenty years, who had served first as Attorney General and then, when Jefferson retired, as Secretary of State. Only Randolph could be classed as a close confidant and now he was to become a source of humiliation and embarrassment to the aging President.

Physically, Washington was in relatively good condition, but his sixty-third birthday found him deeply depressed. As he saw it, he had passed over to "the wrong . . . side of my grand climacteric." And while he remained in this gloomy mood he was informed by Timothy Pickering that Randolph was a traitor. From Britain's ambassador had come an intercepted letter, written a year earlier by France's ambassador, Joseph Fauchet, to the authorities in Paris. The gist of this message was that Randolph had called upon Fauchet to suggest that the American Secretary of State was in a position to put an end to the Whiskey Rebellion, thus bringing relief to the pro-French Westerners, and the inference was that this could be accomplished by the payment of a suitably large bribe to Randolph.

When Washington, in front of Pickering and Wolcott, handed Randolph a translation of the letter, Randolph first attempted to explain what lay behind the apparently incriminating document, then said he would prepare a written statement of the facts, and finally dashed from the room, shouting, "I could not continue in the office one second after such treatment." Before the day was out, Randolph gave Washington a letter denying his guilt, but repeating his intention of resigning as a result of the manner in which he had been humiliated. Although it was not clear at the time, it appeared later that Randolph was probably innocent of the charges that Pickering and Wolcott brought against him. In light of Ambassador Fauchet's subsequent denial that Randolph had suggested a bribe, what seems likely is that Pickering and Wolcott, fearing that Randolph might stand in the way of ratification of Jay's Treaty, had done their level best to discredit him in Washington's eyes, and had succeeded. It was the end of the two Virginians' friendship and some months later, in December of 1795, Randolph published a 103-page *Vindication* defending his own actions, revealing Washington's own lack of enthusiasm for the Jay Treaty, and accusing the President of weakness, indecision, and hypocrisy. Never again did Washington mention his old friend Randolph's name in a letter.

Adding salt to his wounds was a mounting campaign of abuse that appeared in newspapers and in public utterances about him. A Philadelphia journalist called him "a man in his political dotage" and a "supercilious tyrant"; a Congressman wrote that Washington was "the head of a British faction, and gratitude no longer blinds the public mind." The press fastened on the ineptness of his military career and claimed that he had been elected President only because of "the insipid uniformity of his mind." And several articles in one journal charged — embarrassingly and accurately — that he had overdrawn the salary voted him by Congress. Although Washington pointed out that his salary had been used only to defray official expenses (which it did not begin to cover), the fact was that he drew down more than $11,000 in the first three months of his second term although he was entitled to receive $6,250.

Attacked unceasingly for what people regarded as the invidious terms of the Jay Treaty, Washington was further humiliated when he tried to replace Randolph as Secretary of State. Five men who were offered the post refused — among them Charles Cotesworth Pinckney (to whom Washington had written that "the affairs of this country are in a violent paroxysm"), and Patrick Henry. And when he asked Hamilton for help, the reply was: "I wish, sir, I could present to you any useful ideas . . . but the embarrassment is extreme as to Secretary of State. . . . In fact, a first-rate character is not attainable. A second-rate must be taken with good dispositions and barely decent qualifications. . . . 'Tis a sad omen for the government."

There were more such omens ahead. Against his better judgment, Washington finally offered State to Pickering, who refused, forcing the President to beg him to accept. To replace Pickering as Secretary of War, Washington chose John Eager Howard of Maryland and was turned down. Then Patrick Henry and another refusal. His nomination of John Rutledge to be Chief Justice was rejected by the Senate (Rutledge was accused of insanity); a second nominee was confirmed, but declined the seat; and an Associate Justice resigned, leaving two vacancies on the Court. At last, the embarrassing business was settled. James McHenry was named Secretary of War; Charles Lee, Attorney General; Oliver Ellsworth, Chief Justice; and Thomas Chase, Associate Justice. But these were not the giants of old. "The offices are once more filled," John Adams wrote, "but how differently than when Jefferson, Hamilton, Jay, etc., were here."

In September of 1795, when the President received a letter from George Washington Lafayette, the son of the Marquis, he did not dare invite the young man to stay at his home lest he provoke another political storm, and did not even see him until the following April. The House of Representatives, dominated by Republicans, threatened to block implementation of Jay's Treaty by refusing to appropriate the necessary funds and then passed a bill that would have given the House the right to reconsider treaties and to supervise all acts of the Chief Executive, a move that would have placed the so-called "popular branch" of the government firmly in the saddle.

Convinced that the House had brought "the Constitution to the brink of a precipice," Washington decided that the problem confronting him was "one of those great occasions than which none more important has occurred or probably may occur again," and his reaction was unequivocal. In a historic message delivered on March 30, 1796, he informed the House that that body had no right to examine presidential documents except in the case of impeachment, and that treaties ratified by the Senate were law, from that moment on, and as such to be honored. There would be no compromise.

The entire country followed the debate that ensued, as the House went into a Committee of the Whole to discuss the President's reply, and not until the Federalists trotted out their champion orator, Fisher Ames of Massachusetts, who was said to be at death's door, was the issue resolved. In a ringing speech Ames described the hideous consequences that would result from breaking the treaty with England, painting a vivid picture of savage Indians descending on helpless frontier settlements, butchering women and children, predicting that "The darkness of midnight will glitter with the blaze of your dwellings." The day was won, and as Jefferson was quick to see, his party was badly crippled. "Republicanism," he wrote James Monroe, "must lie on its oars, resign the vessel to its pilot, and themselves to the course he thinks best for them."

Ames' dramatic speech was what was remembered as having turned the tide, but there were many other factors involved, most of which had been described by Washington in his annual message to Congress on December 8, 1795. The nation was prospering. Turnpikes were under construction, linking one section of the country to another; coal deposits had been discovered in Pennsylvania; foreign trade was booming. The Federal City on the Potomac was a-building. Three new states had entered the Union — Vermont, Kentucky, and Tennessee. And a treaty signed with Spain in October of 1795 and popularly named for its negotiator, Thomas Pinckney, had at last opened the Mississippi River to Americans on the western frontier, granting them the right to deposit freight in New Orleans for shipment by sea, while settling the southern boundary of the United States at the thirty-first parallel.

Whatever Washington's disappointment at leaving office with the unwanted cries of factionalism ringing in his ears, he could look with gratification upon that list of accomplishments. And there were others, less tangible, but no less significant and enduring. For all his detractors said of him, he had set a standard of probity that would serve as a beacon for most of his successors. He had established what for lack of a better term might be called the majesty of the Presidency. He had set a new nation upon the road to the future in peace and prosperity. And despite the party disputes that aggravated and grieved him, the disparate and often discontented segments of the nation had united behind the Constitution, accepting it, whatever its flaws, as the framework of laws and principles by which they would be governed. As Thomas Jefferson so succinctly described the achievement, Washington had conducted the councils of the nation "through the birth of a government, new in its forms and principles, until it settled

down into a quiet and orderly train . . . ." It had been an immensely demanding and trying task, often filled with sorrow and frustration, and as he had accurately foreseen many years earlier, he had been all but forsaken by some of his friends. Yet the pledge he made then he had kept: as he had written Henry Knox, before taking office, "Integrity and firmness is all I can promise," and he had delivered those in full measure.

Now, as he prepared to leave, he turned once again to a man who had served him loyally in the past. About the end of April, 1796, Washington requested Alexander Hamilton's assistance in preparing a valediction. Before doing so, the President retrieved from his files the farewell address Madison had written for him at the end of his first term and added to it an angry justification of his conduct in office. The criticism had cut deep and his impulse now was to make this his self-defense. For several months he and Hamilton corresponded, sending revised drafts back and forth to each other until Washington was finally satisfied with the result. In mid-September he summoned David Claypoole, the owner of the *American Daily Advertiser,* to his Philadelphia office and handed him the document. (The President concluded that the address should be released to one newspaper, after which he would "suffer it to work its way" into other channels.) On September 19, 1796, it was published on the second page of Claypoole's journal under an inconspicuous headline reading: "To the PEOPLE of the United States, Friends and fellow citizens." At the end of the text appeared the words "G. Washington, United States, September 7, 1796." Neither he nor Claypoole felt the need to explain the document beyond that.

Most of Washington's anger and bitterness had disappeared from the address as it evolved, and what remained was a message of advice to his countrymen. He informed them that he would refuse a third term, thereby setting a precedent that would endure for a century and a half; he reminded them of the importance of union — "The palladium of your political safety"; he warned against allowing factional disputes to divide the nation (he had learned through experience that Madison was right; "the spirit of party," he admitted ruefully, was "Unfortunately . . . inseparable from our nature"); he encouraged the preservation and protection of the nation's credit; and, in what was to become a keystone of public policy until the twentieth century, he cautioned them against making permanent foreign alliances which could "entangle our peace and prosperity in the toils of European ambition, rivalship, interest, humor, or caprice." With that he apologized for his own inadequacies, spoke of his anticipation of retirement, and bid them adieu.

As might have been expected, the address was reprinted again and again in America and abroad, and the reaction in the United States was generally a mixture of deep satisfaction and approval. Washington had, after all, renounced an office whose term had been undefined by the Constitution and he had not only yielded willingly a position of great power and honor but done so in such a way as to establish a principle of orderly succession in the governance of the nation. Above all else, his message was a statement of principles with which most of his countrymen could and did agree — in particular his plea for a posture of neutrality in foreign affairs, through which peace might be attained and preserved.

It was not as though he was leaving office with all the problems solved, however; the country still seethed with controversy over Europe's war, while American vessels were being stopped and searched by ships of the British and French navies. Yet there was a general feeling that the nation was safe for a while at least — had passed a momentous landmark of some kind — and that this was in no small way Washington's doing. On March 3, 1797, he carried out his last official acts as President, by pardoning several men convicted of treason during the Whiskey Rebellion and remitting a fine imposed on a smuggler. A few weeks earlier he had celebrated his last birthday in office — his sixty-sixth — by attending a ball with twelve-thousand persons (including several who were trampled to death in a rush to supper). There, when Martha and George Washington entered the hall, the applause from the huge audience was said to be "indescribable," and the President's lady was moved to tears, while his own emotions "were too powerful to be concealed. He could sometimes scarcely speak." As Washington later wrote his old friend Knox, he had no wish to mix again in politics ever and wanted more than anything in life to retire; yet he was "not without regret at parting with (perhaps never more to meet) the few intimates whom I love."

Most of the regrets had apparently vanished when the time came to turn over the reins of government to his successor on March 4, 1797. John Adams had narrowly won the presidency by an electoral vote of 71 to 68 over Thomas Jefferson, who automatically became Vice-President. Although Adams viewed himself as the man who had created Washington by urging his appointment as commander in chief of the Continental Army, he had been, to his chagrin, in the shadow of the Virginian ever since and he was to have one final demonstration of it even on his triumphal inauguration day. Dressed to the nines for the occasion, Adams was driven to the House of Representatives in the state carriage and entered to find that many of the members were in tears. They had eyes not for the new President but for the old, a man who had come alone to Congress Hall in a plain black coat and was seated by himself on the dais when Adams entered. Always on the alert for a slight, it occurred to Adams that Washington seemed "to enjoy a triumph over me." As he wrote his wife Abigail, "Methought I heard him say, 'Ay! I'm fairly out and you fairly in. See which of us will be happiest!'"

For most of his adult life George Washington had been setting examples for other men, and at the last there was one more instance of this innate quality. After John Adams took the oath of office, delivered his acceptance speech, and departed, Washington and Thomas Jefferson remained on the dais. Washington turned to his fellow Virginian and motioned for him to precede him from the hall. Politely, Jefferson indicated refusal. Washington gestured again, this time with unmistakable authority: the Vice-President should take precedence over the citizen.

When Jefferson had left, Washington walked out of Congress Hall and made his way through the crowd to a nearby hotel to congratulate the new President. The throngs of people watched him enter the building and as he disappeared inside a great roar went up — a noise, one man wrote, like "a sound of thunder."

PEACEFUL
PURSUITS

George Washington, Farmer, PAUL LELAND HAWORTH

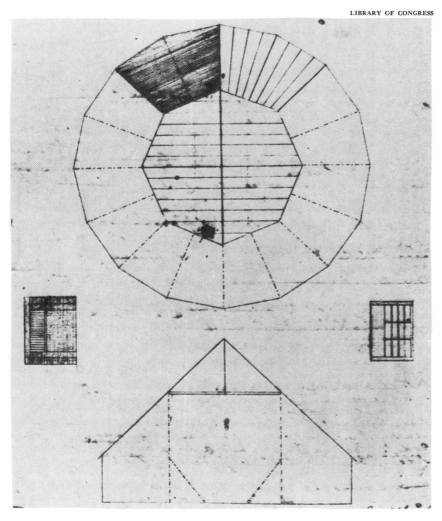

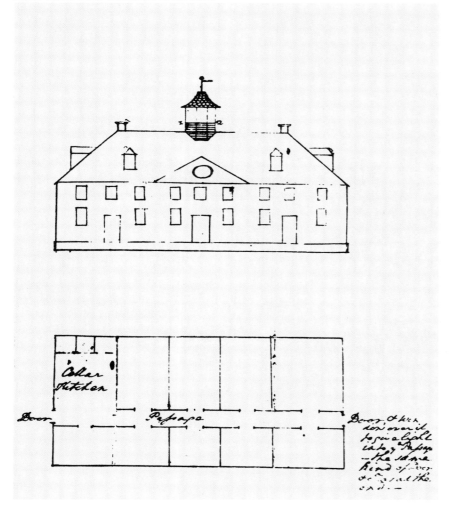

The moment he returned to private life, Washington realized his desperate need for a secretary. He wanted someone who would "live in the family" — a "gentleman who can compose a good letter . . . examine, arrange, and properly methodize my papers," handle accounts, and devote some time to tutoring the small Custis children. In January, 1786, a letter from Benjamin Lincoln brought word of "a Mr. Lear, who supports the character of gentleman and scholar," and six months later young Tobias Lear, son of a Portsmouth shipmaster, walked into Washington's life — to become, eventually, his most intimate assistant. Industrious and highly intelligent, Lear quietly took charge of the chaos of papers at Mount Vernon and performed even more valuable service in 1789, when he served as private secretary to the President. When he resigned in 1793 to go into business, Washington described him to a friend as "a person who possesses my entire friendship and confidence." The portrait of Lear, opposite, is by Sharples. Below it, a bill of lading covers a shipment to Washington from the King of Spain. The Virginian wanted to improve the local mules by breeding American mares to Spanish jackasses; the King sent him two (one of which died in passage); and the survivor took no interest in Washington's mares. Washington, comparing the jackass's "deliberation and majestic solemnity [in] the act of procreation" to those of the elderly Spanish monarch, named him "Royal Gift" and fumed over his "slothful humors" in the paddock. At left, top, is Washington's own plan for a sixteen-sided barn he had built on his Dogue Run farm, and below is an elevation he drew of Mount Vernon, reproduced here for the first time.

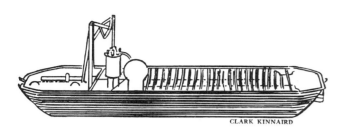

PROPOSALS

For forming a Company, to enable

JAMES RUMSEY

To carry into Execution, on a Large and Extensive Plan, his

STEAM·BOAT

And sundry other Machines herein after mentioned.

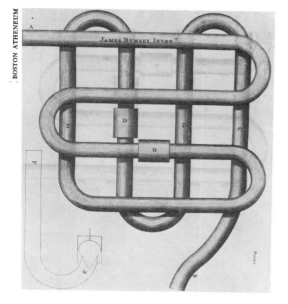

JAMES RUMSEY INVEN.T

THE WEST
BECKONS ANEW

Retired he might be, but projects and plans filled Washington's mind, among them a scheme to provide a practical route for joining the waters of the Potomac with those of the Ohio. In 1784 he saw for the first time a craft devised by James Rumsey, which was capable of traveling upstream. After meeting Rumsey at Bath, in western Virginia, Washington wrote, "I have seen the model of Mr. Rumsey's Boats constructed to work against Stream; have examined the power upon which it acts; have been an eye witness to an actual experiment in running water of some rapidity; & do give it as my opinion (altho' I had little faith before) that he has discovered the Art of propelling Boats, by mechanism & Small manual assistance, against rapid currents." The invention, he concluded, "is of vast importance." A plan of Rumsey's steamboat is shown above, left; below it is a drawing of a boiler invented by the ingenious fellow, who earned a livelihood as landlord of "The Liberty Pole and Flag," a boarding house at Bath. At right is Rumsey's printed prospectus for the sale of stock by which he meant to finance his boat. Among the many obstacles in the way of Washington's dream were the falls and rapids in the Potomac. Benjamin Latrobe's drawings on the facing page show, at top, the bridge over Little Falls, which Washington described as descending "in curling waves thirty-six feet in a quarter of a mile," and below, the Great Falls, whose roar could be heard a mile away. Despite the difficulties, the Potomac project became Washington's passion — to a point where visitors to Mount Vernon complained of "hearing little else for two days." Regrettably, the country had neither engineers nor machinery capable of opening permanent navigable channels in the river or constructing the necessary locks, yet Washington never lost hope. It remained an all-absorbing interest, as James Madison noted in a letter to Jefferson: "The earnestness with which he espouses the undertaking is hardly to be described, and shows that a mind like his, capable of great views and which has long been occupied with them, cannot bear a vacancy." A quarter century after Washington's death the Potomac Company was absorbed into the Chesapeake and Ohio Canal Company, which eventually opened a water passage from Fort Cumberland to the Great Falls.

Castalian Fount.

STANZS

On a Lady's *wearing the* Author's *Cravat.*

ACCOMPLISH'D Mifs, forgive the lay,
   That dare fuch charms as thine to fing :
An eagle fought the fource of day,
   And, blinded, fell on trembling wing.

Oh ! that each Grace would join to wreathe
   A *garland* worthy of thy charms ;
And would the Nine but help to breathe
   Each throb that fills me with alarms.

Bright fhould th' ambrofial foliage glow.
   Ambitious thy fair neck to twine ;
And exquifitely fweet fhould flow,
   The verie new offer'd at thy fhrine.

The lily round thy bofom hung,
   Should vainly emulate its hue :
Each line, foft melting as thy tongue,
   From Love fhall flow, to Beauty true.

Thy ruby'd lips the rofe fhould vie,
   Its perfume like their breathings fweet ;—
Each thought fhould, like thy melting eye,
   With fineft feelings beam replete.

On MARRIAGE.

TOM prais'd his friend, who chang'd his ftate,
   For binding faft himfelf and *Kate,*
     In union fo divine.
" Wedlock's the end of life," he cry'd,
" Too true, alas !" faid Jack, and figh't,
   " 'Twill be the end of mine !"

MISCELLANY.

ANECDOTES of Daniel Shaise, *leader of the Infurgents.*

THIS perfonage, lately fo much talked of, is defcended from a poor family in the County of Worcefter, and ferved his apprenticefhip to the farming bufinefs, at Brookfield—From his youth he was remarkable for fubtlety and duplicity, which, notwithftanding his want of education, was conjectured would one day or other, make him famous—the following occurrence will demonftrate the augury was not ill-grounded—At the commencement of the late war, our hero, then about 23 years of age, entered the Continental army, where his activity gained him a fergeantcy—From a knowledge of his abilities, his Colonel thought him a proper perfon for the recruiting fervice, and as an inducement to his activity, was promifed an Enfign's commiffion provided he enlifted a certain number of men—this was an opportunity which the ambition of our hero would not permit him to pafs unimproved—He applied himfelf with all diligence to his duty, and foon, by promifes and intrigue obtained the number—he had now fomething more in view than an Enfigncy—and continued enlifting men, but upon the exprefs condition that he fhould be their commander—When arrived at camp with his recruits, and the Infpector was proceeding to diftribute them among the feveral regiments, Shaife prefented him the enlifting paper, requefting at the fame time a commiffion to command them, as without it they were not bound to tarry—The army being then in want of recruits, a Commiffion as a Captain, was given him—in which grade he continued, until a new arrangement of the army took place—when an opportunity was given his fuperiours of rewarding his duplicity, by a derangement.

Added to the foregoing, another anecdote related of our hero, places his character as a foldier, and as a man, in a moft difagreeable light—In the year 1780, that diftinguifhed nobleman, the Marquis de la Fayette, prefented the officers of the army, each with an elegant fword—this pledge of his affection, which a man of honour and fpirit would have facredly preferved, and handed down to his pofterity as a jewel of high price, he was mean enough to difpofe of for a trifling confideration.

After our hero left the army, he funk into his original obfcurity, where he probably would have continued, had not the tumult of the times, given him an opportunity to difplay his activity, by joining a miftaken multitude, with the defign, *as he profeffed,* of " reforming government," by obftructing the regular adminiftration of law and juftice—What his *real* defigns are, Time muft bring to light—thus much is certain, his ambition is unbounded—and his fortune fuch as has fometimes urges men to defperation.

Though Shaife's honour has been called in queftion, his perfonal courage is unimpeached—During the time the parties under Gen. *Sheppard* and himfelf, were at Springfield, an interview was appointed by them, to be held in the interval between the lines—At meeting Gen. *Sheppard* complimented our hero with the title of General—to which he inftantly demanded an explanation; adding at the fame time, that as he claimed no other rank than Captain, fhould the General perfift in giving him any other, he fhould confider it as an affront, and would demand immediate fatisfaction.

PHYSICAL ANECDOTE.

THE celebrated Dr. Radcliffe, attending one of his moft intimate friends in a dangerous illnefs, with an unufual ftrain of generofity declared, he would not touch a fee.—One infifted, and the other was pofitive. At laft, when the cure was performed, and the phyfician taken his leave, " Sir," faid the patient, (his friend) " in this purfe I have put every day's fee ; nor muft your goodnefs get the better of my gratitude." The doctor eyes the purfe, counts the days in a moment, and then holding out his hand, replied, " Well, I can hold out no longer ; *fingly* I could have refufed them for a twelve month ; but *all together* they are irrefiftible."

EPIGRAM.

CRIES fober Will, well *Shaife* has fled,
   And peace returns to blefs our days——
Poh ! poh ! cries James, I always faid,
   He'd prove at beft a *fall-back Shaife.*

The Weekly Monitor.

EVERY man *is obliged to endeavour to obtain juft ideas of God—to know his laws—his views with refpect to his creatures, and the end for which they were created : Man, doubtlefs, owes the moft pure love, the moft profound refpect to his creator ; and to keep alive thefe difpofitions, and all in confequence of them, he fhould honour God in all his actions, and fhew by the moft fuitable meafures, the fentiments that fill his mind. This fhort explanation is fufficient to prove, that man is effentially and neceffarily free to make ufe of his own choice in matters of religion. His belief is not to be commanded ; and what kind of worfhip muft that be, which is produced by force ? Worfhip confifts in certain actions performed with an immediate view to the honour of God ; there can then be no worfhip proper for any man, which he does not believe fuitable to that end.*

To be SOLD or CHARTERED,

(If applied for foon.)

SIGNS OF CHAOS

Two symbols of the parlous state of government in 1786 were the ruins of the abandoned capitol at Williamsburg (shown above in Benjamin Latrobe's drawing) and the futile attempt that was made to achieve interstate cooperation in Annapolis that year. Only five of the thirteen states sent delegates to a meeting on trade problems held in the Maryland capitol (below). In December armed insurrection erupted in Massachusetts and troops under Benjamin Lincoln (left) were called out to put down a rebellion led by Daniel Shays. The newspaper on the facing page has a brief and rather biased summary of Shays' career, which included service with a Massachusetts regiment at the battle for Bunker Hill.

A SUMMONS TO PHILADELPHIA

Undaunted by failure in Annapolis, delegates to that convention issued a call for all thirteen states to send representatives to Philadelphia to "render the constitution of the Federal Government adequate to the exigencies of the Union." When Washington arrived in the city — shown here in a 1790 engraving — wildly cheering crowds greeted him, and he accepted Robert Morris' invitation to stay with him in what was acknowledged to be the grandest residence in the town. (Sir William Howe had chosen it for his headquarters during the British occupation of Philadelphia.) The only delegations present on May 14, 1787, were Virginia's and Pennsylvania's and their members included the two most illustrious figures in the country — George Washington and Benjamin Franklin, the latter carried into the newly named Independence Hall in a sedan chair by two convicts.

ARCHITECTS OF THE CONSTITUTION

The cast of characters at the Constitutional Convention included some of the most remarkable men in America. George Mason (lower left), Washington's Virginia neighbor and author of that state's constitution, proposed the plan for dual Federal and state sovereignty upon which the government of the United States is based. His efforts to abolish the slave trade and to include a declaration of rights in the Constitution were voted down, as a result of which he refused to sign the document, saying, "I would sooner chop off my right hand." Later, his suggested Bill of Rights bore fruit as the first ten amendments. Connecticut's Roger Sherman (lower right), the one man who signed all the great Revolutionary documents from the Articles of Association in 1774 to the Constitution, offered the "Connecticut Compromise," providing for equal representation in the Senate and a House of Representatives elected on the basis of population. It was the idea of James Wilson of Pennsylvania (top left) that executive power should be placed in the hands of a single individual — a notion opposed by many delegates, who feared that the President might resemble a king. William Paterson of New Jersey (top right) proposed the "small state" plan, endorsed by Delaware, Connecticut, and New York, which gave each state an equal vote in Congress. When this was incorporated into the Connecticut Compromise, Paterson agreed to sign the document. The senior statesman present was 81-year-old Benjamin Franklin (opposite, in a painting done in 1766 by David Martin), whose great talent was to soothe the delegates' ruffled tempers with homely jokes. A believer in compromise, he helped draft the clause on which the two-house Congress is based.

WE the People of the States of New-Hampshire, Massachusetts, Rhode-Island and Providence Plantations, Connecticut, New-York, New-Jersey, Pennsylvania, Delaware, Maryland, Virginia, North-Carolina, South-Carolina, and Georgia, do ordain, declare and establish the following Constitution for the Government of Ourselves and our Posterity.

ARTICLE I.

The stile of this Government shall be, " The United States of America."

II.

The Government shall consist of supreme legislative, executive and judicial powers.

III.

The legislative power shall be vested in a Congress, to consist of two separate and distinct bodies of men, a House of Representatives, and a Senate; ~~each of which shall, in all cases, have a negative on the other. The Legislature shall meet on the first Monday in December in every year.~~

The Legislature shall meet at least once in every year and that meeting shall be on the first Monday in December unless a different day shall be appointed by law.

IV.

Sect. 1. The Members of the House of Representatives shall be chosen every second year, by the people of the several States comprehended within this Union. The qualifications of the electors shall be the same, from time to time, as those of the electors in the several States, of the most numerous branch of their own legislatures.

Sect. 2. Every Member of the House of Representatives shall be of the age of twenty-five years at least; shall have been a citizen in the United States for at least _____ years before his election; and shall be, at the time of his election, _____ of the State in which he shall be chosen.

Sect. 3. The House of Representatives shall, at its first formation, and until the number of citizens and inhabitants shall be taken in the manner herein after described, consist of sixty-five Members, of whom three shall be chosen in New-Hampshire, eight in Massachusetts, one in Rhode-Island and Providence Plantations, five in Connecticut, six in New-York, four in New-Jersey, eight in Pennsylvania, one in Delaware, six in Maryland, ten in Virginia, five in North-Carolina, five in South-Carolina, and three in Georgia.

Sect. 4. As the proportions of numbers in the different States will alter from time to time; as some of the States may hereafter be divided; as others may be enlarged by addition of territory; as two or more States may be united; as new States will be erected within the limits of the United States, the Legislature shall, in each of these cases, regulate the number of representatives by the number of inhabitants, according to the _____ the rate of one for every forty thousand. *Provided that every State shall have at least One representative.*

Sect. 5. All bills for raising or appropriating money, and for fixing the salaries of the officers of government, shall originate in the House of Representatives, and shall not be altered or amended by the Senate. No money shall be drawn from the public Treasury, but in pursuance of appropriations that shall originate in the House of Representatives.

struck out

Sect. 6. The House of Representatives shall have the sole power of impeachment. It shall choose its Speaker and other officers.

Sect. 7. Vacancies in the House of Representatives shall be supplied by writs of election from the executive authority of the State, in the representation from which they shall happen.

V.

A RECORD
OF COMPROMISE

These careful interlineations, made by the chairman of the Convention on his copy of the final draft of the Constitution, give no clue to the wrangling over which he had to preside in the stifling heat of a Philadelphia summer. Debate began after presentation of the so-called Virginia Plan, calling for a bicameral legislature, an executive, and a judiciary. What outraged small states was the idea that representation in the new government should be based on population; as Gunning Bedford of Delaware pointed out to representatives of the large states, *"I do not, gentlemen, trust you! . . . The small states never can agree to the Virginia Plan, and why then is it still urged?"* Sooner than be ruined, he said, Delaware and other small states would look to foreign powers, "who will take us by the hand." Parliamentary debate had never been one of Washington's strong points, and his colleagues were relying upon his presence and reputation to hold the Convention together during its most trying hours. From the outset, he realized that it would be a long, drawn-out affair; he asked his nephew George Augustine Washington to send certain articles of apparel from Mount Vernon to Philadelphia, "as I see no end to my staying here." As summer wore on, one crisis after another, including a threat of immediate adjournment, was passed, and finally on September 15, just before six in the evening, all but three delegates (including Peyton Randolph, who had put forth the Virginia Plan) agreed to a revised draft; Washington ordered the document engrossed, and his gavel fell for the last time. He had been a passive participant (in four months, he gave only one brief speech), but there was general agreement that his calm, commanding presence had been a significant factor in the Convention's ultimate outcome.

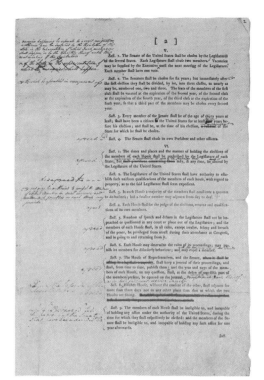
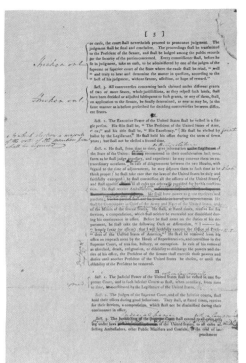
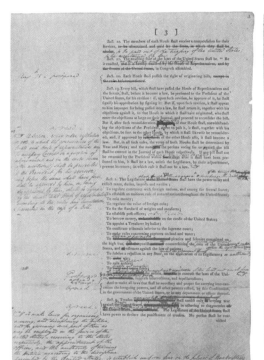
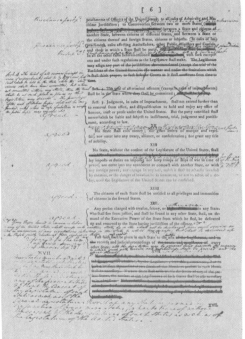
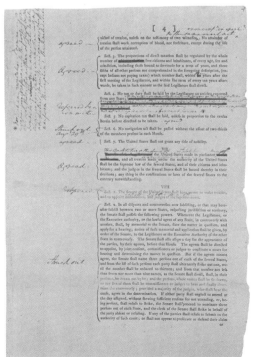
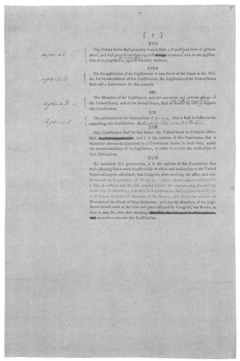

CONVENTION CHAIRMAN

On Friday, May 25, 1787, Washington recorded in his diary that the arrival of delegates from New Jersey provided a quorum, after which, "by a unanimous vote I was called up to the Chair as President of the body." In an early print, below left, Washington is seen presiding over the debates that continued through the summer. On the facing page is the portrait of him done at this time by Edward Savage, and below is the chair he used during the sessions. This chair, with a rising sun painted on the back, was the subject of a famous remark by Benjamin Franklin at the conclusion of the Convention. As the delegates came forward to sign the document they had written, Franklin looked at the chair and observed that he had often wondered, in the course of their deliberations, whether the sun was rising or setting. "But now at length," he said, "I have the happiness to know that it is a rising and not a setting sun." At left is a record of the voting on various questions, including that of whether the new government would have a single executive.

210

GEORGE WASHINGTON
Painted from life by
EDWARD SAVAGE in 1790

THE DRIVE
FOR
RATIFICATION

AN

ADDRESS

TO THE

PEOPLE

OF THE

STATE OF NEW-YORK,

On the SUBJECT of the

CONSTITUTION,

Agreed upon at PHILADELPHIA,

The 17th of September, 1787.

NEW-YORK:

PRINTED BY SAMUEL AND JOHN LOUDON,

PRINTERS TO THE STATE.

REDEUNT SATURNIA REGNA.
On the erection of the Eleventh PILLAR of the great Na-
tional DOME, we beg leave moſt ſincerely to felicitate " OUR DEAR COUNTRY."

Riſe it
will.

The foundation
good—it may yet
be SAVED.

The FEDERAL EDIFICE.

Although a Constitution for a new government now existed, the battle for its adoption had only begun, and as soon as Washington returned to Mount Vernon he began writing to friends, enlisting their support for ratification. The man who had had more to do with the framing of the Constitution than any other at the Convention was his fellow-Virginian James Madison (left, top), who threw himself into the fight for adoption and, in cooperation with Alexander Hamilton and John Jay, published *The Federalist* papers explaining the proposition to the public. Jay (far left) had not attended the Federal Convention, but he was an influential advocate for adoption. With Hamilton, Jay helped push New York into ratifying the Constitution. At left, below, is the title page of a persuasive address written by Jay advocating ratification. By the time New York had registered approval, the "Federal Edifice" lacked only North Carolina and Rhode Island to make ratification unanimous, as the 1788 British cartoon above indicates. An artist named David Grim made the drawing below — a depiction of the elaborate banquet pavilion erected in New York City to celebrate the state's ratification in July of 1788.

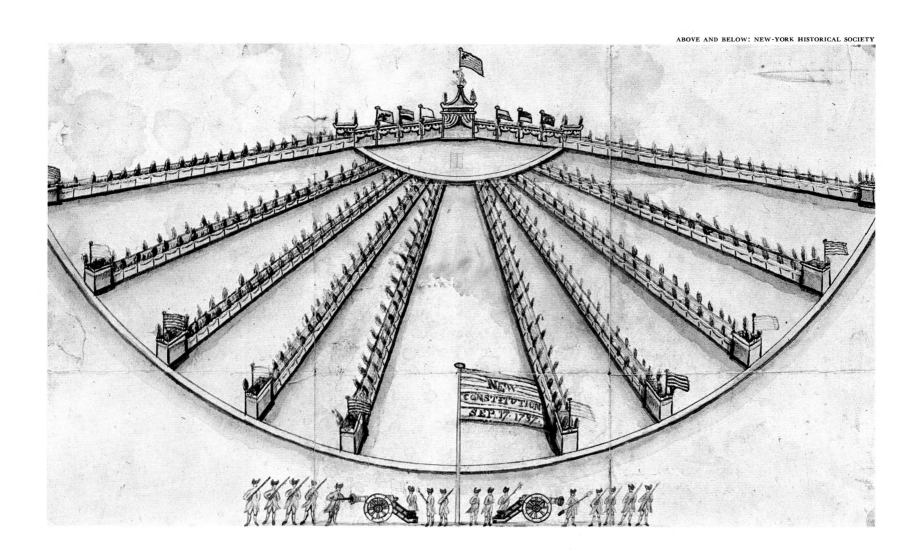

CALL TO THE PRESIDENCY

THE NATIONAL ARCHIVES

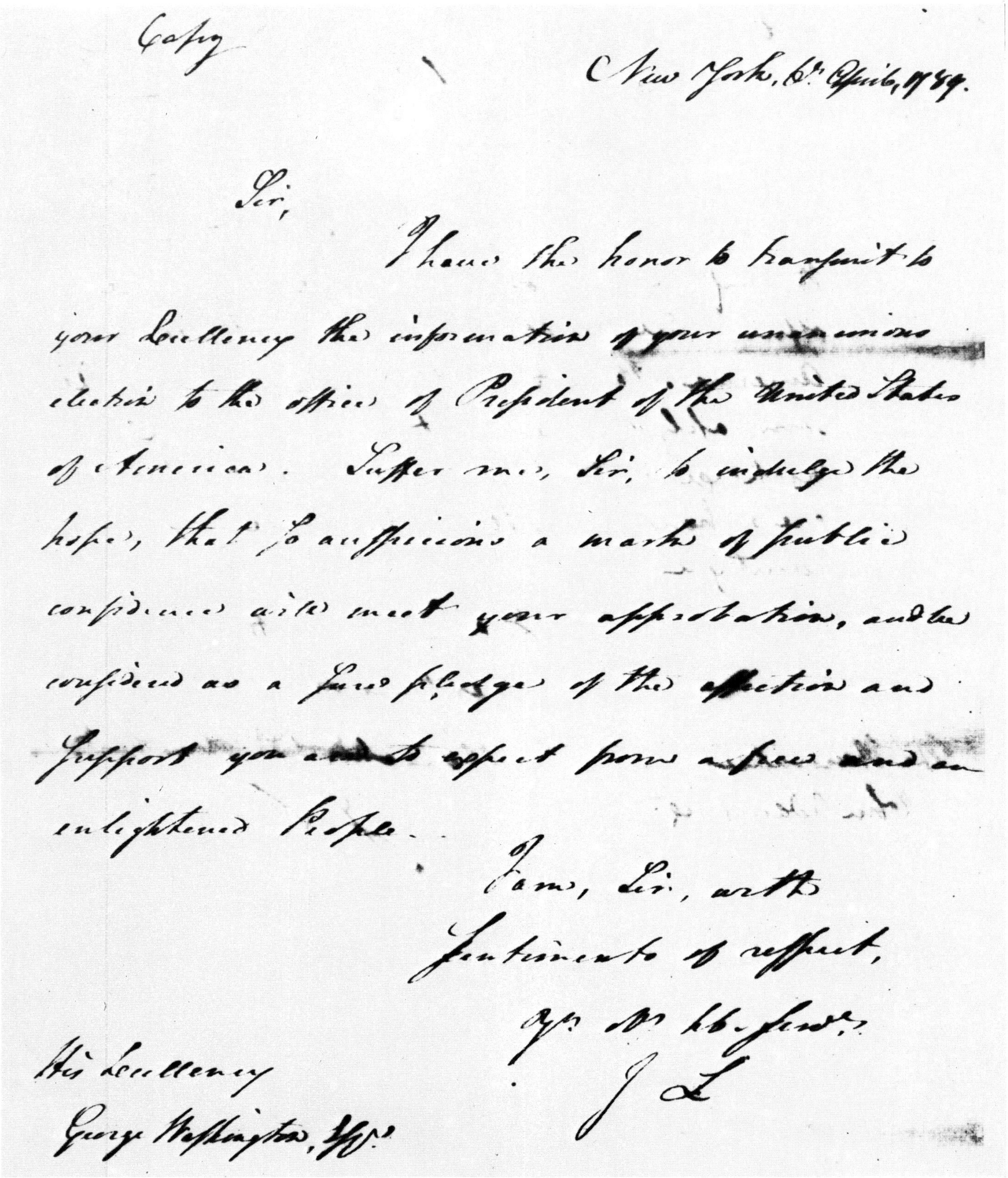

Copy

New York, 6th April, 1789.

Sir,

I have the honor to transmit to your Excellency the information of your unanimous election to the office of President of the United States of America. Suffer me, Sir, to indulge the hope, that so auspicious a mark of public confidence will meet your approbation, and be considered as a sure pledge of the affection and support you are to expect from a free and an enlightened People.

I am, Sir, with sentiments of respect,
Yr. Mt. Ob. Servt.
J L

His Excellency
George Washington, Esqr.

Mount Vernon April 14th 1789.

Sir;

I had the honor to receive your Official Communication by the hand of Mr Secretary Thompson, about one o'clock this day. — Having concluded to obey the important & flattering call of my Country, and having been impressed with an idea of the expediency of my being with Congress at as early a period as possible; I propose to commence my journey on Thursday morning which will be the day after tomorrow. —

I have the honor to be with sentiments of esteem Sir Your most obedt servt

Go Washington

The Honble
Jno Langdon Esqr

Washington's selection as President of the new nation seemed a foregone conclusion, and although he wrote to others indicating that he was undecided about whether to accept if elected, the indications are that he had made up his mind to do so. On February 4, 1789, electors in each state met to cast their ballots, and all sixty-nine voted for Washington for President. The outgoing Congress had set March 4 as the date for the new government to come into being; at that time, it was supposed, Congress would convene at New York, whereupon the president pro tem of the Senate would officially open the ballots and declare George Washington elected. Like its predecessors, however, this body of legislators showed no signs of haste; March 4 came and went, and three weeks later no quorum was present. "The delay is inauspicious to say the best of it," Washington wrote his friend Henry Knox, "and the World must contemn it." Finally enough senators and representatives made their appearance in New York to constitute a quorum, and on April 14 Irish-born Charles Thomson (left), who had served as secretary to the Continental Congress from 1774 until the present, rode up to Mount Vernon, greeted Washington, and solemnly made a speech informing him that he had been chosen President. Thomson handed Washington formal notification of this fact — a letter from John Langdon of New Hampshire, president pro tem of the Senate. (A copy of Langdon's letter appears on the facing page.) Washington, it seems, was well prepared. He took out a paper on which he had written his acceptance, read it to Thomson, and then drafted a reply to Langdon, which is reproduced above. Two days later he stepped into his coach and, accompanied by Thomson and David Humphreys, a wartime aide who has been discussing the possibility of writing his biography, departed from Mount Vernon, bidding adieu to it, "to private life, and to domestic felicity, and with a mind oppressed with more anxious and painful sensations than I have words to express, set out for New York." Those were the thoughts confided to his diary.

A DISPLAY of the UNITED STATES of AMERICA

TRIUMPHAL PASSAGE

America had never seen or imagined anything like Washington's triumphal journey from Mount Vernon to New York. Along the route towns turned out en masse to do the new President honor, greeting him with mounted escorts, parades, dinners, fireworks, speeches, fêtes of every description. For eight days it went on. In Chester, Pennsylvania, he was welcomed at ten o'clock one morning with a parade that accompanied him into Philadelphia. An afternoon banquet was followed by an evening of fireworks and five interminable addresses, and Washington was unable to continue on his way until the next day. The engraving below, after a drawing by Charles Willson Peale, shows the eastern terminus of Gray's Ferry near Philadelphia festooned with greenery, a flag, and liberty cap in tribute to him. For Washington, the high point of the trip was an "affecting moment" on the bridge over Assunpink Creek at Trenton. Decorated with greens, the bridge wore a banner stating that the hero who had protected America's mothers would now defend her daughters as well. Crossing the bridge, he was surrounded by women and girls dressed in white who sang an ode and strewed flowers in his path — a far cry from his visit to the same place in January of 1777. Opposite, a 1789 print by Amos Doolittle shows Washington in civilian dress, encircled by the coats of arms of the thirteen original states and that of the new Federal government. A similar design is used in the brass button at left, struck in 1789 and decorated with the initials of the new President surrounded by those of the thirteen states.

An East View of GRAY'S FERRY, near Philadelphia with the TRIUMPHAL ARCHES, &c. erected for the Reception of General Washington, April 20th 1789.

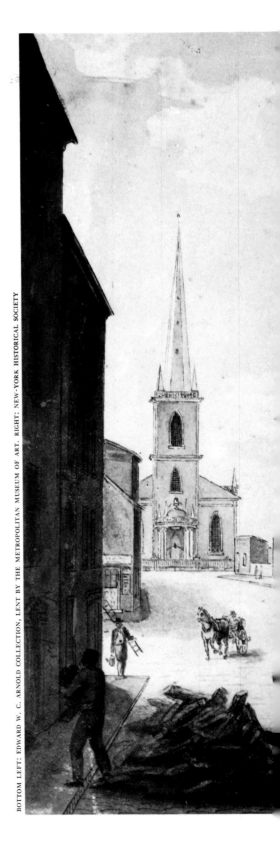

Fellow Citizens of the Senate
and
of the House of Representatives.

Among the vicissitudes incident to life, no event could have filled me with greater anxieties than that of which the notification was transmitted by your order, and received on the fourteenth day of the present month: —— On the one hand, I was summoned by my Country, whose voice I can never hear but with veneration and love, from a retreat which I had chosen with the fondest predilection, and, in my flattering hopes, with an immutable decision, as the asylum of my declining years: a retreat which was rendered every day more necessary as well as more dear to me, by the addition of habit to inclination, and of frequent interruptions in my health to the gradual waste committed on it by time. —— On the other hand, the magnitude and difficulty of the trust to which the voice of my Country called me, being sufficient to awaken in the wisest and most experienced of her citizens, a distrustful

FIRST INAUGURATION

Dense crowds lined the foot of Wall Street and vessels in New York Harbor were decked with flags; the ships fired off thirteen-gun salutes, cannon at the Battery roared, church bells pealed, and the crowd cheered itself hoarse as Washington arrived by barge on April 23, 1789. Six days later, after having his hair powdered and dressing himself in a suit of brown Hartford broadcloth, he was escorted to Federal Hall for his inauguration. There, on a portico overlooking Wall and Broad Streets, he took the oath of office, as shown (below left) in a detail from Amos Doolittle's engraving. At left is the first page of the address he wrote in his own hand to be delivered to members of Congress. He had composed it some weeks before at Mount Vernon, calculating that it would take about twenty minutes to deliver. (It was not heard by the crowd outside the hall; even had he wanted to address them, his voice would not have been audible over the din.) Below is a view of Federal Hall (center), looking along Wall Street toward Trinity Church; at right is the Verplanck mansion.

THE PRESIDENT AND HIS LADY

In 1790 Vice-President John Adams commissioned Edward Savage to paint these portraits of the first President and his lady (attired in one of the elaborate headdresses she habitually wore), and when Adams himself retired from the presidency in 1801 he took them to his home in Quincy, Massachusetts, where they have hung ever since. The portrait of Adams on the facing page was done in 1798 by William Winstanley, the Englishman from whom Washington had purchased two Hudson River views (see pages 268–269). Adams was no man to be carried away by the tide of reverence for Washington. In 1790 he wrote a friend, "The history of our Revolution will be one continued lie from one end to the other. The essence of the whole will be that Dr. Franklin's electrical rod smote the earth and out sprang General Washington; that Franklin electrified him with his rod — and thence forward these two conducted all the policy, negotiations, legislatures, and war." In most matters, Adams supported the administration, but as the vice-presidents who followed came to realize, his was no enviable position. "My country," he wrote acidly, "has in its wisdom contrived for me the most insignificant office that ever the invention of man contrived or his imagination conceived." A man with a sharp tongue and pen, a keen mind, and independent attitude, Adams was contemptuous of "all parties and all men," as Jefferson observed. He was not slightly awed by Washington, for whose eminence he felt largely responsible, having nominated him as commander in chief of the Continental Army; he referred to him sarcastically as "His Majesty" and, on one occasion, as "an old mutton head." His wife Abigail was more kindly disposed toward the President, whom she described as "affable without familiarity, distant without haughtiness, grave without austerity, modest, wise, and good." Martha, Abigail noted, "is plain in her dress, but the plainness is the best of every article. . . . Her hair is white, her teeth beautiful."

HOUSE OF WORSHIP

Immediately following his inauguration, Washington walked
from Federal Hall to Saint Paul's Chapel, where the
Episcopal Bishop of New York offered prayers for divine
guidance. Representative Fisher Ames of Massachusetts,
who occupied a pew near Washington's, evidently concluded
that heavenly assistance might be needed: "Time," he
concluded after seeing the weary President at close range,
"has made havoc upon his face." The chapel is shown at
right in the view above; the other edifice is the Brick
Presbyterian Church. The coat of arms of the United States
(right) hung on the wall over Washington's pew at St.
Paul's, where he worshiped until the capital was moved to
Philadelphia. A companion painting (below) shows the coat
of arms of the state of New York; this hung above Governor
George Clinton's pew, in the south aisle of the chapel.
Built of native stone, the church was completed in 1766,
and much of its ornamentation was the work of Major
L'Enfant, the French architect and engineer who later
designed the Federal City on the Potomac. The elaborately
carved pulpit, surmounted by a coronet and six feathers,
was one of the few symbols of British royalty to
survive the ravages of revolution in the city.

LEFT AND RIGHT: ST. PAUL'S CHAPEL

THE FIRST CAPITAL: NEW YORK

New York's ascending commercial eminence was nowhere more evident than at the corner of Wall and Water Streets. Here, at the Tontine Coffee House (the building on which the flag flies in the 1798 view above), every ship's arrival and clearance was registered. The Tontine housed the stock exchange and insurance offices, and merchants met here every day between eleven and two o'clock to do business "in a large way." Not far away, at the corner of Pearl and Cherry Streets, was the first presidential residence (left). Known as the Franklin House, it had been used by the president of Congress, and Washington discovered that it offered him no privacy whatever. "From the time I had done breakfast and thence till dinner and afterwards till bedtime I could not

get relieved from the ceremony of one visit before I had to attend to another," he complained. He also learned that he would have to alter the public attitude toward the Chief Executive: the presidents of Congress, he decided, had been regarded "in no better light than as a maître d'hôtel . . . for their table was considered as a public one and every person who could get introduced conceived that he had had a *right* to be invited to it." The structure at right, intended as the new presidential mansion and known as Government House, fell on evil days when the government was moved to Philadelphia. Later it became the Elysian Boarding and Lodging House, then the Custom House, and it was torn down in 1815.

225

JOURNEY TO THE NORTH

On October 15, 1789, the President set out on a tour of New England — the first of several such journeys he planned as a means of seeing the country and being seen by the people who had elected him. When he arrived in Boston he received a glorious welcome from the citizens of the town where he had won his first victory over the British. A triumphal arch and colonnade (right) had been erected in front of the State House (shown above in a 1793 view), but the governor of Massachusetts, John Hancock, was not among the greeters. A staunch states' right advocate, Hancock sent word that he was indisposed, implying that the President — as a guest of the state — should call upon him. Washington immediately cancelled his dinner engagement with Hancock, whereupon the latter capitulated and came to pay his respects. The matter of precedence settled, President and governor broke bread together "at a large and elegant dinner at Faneuil Hall," after which Washington consented to sit for a portrait, destined for Harvard College, painted by Edward Savage. The same artist portrayed John Hancock and his wife, the former Dorothy Quincy (opposite). Their first-born child, christened George Washington Hancock, died at the age of nine.

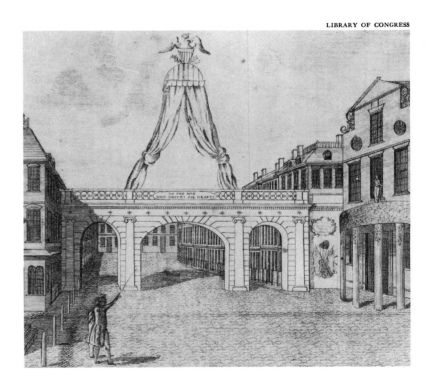

227

A TRANSFER TO PHILADELPHIA

To the dismay of New Yorkers who had counted on retaining the Capital, the government moved in 1790 to Philadelphia, long the richest and largest city in America. The popular belief was that the move had been instigated by Robert Morris, the financier, who appears at left in a 1790 cartoon dragging a small minority of Congressmen on his "ladder of money and preferment" while the majority follows tamely in his wake. Above, a pencil and watercolor sketch shows Morris' elegant town house, which was put at Washington's disposal; and at right a page from *Stephens's Directory* of the city includes an entry for the President of the United States. In 1793 Washington, who had seen the advent of Rumsey's steamboat, witnessed the beginning of airborne transportation in America when he went to Germantown to see France's Jean Pierre Blanchard and a black dog make a balloon ascension that took them to New Jersey. The balloon (above right) carried an American flag and Blanchard had with him the first and only passport ever issued personally by a U.S. President, requesting that he be permitted "to pass in such direction and to descend in such places as circumstances may render most convenient."

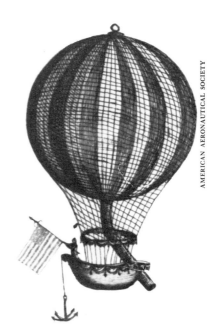

Walter John, painter & glazier, Margaret ft. between Front and Second.
Walter Philip, mariner, Stillhouse alley.
Walter Philip, fhoemaker, 198, No. Second ft.
Walters George, fhoemaker, Shippen ft. near Vernon ftreet.
Walters Jacob, tin plate worker, 177, No. Third ft.
Walters Nicholas, gentleman, 4, Cable lane.
Walters Peter, baker, No. Water ft. near Callowhill ftreet.
Walfham,   widow, huckfter, German ft. near Third ft.
Walfh John, fea captain, 165, No. Third ft.
Walfh Michael, grocer, So. Fifth ft. near Oak ft.
Walton Elizabeth, widow, huckfter,   Race ft.
Walton Samuel, huckfter, 28, Spruce ft.
Walton Samuel, cabinet maker, 248, No. Front ft.
Wample Ifaac, fcrivener, 124, No. Third ft.
Wann William, mariner, Chriftian ft. near Church alley.
Ward John, Smith's alley.
Ward Sufanna & Sarah, huckfters, 15, No. Fourth ft.
Warden John, barber, 54, Vine ft.
Warder Jeremiah, Parker & co. merchants, 12, No. Third ft.
Warder John, merchant, 103, Market ft.
Wardner Margaret, widow, 25, Saffafras alley.
Ware Ann, boarding-houfe, 176, So. Water ft.
Ware John, fhip-joiner, 123, Callowhill ft.
Ware William, labourer, 70, Sugar alley.
Warens Frederick, coach-maker, German ft. near Second ft.
Warner Anna, gentlewoman, 20, Arch ft.
Warner Hieromius, brafs founder, 26, No. Eighth ft.
Warner John, ivory turner and whalebone manufacturer, 28, No. Fourth ft.
Warner Jofeph, laft and heel maker, 14, Chefnut ft.
Warner Margaret, widow, wafher, bet. 50 & 133, Pine ftreet.
Warner Mary, widow, fieve maker, near No. 9, Comb's alley.
Warner Philip, fhoemaker, Sugar alley, No. Sixth ft.
Warner Swen, laft maker, 24, Chefnut ft.
Warner William, tavern keeper, No. Water ft. near Callowhill ft.
Warr, Valentine, fhopkeeper, 32, Chriftian ft.
Warrant James, boarding-houfe, 320, So. Second ft.

Warren Mary, fchool-miftrefs, Shipherds court.
Warrington Cefar, labourer, 73, So. Fifth ft.
Wartman Sarah, widow, boarding-houfe, 15, Branch ft.
Warts John, fea-captain, near 19, Vernon ft.
WASHINGTON GEORGE, PRESIDENT of the UNITED STATES, 190, High Street.
Waftlie John, fkin-drefler, 53, So. Fifth St.
Waterman Jeffe, fchool-mafter, 28, North alley.
Waters Mary, widow, doctorefs, Willings alley.
Waters Nathaniel, fcrivener, 52, Walnut ft.
Waters Patrick, currier, Merediths court.
Waters Thomas, labourer, 150, Spruce ft.
Watkins John, fhoemaker, Cedar ft. bet. 13 & 21.
Watkins Jofeph, gentleman, 121, Arch ft.
Watkins Thomas, brufh-maker, 13, Strawberry ft.
Watkins William, tobacconift, 166, So. Water ft.
Watman Adam, tavern-keeper, 240, No. Second ft.
Watman George, butcher, Beach ft.
Watfon Arabella, widow, feamftrefs,   German ft.
Watfon Charles C. taylor, 24, So. Fourth ft.
Watfon John, merchant, 254, Market ft.
Watfon Margaret, millener, 177, South Second ft.
Watfon Mary, widow near 84, No. Eighth ft.
Watfon Thomas, grocer, 48, Lombard ft.
Watfon Thomas, chimney fweeper, Old Fourth ft.
Watfon William, coachmaker, Black horfe alley.
Watfon William, fea-captain, 58, Artillery lane, bet. Front & Second ft.
Watts Stephen, mariner, near 98, So. Fifth ft.
Watts William, grocer, 8, Moravian alley.
Watt Samuel, merchant, 5, So. Front ft.
Way Andrew, taylor, 1, Quarry ft.
Way George, coachmaker, 152, Arch ft.
Way Jofeph, pilot, 481, South Front ft.
Way Nicholas, M. D. 83, So. Second ft.
Wayne Jacob, carpenter & chairmaker, 164 & 166 No. Front ft.
Wayne Jofeph, carpenter, South Front ft. near Mead alley.
Wayne Samuel, houfe-carpenter, 17, Keys alley.
Wayne Thomas, cooper, 481, South Front ft.
Weafley John, cooper, 386, No. Front ft.
Weatherby Margaret, widow, midwife, Strawberry lane.
Weatherall Benjamin, tin man & copperfmith, 187, Market ft.
Weatherer Alexander, fruiterer, 93, No. Front
R

TRAVELS
TO THE SOUTH

Washington's next extended tour as President took him, in the spring of 1791, to the South. Leaving Philadelphia in March, he traveled along roads like the one below, which he found "exceedingly deep, heavy & cut in places." This engraving is from *The Columbian Magazine* and shows the "view from Bushongo Tavern five miles from Yorktown on the Baltimore road." In Charleston, South Carolina (in the 1762 engraving above, showing the city as it appeared while it was still under British control), he was treated to a sample of the area's noted hospitality, including a visit from "a great number of the most respectable ladies . . . the first honor of the kind I had ever experienced and it was as flattering as it was singular."
The City Council commissioned John Trumbull to paint his portrait and the artist obliged by providing a likeness of Washington on the eve of the battle of Princeton.
This was rejected by the city fathers, who told Trumbull they preferred to see the President in a "calm, tranquil, peaceful light," and when the artist asked Washington if he would pose again, the latter "cheerfully submitted to a second penance," and the portrait here resulted. Washington suggested that Trumbull keep the first picture.

JEFFERSON VS.

The Cannibals are landing

Triumph Gove

Above all else, Washington had hoped to avoid the outbreak
of factionalism in his administration, but his first term was
hardly under way in earnest before a bitter dispute between
Alexander Hamilton, his Secretary of the Treasury, and Thomas
Jefferson, Secretary of State, erupted. The portraits of
Jefferson, above, and Hamilton, on the facing page, were done
by Charles Willson Peale, but that was virtually all they
had in common. By the time the President returned from
his journey to the South in 1791, the battle lines had been
drawn between these two brilliant men and their followers, and
their continuing struggle was to be the bane of Washington's
two terms in office. Simply put, the differences between them
were based on antipathetic philosophies. Hamilton's Federalists
favored the encouragement of industry, commerce, and finance,
and supported a strong central government dominated by propertied
men, on the theory that the masses were unfit to govern

HAMILTON

themselves. Jefferson's Antifederalists, or Republicans, believed that government should be decentralized and that the new nation's future prosperity lay in remaining agrarian, with little industry, its strength based upon small farmers, artisans, and democratic institutions. Among Jeffersonians there was a strong suspicion that Washington was overly fond of pomp and that he and Hamilton were taking the nation down a road to monarchy. For their part, Hamiltonians were convinced that Jefferson and his followers would turn the country over to the rabble, following France's example. The conflict between the two factions was exacerbated by rival newspapers, which printed the most scurrilous attacks on the opposition. In the cartoon here, from a pro-Hamilton paper, Washington is shown driving the Federal chariot, leading his troops against French "cannibals" who would invade America, while Jefferson, at far right, tries to stop "de wheels of de gouvernment."

BANNAKER.

THE FEDERAL CITY

One positive result of the Hamilton-Jefferson feud was agreement on a site for the new permanent Capital. In return for Jefferson's support of his debt refunding measures, Hamilton decided to sacrifice "the dearest interest of New York" (which had invested substantially in making President and Congressmen comfortable, so that they would not want to move) and agreed that the seat of government would be located on the Potomac, at a spot to be selected by Washington. By 1791, when the President returned from his southern journey, plans were under way. He had fixed on a 100-square-mile area, and one of the men named to survey the city was Benjamin Banneker (left), the first Negro to receive a presidential appointment. The Great Columbian Federal City, as some called it, would be built just east of the town of Georgetown, in Maryland (the 1794 view above is from Georgetown looking toward the site). Major Pierre Charles L'Enfant, whose likeness appears on the medal, opposite, was engaged to lay out the city, and he devised a plan incorporating broad avenues that ran at angles through a street pattern of rectangular squares, as shown in the reproduction of his scheme on the facing page. What L'Enfant

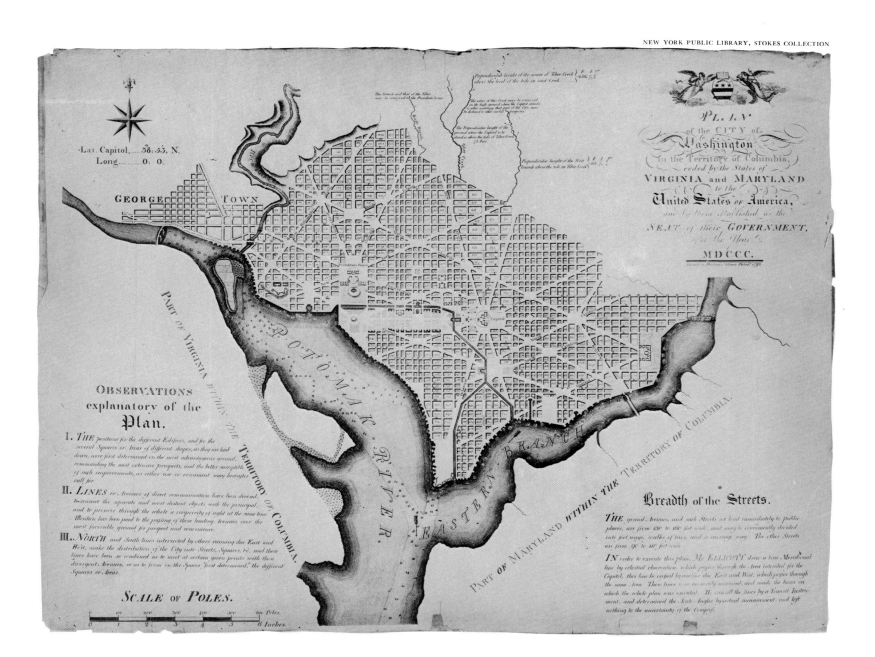

PLAN
of the CITY of
Washington
in the Territory of Columbia,
ceded by the States of
VIRGINIA and MARYLAND
to the
United States of America,
and by them established as the
SEAT of their GOVERNMENT,
after the Year
MDCCC.

OBSERVATIONS
explanatory of the
Plan.

Breadth of the Streets.

SCALE OF POLES.

termed the "Presidential Palace" overlooked the Potomac and one end of a "vast esplanade," at the eastern end of which was the "Congress House." Although the Secretary of State was supposedly responsible for arrangements for the capital, Washington took matters into his own hands and, working closely with L'Enfant, plunged into designing a city whose grandeur appalled Jefferson, who envisioned a capital one-half or one-third the size of what L'Enfant had in mind. Regrettably, the Frenchman refused to cooperate with commissioners appointed to oversee the work; he lost patience with a government unwilling to provide the huge funds for his grand plan; and finally became so unconciliatory that Washington ordered his dismissal. The following year Washington approved a design for the President's house submitted by an Irish architect named James Hoban; and in 1792 an English physician, William Thornton, adapted some drawings done by Jefferson and the architect Stephen Hallet to produce a plan for the Capitol. By 1800, when the government moved to its new quarters, there was nothing to suggest the magnificence L'Enfant had imagined; the grand Federal City was little but a sea of mud and vacant lots.

M. Gen. Butler. Col. Oldham. Maj. Ferguson. Maj. Clark. Maj. Hart. Capt. Bradford. Capt. Phelon. Capt. Kirkwood. Capt. Price. CV. Swearingin. Capt. Tipton. Capt. Smith. Capt. Purdy. Capt. Pratt. Capt. Guthrie. Capt. Cribbs. Capt. Newman. Lt. Spear. Lt. Warren. Lt. Boyd.

Lt. M'Math. Lt. Burgess. Lt. Kelso. Lt. Read. Lt. Little. Lt. Hopper. Lt. Lickins. Enf. Cobb. Enf. Balch. Enf. Chace. Enf. Turner. Enf. Wilson. Enf. Brooks. Enf. Beatty. Enf. Purdy. Q.M. Reynolds. Q.M. Ward. Adj. Anderson. 39 Dr Grafton.

Maj. Gen: RICHARD BUTLER,
Slain in the *Battle* at *Miami-Village*, Nov. 4.

BLOODY INDIAN BATTLE,
Fought at MIAMI VILLAGE, Nov. 4. 1791

THE
COLUMBIAN TRAGEDY:
CONTAINING A PARTICULAR AND OFFICIAL
ACCOUNT
Of the BRAVE and UNFORTUNATE OFFICERS and SOLDIERS, who were
SLAIN and WOUNDED in the EVER-MEMORABLE and
BLOODY INDIAN BATTLE,
Perhaps the most shocking that has happened in AMERICA since its first Discovery; which continued *Six Hours*, with the most unremitted *Fury* and unparalleled *Bravery* on both Sides, having lasted from day-break, until near ten o'clock on *Friday Morning, Nov. 4, 1791*; between *Two Thousand* AMERICANS, belonging to the UNITED ARMY, and near *Five Thousand Wild Indian Savages*, at *Miami-Village*, near *Fort-Washington*, in the *Ohio-Country*, in which terrible and desperate *Battle* a most shocking Slaughter was made of *Thirty-nine gallant* AMERICAN OFFICERS and upwards of *Nine Hundred brave youthful* SOLDIERS, who fell *gloriously fighting* for their COUNTRY.—These *Particulars* and *Elegy* are now published in this SHEET by the earnest Request of the *Friends* to the DECEASED WORTHIES, who died in Defence of their COUNTRY, not only as a *Token* of *Gratitude* to the DECEASED BRAVE, but as a PERPETUAL MEMORIAL of this *important Event*, on which, perhaps may very essentially depend the future FREEDOM and GRANDEUR of *Fifteen* (or *Twenty* States, that might, at some Period, be annexed to the AMERICAN UNION.

List of KILLED and Wounded OFFICERS
KILLED; 1 Maj. Gen. RICHARD BUTLER.—1 Col. Oldham.—Majors; 3 Ferguson—4 Clark—5 Hart.—Captains; 6 Bradford—7 Phelon—8 Kirkwood—9 Price—10 Van Swearingit—11 Tipton—12 Smith—13 Purdy—14 Pratt—15 Guthrie—16 Cribbs—17 Newman—Lieuts. 18 Spear—19 Warren—20 Boyd 21 M'Math—22 Burgess—23 Kelso—24 Read—25 Little—26 Hopper—27 Lickins.—Ensigns; 28 Cobb—29 Balch—30 Chace—31 Turner—32 Wilson—33 Brooks—34 Beatty—35 Purdy.—36 Q. Mast. Reynolds—37 Ward.—38 Adj. Anderson.—39 Dr. Grafton. WOUNDED; 1 Adj. Gen. Sargent—2 L. Col. Gibson—3 Dark—4 Major Butler.—Capts. 5 Doyle—6 Trueman—7 Ford—8 Buchanan—9 Dark—10 Slough.—Lts. 11 Greaton 12 Davidson—13 DeButts—14 Price—15 Morgan—16 M'Crea—17 Lysle.—18 Thompson.—19 Adj. Whistler—20. Crawford. 21. Enf. Bines. 22. Vis. Malertie, Volunteer, Aidecamp to Gen. St. CLAIR.

A
FUNERAL ELEGY on the Occasion.
2 SAMUEL, chap. i.

Ver. 19. *The Beauty of Israel is slain upon thy high places: How are the Mighty fallen!—20. Tell it not in Gath, publish it not in the streets of Askelon: Lest the Daughters of the Philistines rejoice, lest the Daughters of the uncircumcised triumph.—21. Ye Mountains of Gilboa, let there be no dew, neither let there be rain upon you, nor fields of offerings; for there the Shield of the Mighty is vilely cast away.*

YE Friends to men attend the Tale,
Ye brave ones all give ear,
With sympathetic grief bewail
And shed a sorrowing tear.

2. Behold the various scenes of
This hour is mirth and glee, (life
The next we're free'd from care and strife,
And in eternity.

3. Joyful from *Boston*'s happy Town,
These brave Men took their way,
Ah! soon were slain upon the ground,
To BLOODY BRUTES a prey!

4. Adieu to wanton songs and joys,
To idle tales that fill the ear
A mournful theme my heart employs,
And hope the living will it hear.

5. A horrid *Fight* there hap'd of late,
The fourth day of November,
When a vast number met their fate,
We all shall well remember.

6. 'Twas on renown'd *Ohio*'s Land,
And fatal prov'd of old,
Sad to relate! our FEDERAL BAND,
Were slain by INDIANS bold!

7. Ah cursed *Spot!* Ah rueful *Land!*
New-England will rejoin,
Where thousands of our *Countrymen*
Their wasted bones inshrine.

8. By much too dear the *Land* was bo't,
It's stain'd with *English* gore,
Where BRADDOCK fell 1 O sad to tell!
Full thirty years before.

9. Our WASHINGTON with chosen Men,
All ruddy, youthful too,
There rally'd some of *British* Train,
Coop'd by infernal Crew.

10. A horrid covert, where there lay
Whole legions of *black Men*,
But by the courage of that YOUTH,
They're hunted from their den.

11. A handful of *Columbians* led,
Their *Standard* sav'd from harm,
Full tatter'd when fam'd *Berwick* bled,
And *Tallard* felt its arm.

12. The flower of *British* pride was lost,
In one great day they fell!
BRADDOCK's defeat, young SHIRLEY's loss
Our Annals all can tell!

13. Such scenes apart! my Muse still hear
The groans of dying *Friends*;
The horrid shrieks do fill the air,
Of wounded, dying Men.

14. Will not *Columba*'s *Youth* now rouse,
And cheerful take the *Field*,
Columba's *Cause* they will espouse,
Nor to those BLOOD HOUNDS yield.

15. My Muse must quit that mournful Tale,
A worse one to record,
BOSTON shall weep and sore bewail
The stroke sent by the LORD.

16. Our COUNTRYMEN in youthful bloom,
Must in their vigrous prime,
Are summond hence to meet their GOD,
And snatched out of time.

17. Brave General BUTLER's Loss we feel,
And OLDHAM's Death bemoan,
Let's drop a tear when in we tell,
And view their hapless urn.

18. Young NEWMAN fell! and TURNER
With PHELON at their Head, (brave
No friendly arm there was to save,
They're number'd with the dead.

19. The names of WARREN, BALCH and
Let's mourn now o'er their grave, (COBB,
Who late with courage spilt their blood,
And fell with many brave.

20. Ah! WARREN's valor full was shewn,
A *Name* we'll now renew,
Who fell too soon! ah! much too soon!
Tho' twelve fierce Brutes he slew.

21. Let's sing of BRADFORD and whole
Of *Officers* so brave, (scores
They're call'd to the *Elysian* shores,
And mingled in one grave.

22. We must relate the *Warrior*'s fate
Of GREATON, young and brave!
A cruel shot his body pierc'd,
But yet his life was sav'd.

23. Of *Thirty* brave *Youth* in his corps,
But *Three* surviv'd the Brunt,
Was ever such a scene before?
Ah! fatal *Indian Hunt!*

24. *Columba*'s Land a scene presents,
Of blood and slaughter too,
The *Widow*'s heart doth sore lament,
To bid their *Friends* adieu.

25. What shall we say when 'tis decreed,
By fate it must be so,
To see our dearest *Brethren* bleed,
And ev'ry vein to flow.

26. What heart that feels for others woe,
Can stop the gushing tear,
Or not the pangs of pity show,
When such scenes they hear.

27. But if such pity here imparts,
Think O! what griefs assail,
Their *Widow*'s and their *Children*'s hearts,
When they shall hear the tale!

28. The thought already fills each breast,
With kind condoling care,
And hope in Heav'n they'll meet at rest,
Their *Friends* and *Fathers* there.

29. We feel and sympathize for them
Who late in battle fell,
We mean those hardy, youthful man,
Their names to ages tell.

30. Though *Powers Immortal* are averse,
O LORD! the praise is thine!
The scene, O GOD, O GOD rehears'd
And make our arms to shine!

31. We'll scour all their *Thickets* then,
Make INDIANS sue for peace,
Hunt *lurking Savage* from his den,
When we shall win the chace.

32. If great JEHOVAH takes the shield,
And guards us round about,
No INDIAN will his *Tomax* wield,
Nor arrow dare to shoot.

33. My trembling hand can scarcely hold
My faint, devoted quill,
To write the actions of the Bold,
Their valor and their skill.

34. Let's not forget the SOLDIER brave,
Who fell with Indian ax,
Who scorn'd to flinch their lives to save,
Nor on them turn'd their backs.

35. NINE HUNDRED hardiest of our Sons,
Some in their *early* prime,
Have fell a *victim* to their rage,
And are cut off from time.

36. Yes, numbers met an awful death,
In battle they were slain,
But we that live upon the earth,
Their mem'ry will sustain.

37. If that the LORD is on our side,
We need not fear our foe,
And if that gracious Isr'el's GOD
Now with our armies go;

38. Our heads he'll cover when in fight,
From harm he will us keep,
If that we seek his face aright,
Nor let our feet to slip.

39. With conq'ring might he will us shield,
And INDIANS all destroy,
He'll help us thus to win the field,
And slay those that annoy.

40. Our *Country* calls us far and near,
Columba's Sons awake,
For helmet, buckler and our spear,
The LORD's own arm we'll take.

41. His shield will keep us from all harm,
Tho' thousands 'gainst us rise,
His buckler we must sure put on,
If we would win the prize.

AMERICA:
BOSTON; Printed by E. RUSSELL,
for THOMAS BASSETT, of Deerborton, (New-Hamp.)—[Pr. Six Pence.]
☞ Said BASSETT sells Bickerstaff's Almanack,
for 1792, as CHEAP as at this Office.

FRONTIERS AFLAME

A problem that absorbed Washington's attention throughout two
terms in office was the sensitive one of how to deal with the Indians
on the western and southern frontiers. In the northwest the British
were stirring up the red men against Americans pushing into their
lands; to the south, the Spanish were doing the same; and while
Washington did what he could to guarantee the treaty rights granted to
various tribes, there was almost no way the administration could
prevent white settlers from encroaching on Indian lands. In the fall
of 1790 General Josiah Harmar marched into Ohio country and suffered
a humiliating defeat at the hands of the Indians. A year later
another American expedition under General Arthur St. Clair headed
into the same territory and met with even more disastrous consequences,
detailed in the broadside on the facing page as "the most shocking
that has happened in America since its first Discovery." Two-thirds of the
men engaged were lost. Not until Anthony Wayne's army conquered
the Indians at Fallen Timbers in 1795 did a generation of fighting
end in the Ohio Valley. Unfortunately the treaties negotiated by the
government were almost never observed by the restless, land-hungry
American frontiersmen, and although the Indians were guaranteed
"Perpetual peace," it was little wonder that they referred to the
surveyor's compass as the white man's "land stealer." At right is a
medal presented to a Shawnee chief as a token of peaceful intentions
in 1792; a peace pipe changes hands, the tomahawk lies on the ground,
and the background suggests that the chief would do well to practice
agriculture. Above are portraits of two Creek chiefs who visited
Washington in New York in 1790 to discuss land cessions. John
Trumbull, who drew them, had to work surreptitiously because the
Indians feared his "magic"; he described them as having "a
dignity of manner . . . worthy of a Roman senator."

GEORGE WASHINGTON
PRESIDENT.
1792.

THE GENET AFFAIR

Of all the ugly effects of the Hamilton-Jefferson contretemps,
none exasperated Washington more than the episode in which
Edmond Charles Genêt, France's first minister to the United
States, attempted to turn the American people against their
President. France's Revolution, and the outbreak of war between
France and England, pitted Federalists and Republicans against
each other anew — the Jeffersonians siding with the old wartime
ally, the Hamiltonians eager to avoid any split with Great
Britain and loss of the essential trade with that country. By the
time Genêt (shown here in a contemporary silhouette) arrived
in 1793, the feud between the two American political antagonists
had reached white heat, and the partisan newspapers they sponsored
were exploiting every possible situation. In Washington's
estimation, the pro-Jefferson attacks published by journalist
Philip Freneau were "outrages on common decency," but certainly
the Federalist press was no better. At bottom left is a
typical cartoon produced by the Hamiltonian side, showing
Jefferson on a table top — in league with the Devil, at lower
left — speaking to the rabble in an Antifederalist club.
Although the Genêt controversy subsided when even his supporters
recognized that the Frenchman had gone too far, the scars it
left were apparent in 1794, when farmers in western Pennsylvania,
led by members of a "Democratic Society," rose up in opposition
to Hamilton's fiscal policies and attacked government officials.
Above, on the facing page, is a Republican cartoon of the
unpopular exciseman, suffering the consequences of confiscating
whiskey from back country distillers.

CULVER

239

REBELLION IN PENNSYLVANIA

An unknown artist depicted the aging Washington, in uniform once again, reviewing the army of militiamen summoned to put down the Whiskey Rebellion in 1794. During November the western Pennsylvania countries were occupied without bloodshed and prisoners were sent to Philadelphia (to be acquitted, pardoned, or dismissed for lack of evidence). Washington was convinced that the insurrection was inspired by newcomers as yet unconverted to American institutions — the handiwork of Democratic Societies created to support Genêt. Jefferson, believing that the calling up of an army was Hamilton's doing, called the expedition "an armament against people at their ploughs."

A CORNERSTONE IS LAID

September 18, 1793, was designated as the day for laying the cornerstone of the United States Capitol, but the occasion was neither as orderly nor as auspicious as the drawing by Latrobe at the top of the opposite page made it out to be. Washington's fellow Masons had been entrusted with arrangements for the parade, and Lodge Number 22 of Alexandria turned out in all their regalia and symbols of office, accompanied by dignitaries from the town of Georgetown, the city of Washington, and the Virginia Artillery. Unfortunately, the presidential mansion, where the parade began, was but a partially excavated foundation; trees or stumps stood in the grand avenues conceived by L'Enfant; the city's lots were still being cleared; and the procession was forced to make an ungainly crossing of Goose Creek, since the commissioners of the District of Columbia had been unable to raise the funds to build a bridge there. Above is William Williams' 1794 portrait of Washington in Masonic robes and apron; the President wore the Masonic apron at right, made for him by nuns of a religious order in Nantes, France, to the September 18th ceremony at the Capitol.

BOTH: ALEXANDRIA-WASHINGTON LODGE NO. 22, A.F. & A.M., ALEXANDRIA, VIRGINIA

244

CAPITAL SOCIETY

In Philadelphia the Washingtons found themselves at the vortex of a
social scene that was without rival in the country, and since their
taste in friends ran to families of wealth and sophistication, democrats
like Jefferson worried increasingly about the trend to monarchical
ways. At the center of this social whirl was Mrs. William Bingham
(left), the daughter of Robert Morris' senior partner and the wife of a
man who had made a mysterious fortune abroad during the Revolution.
Abigail Adams thought her "the finest woman I ever saw," but regretted
her "passion and thirst after all the luxuries of Europe." Washington's
favorite female companion in Philadelphia was Mrs. Samuel Powel,
whose husband was said to be the richest young man in the city. Eliza
(far left) was a saucy, intelligent, interesting woman who flirted
with Washington, teased and amused him, and became almost at once his
confidante and adviser in matters social and political. (It was she who
wrote him a letter in 1793 that may have persuaded him not to reject a
second term.) These confident, glittering ladies were quite a contrast
to Martha, shown below left in an engraving after a lost portrait by
Charles Willson Peale; known as "Lady Washington," she was a trifle
dowdy, naive, and grandmotherly by comparison with the Philadelphia
beauties. Below is a dinner invitation from the Washingtons (these
were sent in rotation to various officials), and at right is a
silhouette of the President in evening dress, made about this time.

*The President of the United States
and Mrs Washington, request the Pleasure of
Mr & Mrs Gilbert's
Company to Dine, on Thurs next, at 4 oClock.
5 May 1794
An answer is requested.*

CLARK KINNAIRD

Washington liked a well-appointed house, and one of the glories of Mount Vernon was a set of "elegant China" presented to him by the Comte de Custine-Sarreck, owner of the Niderviller porcelain factory in France, who had served with him at Yorktown. (On the facing page is a covered cream pitcher from the set, which was later given to Dolley Madison by Martha.) While the luxury he saw on all sides in Philadelphia made Mount Vernon seem pallid by comparison, he had endured enough criticism from the Republicans to be cautious about his dwelling there and its furnishings. It would be unwise, he concluded, "to stir any question that would tend to reanimate the dying embers of faction." Although he had had a number of alterations made to the Morris house, he still found it cramped, and complained that visitors who came on business matters "have to ascend two pairs of stairs and to pass by the public rooms." Nonetheless, there were certain niceties he found impossible to resist. When the carriagemakers David and Francis Clark were engaged to refurbish his "state" coach (opposite, lower left), Washington specified the paint color, chose the interior fabric, and even made a sketch of the "cypher" he wanted on the doors — his initials surmounted by a griffon (lower right). Inevitably, prominence had its hazards. After he had employed the silversmith Joseph Cook to make some wine bottle holders, it was discovered that Cook was preparing to advertise himself as "silver Smith to the President," and Tobias Lear addressed the letter at right to the fellow, telling him to cease and desist. Cook had recently come from London, where service to royalty was an accepted distinction, and he was not entirely daunted by Lear's instructions. Two years later he was still publicizing "The very great honor already done him by some of the first characters of the United States in visiting his manufactury, and honoring him with their employment."

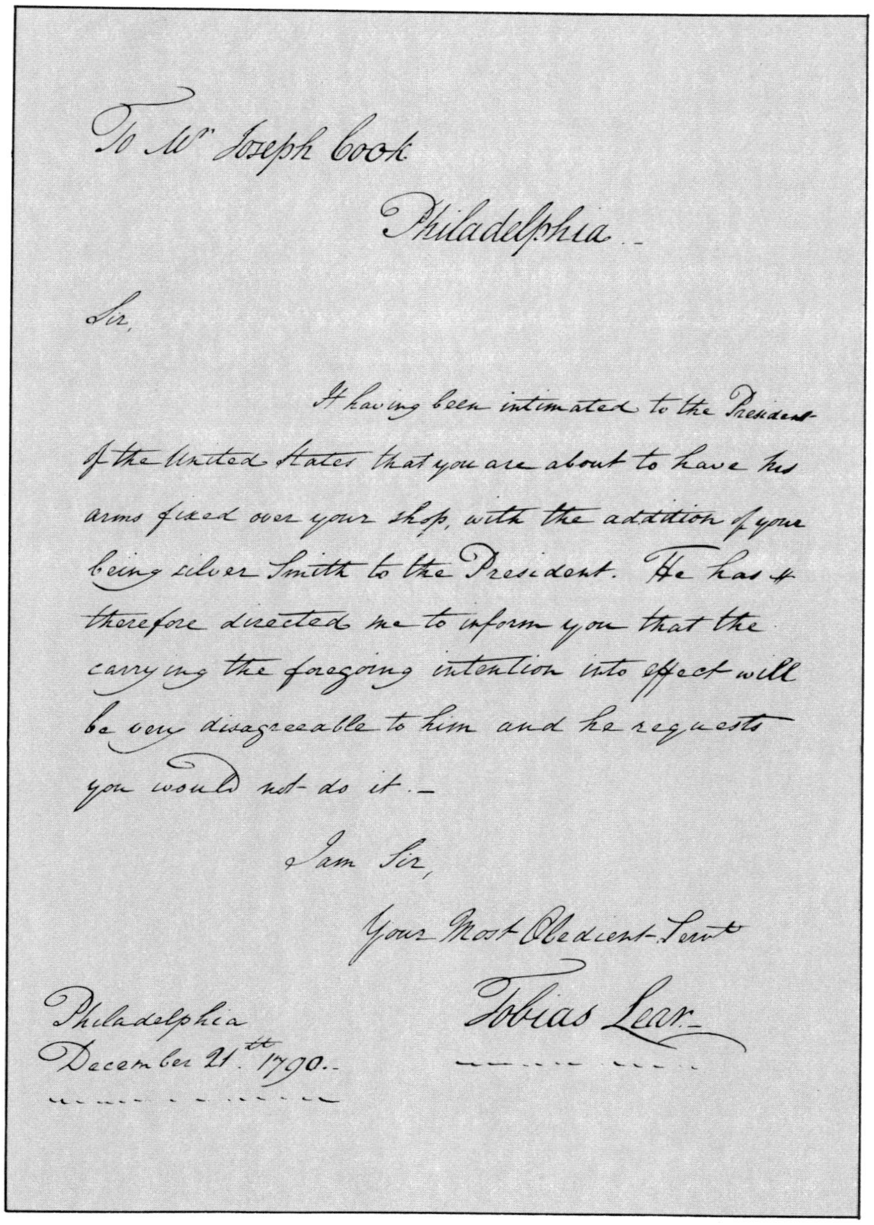

To Mr Joseph Cook

Philadelphia.

Sir,

It having been intimated to the President of the United States that you are about to have his arms fixed over your shop, with the addition of your being silver Smith to the President. He has & therefore directed me to inform you that the carrying the foregoing intention into effect will be very disagreeable to him and he requests you would not do it. —

I am Sir,

Your Most Obedient Servt

Tobias Lear

Philadelphia
December 21st 1790. —

FRANCE IN REVOLT

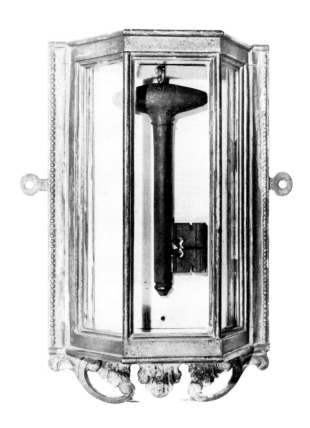

The convulsions of France's revolution found Washington concerned, above all, for his younger friend and protégé, the Marquis de Lafayette. At first, all had gone well; when the Bastille fell, Lafayette sent Washington the "main key" of that "fortress of despotism" and a picture of the historic event, and these items were proudly displayed by the recipient in his house in Philadelphia (and later at Mount Vernon) along with an engraving of the French King. To the dismay of aristocratic refugees from France, Washington removed the portrait of Louis XVI from the wall after the monarch was imprisoned — leaving only the two symbols of anarchy and terror. On the facing page are the engraving of Louis and the key to the Bastille, above which appears a letter the President wrote to Lafayette's wife in January, 1793, when he learned that her husband had been imprisoned in Austria. His position made it impossible for him to do anything about Lafayette's plight, and although he did not know the Marquise's whereabouts, he sent the letter and two hundred guineas to a banker in Holland, requesting that the man forward them to the lady as a small payment of Washington's debt "for services rendered me by Mr. de la Fayette, of which I never yet received the account." When the Frenchman's fourteen-year-old son, George Washington Lafayette, arrived in the United States in 1795 hoping to be welcomed as a member of his namesake's family, the President faced an agonizing decision, knowing that he would offend both France and that country's American partisans by doing so. For a year he had to avoid the boy; at last he felt able to take him in and the young man went with the Washingtons to Mount Vernon, where Benjamin Latrobe sketched him (at left) in the group below.

THE FIRST FAMILY AT HOME

All that was closest to Washington's heart is suggested
in this warm family portrait done by Edward Savage between
1789 and 1796. Although the presidential residence during
most of those years was in Philadelphia, the scene here is
Mount Vernon. Once again, as during the Revolutionary War,
Washington was obliged to be away from his farm more often
than not, forced to rely on correspondence with his overseer
as the means of accomplishing work that was to be completed
during prolonged absences. Lacking any children of his own,
he had adopted Martha's two young grandchildren shown here —
George Washington Parke Custis and Eleanor Parke Custis
(Nelly), who came to live at Mount Vernon after the death
of their father, Jacky Custis. Nelly possessed all the
social graces and was already showing signs of the beauty
she acquired, and she was everything a doting stepgrandfather
could wish. Her brother had already displayed, Washington
noted, "an almost unconquerable disposition to indolence in
every thing that did not tend to his amusements," but the
General was forced to admit that he was "the pet of the
family." (To a point, Nelly complained, that "Grandmama
always spoiled Washington.") Like his father, young Custis
was not much for schooling; he attended Princeton, where
he was embroiled almost at once in a "contest with the
passions," and subsequently transferred to St. John's College
in Annapolis, where he stayed only a few months. Both
George and his sister Nelly were not without talent as
artists. The charming sketch of Mount Vernon, below,
was drawn by George when he was a young boy.

The portrait of George Washington that came to be accepted by later generations as the calm, remote image of the father of his country was painted, alas, when age, ill health, the loss of his teeth, and sadness had greatly changed his face and expression. Painted in 1796 by the brilliant and alcoholic virtuoso Gilbert Stuart (whose unfinished self-portrait appears below), the so-called Athenaeum portrait on the facing page was commissioned by Martha Washington, but Stuart never delivered it to her. It was his intention to make a fortune out of copying this and other life portraits in order to sell "a plurality of portraits" of America's hero, and he never finished the background, so that he could truthfully tell Martha it was incomplete whenever she requested it. Indeed, he made so many copies no one has been able to count them. There was a streak of cruelty in Stuart that made him deliberately exaggerate the distorted mouth (his sitter, Stuart observed, "had just had a [new] set of false teeth inserted") and poor Martha received only an inferior copy, for which she never forgave the artist. Asked for a candid opinion of the various likenesses of Washington, Stuart answered, "Houdon's bust [see page 255] came first, and my head of him next." Houdon's work, he admitted, did not suffer from the distortion of the mouth; but he added defiantly, "I wanted him as he looked at that time." The portrait of Mrs. Perez Morton of Philadelphia (left) is also by Stuart. Resentful of the lady's open admiration of Washington, he showed her clasping a piece of jewelry to her wrist, while a grim, shadowy bust of the President looks on disapprovingly. In this imaginary bust, even more than the portraits he did, Stuart cruelly misshaped Washington's mouth.

STUART PAINTS A PORTRAIT

WASHINGTON TO THE LIFE

In 1785 the French sculptor Jean Antoine Houdon arrived at Mount Vernon — "After we were in bed (about 11 o'clock in the evening)," Washington noted ruefully — to make a bust of the hero of the Revolution for the state of Virginia. For several days Houdon observed his subject, watching for the pose he wanted, and according to one account, saw it at the moment Washington was being offered some horses by a dealer. When the General heard the asking price he was indignant, and the determined tilt of the jaw was just what the sculptor sought. Despite his impatience of artists, Washington submitted to having his face smeared with plaster for a life mask, and little Nelly Custis, who was then six years old, remembered walking by the room and seeing him "as I supposed, *dead*, & laid out on a large table cover'd with a sheet . . . except his face, on which Houdon was engaged in putting on plaster to form the cast. Quills were in the nostrils. I was very much alarmed until I was told that it . . . would not injure him." The life mask, which is the most precise documentation we have of Washington's face, appears at left. Houdon then modeled a bust in clay, which he left at Mount Vernon after having a plaster cast made of it; and when he returned to Paris began work on the magnificent marble bust illustrated on the facing page. When Lafayette saw the finished statue years after Washington's death tears came to his eyes as he cried out, "That is the man himself!" Even the critical eye of Gilbert Stuart perceived that this was the foremost likeness ever done of the man — the closest approximation we have of a living, breathing George Washington.

6

⚬

RETIREMENT

The old warrior was going home to rest at last, but first the accumulation of eight years had to be dealt with as the household in Philadelphia was broken up. Most of the furnishings, china, and glassware supplied him by Congress had been broken or worn out by hard use and had been replaced by Washington out of his own pocket on the theory that it would not do for the President of the United States to be surrounded with shabby household effects. By now, however, everything was in a bad state: as Abigail Adams noted when she moved into the house, there was not a chair to sit on and "The beds and bedding are in a woeful pickle." Washington wanted to sell the Adamses what he could—including a chandelier, hangings, various pieces of furniture, and a pair of horses, but Adams cast a sharp Yankee eye on the goods and backed away from the transaction at the last moment. Some objects were sold to others, some were given to friends, but there remained for shipment to Mount Vernon about two hundred packing cases, trunks, and assorted parcels containing everything from a ton of iron and a safe to trivets, venetian blinds, carpets, a tin shower bath, and a bidet. All this went off aboard a sloop rented by Washington while he and Martha, her eighteen-year-old granddaughter Nelly Custis, young Lafayette, and his tutor embarked by coach, surrounded with countless small packages. The move was not all that different from what less exalted Americans experienced: as Washington wrote Tobias Lear, "On one side, I am called upon to remember the parrot; on the other, to remember the dog. For my own part, I should not pine if both were forgot." On March 15, 1797, the family arrived at Mount Vernon, having endured tributes in their honor in Baltimore, Georgetown, Alexandria, and the new Federal City (where they were greeted with an eighteen-gun salute).

Once at home, Washington fell into the slow rhythm of plantation life, much pleased, Nelly Custis wrote, with the idea of being "once more *Farmer Washington.*" As usual, he found innumerable matters requiring his attention—among them the deteriorating main house and outbuildings, and soon he was surrounded by so many joiners, masons, and painters that he had "scarcely a room to put a friend into or set in myself without the music of hammers or the odiferous smell of paint."

He and Martha were both feeling their age and often were reluctant to entertain company (it was at this time that he wrote Lear saying that "Unless someone pops in unexpectedly, Mrs. Washington and myself will do what I believe has not been done within the last twenty years by us, that is to set down to dinner by ourselves"), and Washington invited his nephew Lawrence Lewis to stay with them and take some of the duties of hospitality off his hands. Lewis and Nelly Custis were soon spending much time together, and they brought to the household many youthful companions whose company Washington enjoyed thoroughly—but only for a while. He would withdraw after a time, Nelly wrote, aware that "his presence created a reserve they could not overcome." Another member of the household was George Washington Parke Custis, who was as much of a problem as his father, Jack, had been. What bothered the boy's grandfather was that he was lazy and lacked ambition —"inert," was the way Washington described him— and like his father had little aptitude for school. He had failed at the University of Pennsylvania and the College of New Jersey (later Princeton) before being sent off to St. John's College in Annapolis, and when he decided to leave the latter place Washington wrote him in despair, saying "it would seem as if *nothing* I could say to you made more than a *momentary* impression." Reluctantly, he allowed the young man to come home to Mount Vernon, where Custis was to suffer by comparison with Lafayette's son, still a visitor, whom Washington found "aimiable and sensible."

One of the best descriptions of the aging George Washington at Mount Vernon comes from Benjamin Henry Latrobe, the young English engineer, architect, and artist who visited the plantation in the summer of 1796. "Washington," Latrobe wrote, "has something uncommonly majestic and commanding in his walk, his address, his figure, and his countenance. His face is characterized, however, more by intense and powerful thought than by quick and fiery conception. There is a mildness about its expression, and an air of reserve in his manner lowers its tone still more. . . . He was frequently entirely silent for many minutes, during which time an awkwardness seemed to prevail in everyone present. His answers were often short and sometimes approached to moroseness. He did not at any time speak with very remarkable fluency; perhaps the extreme correctness of his language, which almost seemed studied, prevented that effect. He appeared to enjoy a humorous observation, and made several himself. He laughed heartily several times in a very good-humored manner. On the morning of my departure he treated me as if I had lived for years in his house, with ease and attention."

Try as he would, Washington could never fully escape the problems of the world beyond his Potomac domain. The situation in France had worsened. The credentials of Charles Cotesworth Pinckney, whom Washington had appointed minister to that country, had been refused by the Directory and John Adams then sent John Marshall and Elbridge Gerry to Paris to join Pinckney in an effort to establish some sort of amicable relations. (While America awaited news of their success or failure, Washington paced the porch at Mount Vernon in a dark mood, wondering if the commissioners had been guillotined.) After a chilly reception by France's foreign minister, Tallyrand, the men were told by his subordinates that the road to negotiations would have to be paved with a payment of a $250,000 bribe to Tallyrand, a loan of ten million dollars, and retraction of certain "insults" against France made in one of Adams' speeches to Congress. In their report the three American diplomats referred to the French agents who specified the terms as "X, Y, and Z," from which the episode became popularly known as the XYZ Affair, which marked the end of the honeymoon with France. Americans of all political colorations supported the position of Pinckney, who had replied to the astonishing proposal by crying, "No, No! Not a sixpence," but Washington did not believe that ardent Francophiles would change their views. The infamy of the affair and the corruption it revealed, he wrote Secretary of State Pickering, should "open the Eyes of the blindest," yet he thought that the leaders of the French party in America would remain unconvinced.

May of 1798 brought a disturbing letter from Alexander Hamilton, suggesting that "In the event of an open rupture with France, the public voice will again call you to command the armies of your country." Replying, Washington expressed the opinion that matters had certainly not reached the stage where France would contemplate an invasion of the United States, nor was there appreciable popular support in this country to encourage the French in such an adventure. But he viewed Hamilton's suggestion that he take up his sword again with profound misgivings. If the call from his country "should become so imperious as to leave me no Choice," he wrote, he would answer it, but would go from his present peaceful abode with "as much reluctance . . . as I should do to the tombs of my ancestors."

Hamilton's was no isolated thought. In July Washington received a letter from Secretary of War McHenry asking if the "ancient pilot" would, "in a crisis so awful and important . . . accept the command of all our armies?" And that same day came a request from President Adams on the same subject. Despite the immense reluctance he felt, Washington told McHenry that "the principle by which my conduct has been actuated through life, would not suffer me, in any great emergency, to withhold any services I could render, required by my Country," and went on to suggest how able general officers should be chosen. (His mind turned back to the early days of the Revolution and to the aging militia officers who had proved so ineffective, and he urged both Adams and McHenry to disregard the claims of Revolutionary veterans to seniority.)

Although Washington responded to both letters on July 4, 1798, he learned to his irritation that Adams had appointed him lieutenant general and commander of U.S. military forces on July 2—an appointment unanimously ratified by Congress at once. Adams apologized in a subsequent letter, assuring Washington that if he had had the power to nominate him President he would have done so with "less hesitation and more pleasure" and Washington began formulating his plans, selecting as major generals Hamilton, Pinckney, and Knox in that order of rank. There followed a protracted sequence of arguments and embarrassments—Knox humiliated because junior officers were ranked over him; Adams refusing to let Hamilton outrank the other two because he feared him; Washington angry because Adams had refused to honor his request: and not until Washington finally threatened to resign publicly did he get things his own way. It was not a pretty sight, but at last the impasse was resolved and Washington went to Philadelphia on November 10 to meet with Hamilton and Pinckney (Knox had refused a commission as major general but said he would serve as Washington's aide-de-camp if it came to fighting). Then, and for some months after his return to Mount Vernon, Washington was engaged in the business of organizing a Provisional Army, preparing tables of organization, making up lists of officers, and drawing up plans for recruiting.

It came to no more than that because, for one thing, there was no discernible public enthusiasm for war or for an army in the absence of a clear threat of invasion. For another, the quasi war that followed took place at sea, with American privateers attacking the few French ships that could be spared for duty in American waters. Some ninety French vessels were eventually captured, against a loss of only one American ship, before the undeclared war sputtered out inconclusively in the fall of 1800.

Washington had the opportunity, therefore, to devote most of his attention to Mount Vernon where, as ever, difficulty seemed to be the handmaiden of everyday life. His mind turned frequently to his slaves, whose offspring often appeared to be the plantation's most reliable crop. He estimated that he had half again as many blacks as "can be employed to any advantage in the farming system" and he wanted, for practical considerations and as a matter of conscience, to set them free. But where was the means of doing so, and what would become of these unfortunate people if he did? Beyond that there was the question of Martha's future; she might well outlive him, even though she was not in robust health and was older, and how was she to cope with finding a new livelihood for one hundred and fifty healthy blacks, plus an equal number who were too old or too young to work? What finally emerged from this internal struggle was a decision to free his slaves at the death of his wife. Those who were old and infirm were to be cared for by his heirs as long as the slaves lived; the little children were to be supported until the age of twenty-five, during which time they would be taught to read and write "and brought up to some useful occupation." He was at a loss, however, as to what to do with the able-bodied men and women and had no solution for them once they were freed. As it turned out, his anxiety was confirmed a year after his death when Abigail Adams, who visited Mount Vernon, wrote that "Mrs. Washington with all her fortune finds it difficult to support . . . three hundred slaves. One hundred and fifty of them are now to be liberated, men with wives and young children who have never seen an acre beyond the farm are now about to quit it, and go adrift into the world without horse, home, or friend. Mrs. Washington is distressed for them . . . and very many of them are already miserable at the thought of their lot. The aged she retains at their request; but she is distressed for the fate of others. She feels a parent and a wife."

During his second term, Washington had realized that the acreage collected during the early years of his life was too much for an aging man and he had determined to rent certain parcels of land "to *real* farmers of *good* reputation." None others, declared the advertisements he placed in American and English newspapers, need apply. Parting with the land—even though it would still be tied to him by a lease—was agonizing for a man who loved it so well, and perhaps he deluded himself into thinking he could do it, for he never did find a tenant who suited him. Yet the problem remained: too much land,

land that was not sufficiently fertile, inefficient farm managers, incompetent field hands, work that needed doing that never got done, the never-ending frustration of the owner who desired perfection and found himself always having to settle for less.

Determined to remedy the situation, Washington spent weeks, if not months, concocting a plan by which "everything [would] move like clockwork," spelling out in minute detail what everyone's job was to be. Systematically noting how the crops would be rotated during the years 1800 through 1803 (after which time the cycle would be repeated), he reasoned that a program of this sort "would be less harassing to those who labor and more beneficial to those who employ them." This ambitious scheme for the employment of his people and the use of his land ran to more than thirty thousand words and suggests how fully his mind was occupied with the operation of the plantation.

Neither book work nor advancing age kept him from spending days in the saddle, inspecting the several farms attached to Mount Vernon, checking on boundary lines that were in dispute, attempting to collect rents that were past due. Occasionally he went out surveying and he traveled now and again to the Federal City to see what progress was being made on a house he was building there, which he intended to rent. The house at Mount Vernon, as always, was filled with visitors — guests arriving for a meal and staying the night, to be replaced the following day with someone else.

Lawrence Lewis and Nelly Custis had been married on Washington's birthday, February 22, 1799, and when Nelly hinted broadly that they would be happy to remain at or near Mount Vernon, Washington invited Lewis to take over the Dogue Run farm, the mill, and the distillery, which he intended to leave them in his will. The old man knew there was not much time left to him, and on July 9, 1799, he signed a new will which he had written himself, aided, he said, by "no professional character." It included extraordinarily detailed tables listing all his slaves, their family relationships, where they were housed, and how employed. All his land holdings outside Mount Vernon were described fully and he even provided a record of how he had come by each parcel and his estimate of their present value. In addition to a dozen tracts in Virginia, there were two each in Maryland and Kentucky, one each in New York and Pennsylvania (the latter being the site of Fort Necessity), lands along the Ohio and Great Kanawha Rivers, and several tracts in the Northwest Territory.

Friends, dependents, and servants were among the beneficiaries; he provided freedom and an annuity for Will, his body servant of many years; to Tobias Lear went lifetime use of the farm where he resided; provision was made for support of those slaves who were to be freed who were incapable of earning a living; and there were charitable bequests for education, which he wanted to be used for the poor, and for training future leaders of the country. Various relatives were to receive the property outside Mount Vernon.

The major part of his estate was willed to Martha, and he provided that after her death Mount Vernon should be divided into three sections. One of these consisted of the farm, mill, and distillery given to Nelly and Lawrence Lewis; another went to the two sons of George Augustine Washington and his wife, Fanny Bassett; and the third was bequeathed to Bushrod Washington, his nephew. Bushrod's share included Washington's papers, acreage contiguous to Mount Vernon, and the mansion house itself. Long ago, Washington had promised his favorite brother, John Augustine, that he should have the house if George was killed during the French and Indian War and now, remembering that pledge, he left the place to John Augustine's son Bushrod.

I t was symptomatic of Mount Vernon's condition that the place where Washington wished to be buried had not been maintained properly. "The family vault at Mount Vernon requiring repairs and being improperly situated besides," he wrote, "I desire that a new one of brick, and upon a larger scale, may be built at the foot of what is commonly called the vineyard enclosure. . . ." Here he wished his remains interred, along with those of relatives who had already been buried in the old vault, and, anticipating what might otherwise happen, he requested that the burial be a quiet one — done "in a private manner, without parade or funeral oration."

An interesting aspect of the will was Washington's evident desire that it be recorded with some style. He wrote it on special paper with a circular watermark — a device with the words "GEORGE WASHINGTON" within concentric circles, in the center of which the goddess of agriculture, seated on a plough, held in one hand a staff topped with a liberty cap and in the other a leafy twig. At the top of the device was a griffon. The will itself was written in his own hand, inscribed with extreme care so that the left- and right-hand margins were both neatly aligned.

As Martha was to write, George Washington had no

wish "to quitt the theatre of this world until the new century had been rung in," but he fell short of his ambition by a little over two weeks. On December 12, 1799 — a day when snow began falling at ten in the morning, changed to hail, and then to a steady, cold rain — he spent nearly five hours riding on an inspection tour of his farms. Tobias Lear met him upon his return with some letters to frank and Washington observed that the weather was too bad to send a servant with them to the post office. Lear asked if Washington was not wet from long exposure to the storm but the latter replied that he was not — his greatcoat had kept him dry. Even so, Lear noticed, "his neck appeared wet and the snow was hanging on his hair." The next morning it was snowing again, clearing in the afternoon, and Washington told Lear that he had a sore throat. But characteristically he "took no measures to relieve it," regarding it as a trivial matter, and although he did not ride out in the storm he did take a walk toward the river to mark some trees he wanted cut. That evening he sat talking with Lear and Martha, reading some newspapers aloud to them in a hoarse voice. "He was very cheerful," Lear remarked, until he read an account of the debates in the Virginia legislature which indicated that Madison was supporting James Monroe for the Senate. This seemed to exasperate him, but Lear managed to calm him down and suggested that he take some medicine for his throat before retiring for the night.

"No," Washington replied. "You know I never take anything for a cold. Let it go as it came."

Sometime after two in the morning, Washington aroused Martha to tell her he was ill, suffering from an acutely sore throat and difficulty in breathing; but the room was cold and he would not allow her to get out of bed to call a servant. Apparently it occurred to him then that he was going to die; as his doctors reported later," He was fully impressed at the beginning of his complaint . . . that its conclusion would be mortal. . . ." When a maid came to the room at sunup to make a fire she was sent at once to fetch Lear and an overseer who looked after ailing slaves; Washington wanted the latter to bleed him at once, even though the doctor would not arrive for some time. This was done, over Martha's protests, and when Washington's old friend James Craik appeared at about 9 A.M., he diagnosed the illness as inflammatory quinsy, drew more blood from the patient's arm and, when two more physicians who had been summoned turned up in mid-afternoon, bled him again.

The doctors were not fully agreed on the nature of the illness or the treatment — Dr. Elisha Dick of Alex-andria, youngest of the three, arguing that it was a violent inflammation of the throat membranes, not quinsy, and urging that the trachea be opened to facilitate breathing. Dick opposed further bleeding on the grounds that the patient needed all his strength, but Craik and the other physician, Dr. Gustavus Brown, persisted in the only treatment they regarded as proper in the circumstances — more bleeding and purges. (Later Craik wrote Brown to say he thought Dick had probably been correct. Had they taken no more blood, "our good friend might have been alive now. But we were governed by the best light we had; we thought we were right, and so we are justified.")

Through it all, Washington seemed resigned to his fate. He sent Martha to locate two wills in his desk and had her burn the version he had superseded in July. To Lear he mentioned several matters he wished he had had time to attend to and inquired if there was anything essential he must do now, before the end came, "as he had but a very short time to continue with us." Once, when Craik re-entered the room, Washington managed to say, "I die hard, but I am not afraid to go," and later, when the other doctors tried to get him to change his position, he asked them to let him die in peace, without further trouble. Thanking them for their attention, he said, "Let me go off quietly; I cannot last long." Sometime around midnight he spoke with great effort to Lear: "I am just going," he said. "Have me decently buried, and do not let my body be put into the vault in less than three days after I am dead."

Lear nodded agreement, but Washington wanted to be certain he had been heard.

"Do you understand me?"

"Yes, sir," Lear replied.

" 'Tis well."

Those were the last words he spoke. The night wore on and the death watch continued, Martha sitting near the foot of the bed, Craik staring into the fire, Lear at the head of the bed holding one of Washington's hands, and a cluster of house servants standing silently near the door. At the end there was a slight movement from the bed. Washington withdrew his hand from Lear's and started to raise his arm. Then it fell to his side, limp. When Craik passed his hand over Washington's eyes there was no reaction, no sign of life.

"Is he gone?" Martha asked.

A gesture from the grief-stricken Lear answered her question.

In what direction George Washington's mind wandered at the end, no one can say. From Tobias Lear's account it would seem that his lucid thoughts focused on unfinished business — matters to which he had been unable to give undivided attention, plans unfulfilled or as yet unformed, and it was characteristic of the man that he should have been thinking of duty and responsibility. He had seldom thought of anything else in his maturity, whether it had to do with the small world of his plantation or the larger one of the nation he had done so much to form.

It would be satisfying to know that he looked with some degree of gratification on his accomplishments, and perhaps he did, at that. Although his standard of obligation was higher than that of most men, whatever debt he owed society had been paid many times over, by giving his countrymen a birthright they could call their own and leaving them with a sense of pride in what they had achieved together. There is no reason to suppose that he faced death with anything but equanimity and courage and when it came he was ready, comforted by his wife of forty years and two old friends, knowing that he would meet his Maker in the house he had loved above almost everything else for as long as he could remember.

The end of his century echoed his passing, but in the assessments of that era which followed, George Washington was not usually ranked with the minds that had made it the age of enlightenment. He was not a philosopher, yet he was as much a child of the century as Thomas Jefferson was. Eminently practical, Washington was also an innovator in his own way, as had been shown during the Revolution when, confronted with a situation that demanded an unconventional response, he had improvised and fought an unorthodox kind of war — the only kind that had a chance of success, given the circumstances in which he found himself. He had participated in and led the great experiment that was America's gift to the world and through it all had remained what he was — an honorable man with no pretensions to genius or brilliance, but rather a straightforward, competent, and honest one.

The aura of sainthood that surrounded his name and memory after his death would surely have embarrassed him, for no man knew better than he what his limitations and shortcomings were. He had simply done the best he knew how, always walking on a straight line, and in so doing had fathered a nation.

TWILIGHT AT
MOUNT VERNON

Home at last, George Washington could contemplate his estate on the Potomac in serenity, confident that he would never again have to leave it on public business. In 1792, some years before Washington's retirement, an unknown artist had painted this leisurely view of Mount Vernon, showing the President out for a stroll, with Martha on his arm. The young lady is Nelly Parke Custis, Martha's granddaughter, and the young man summoning his dog is probably her brother, George Washington Parke Custis, with his uniformed tutor. A classical version of the same milieu (left) was done by Benjamin Latrobe, who visited Mount Vernon in 1796 and sketched Nelly at tea-time, standing next to one of the pillars on the piazza. It is not difficult to imagine the General seated behind his brass telescope (right), surveying the majestic sweep of the Potomac.

CHILDREN OF THE HOUSE

WOODLAWN PLANTATION

During the many years the Washingtons lived at Mount Vernon the house seldom lacked for young people. A second generation of children came along to fill the places of Martha's own Patsy and Jack, and among them were the two young ladies portrayed here — Martha's youngest granddaughters, whose father had been the lamented John Parke Custis. The portraits were painted at Mount Vernon by Robert Edge Pine in 1785, and the likeness of Eleanor, known as Nelly (above), now hangs beside the fireplace in the Washingtons' bedroom, and that of Martha, or Patty (facing page), over Mrs. Washington's desk. Nelly was a talented child; at left is a painting she made of a bird, and below, opposite, are the silhouettes she cut of her grandparents. The butterfly, below, was painted by Mrs. Washington. The Windsor high chair on the facing page, made of yellow poplar and red maple, may have been one of the many

ALEXANDRIA-WASHINGTON LODGE NO. 22, A.F. & A.M., ALEXANDRIA, VIRGINIA

items of furniture purchased by George Washington in Philadelphia. The black walnut crib belonged to Nelly — by tradition, a present from Martha. Before her marriage to Washington's nephew, Lawrence Lewis, Nelly's attitude toward the opposite sex was the subject of some amusement at Mount Vernon. She had resolved, she said at the time of her sister Patty's wedding to Thomas Peter, "never to give herself a moment's uneasiness on account of any [young men]." She was content, it seemed, with the homely amusements she found at the farm. "I am not very industrious," she wrote a friend," but I work a little, read, play on the harpsichord, write and talk, and find my time fully taken up with the several employments." The proximity of Lewis altered her outlook, however; they were married, and a few weeks before Washington's death in 1799 Nelly gave birth to her first child. The crib became hers in anticipation of that event.

THE FAMILIAR

OBJECTS OF HOME

In their retirement, George and Martha Washington were surrounded by family possessions they loved, many of them with sentimental attachments. In the "Common Parlour" was the harpsichord (left) ordered in 1793 from London for Nelly, who played and sang with considerable accomplishment. Before leaving Philadelphia at the time of his retirement, Washington bought the "tambour Secretary & book case" (left, top) for $145; later he bequeathed it to his old friend Dr. James Craik. *The Bull-Finch*, a popular little book of English songs in which love is the recurring theme, is identified as Martha's by Washington's inscription; she acquired it shortly after her marriage to him in 1759. The mahogany Hepplewhite sideboard above was made in Philadelphia by John Aitken, the craftsman who also fashioned the secretary. In 1786 Washington acquired the covered tureen (top, right) as part of a 302-piece set, decorated with motifs of the Society of the Cincinnati, for which he paid $150. Below it is a silver tea urn, made by John Carter of London for John Parke Custis and his bride, Eleanor Calvert. At right is a dressing glass, made in China of oriental cypress and ornamented with lacquer and gilt; in the drawer are small fitted lacquer boxes.

Washington's taste in art was considerably ahead of
its time; not until the Hudson River School came into its own
half a century later was his judgment confirmed. He had little
use for the prevailing neoclassicism, preferring instead
"fancy pieces of my own choosing," which were almost inevitably
landscapes. Two canvases he bought in 1793 from a "little
pert young" Englishman named William Winstanley are reproduced
here — at left and right, above. Purportedly scenes of the Hudson,
they were among the furnishings in the presidential household
in Philadelphia which he offered to sell to his successor, John
Adams — who turned them down. Later Washington suggested
that Winstanley try his hand at an oil showing "the passage of
the River Potomac through the Blue Mountains" — the scene
of the long-hoped-for canal — but when nothing came of this
he purchased what was for the time a highly unconventional
canvas (right) from another Englishman, George Beck. This
view of "The Great Falls of the Potomac" was probably in
keeping with Washington's conception of the outdoors. The
porcelain mantel garniture at left — a gift from a British
friend, Samuel Vaughan — is one of three left by Martha to
her grandson, George Washington Parke Custis, and is described
in her will as the "fine old china jars which usually stand
on the chimney piece in the new room."

AN EYE FOR NATURE

John Adams

PRESIDENT of the UNITED STATES of AMERICA.

To all who shall see these Presents Greeting:

Know Ye, That reposing special Trust and Confidence in the Patriotism, Valour, Fidelity and Abilities of George Washington I have nominated and by and with the Advice and Consent of the Senate, do appoint him Lieutenant General and Commander in Chief of all the Armies raised or to be raised for the Service of the United States: He is therefore carefully and diligently to discharge the Duty of Lieutenant General & Commander in Chief by doing and performing all Manner of Things thereunto belonging. And I do strictly charge and require all Officers and Soldiers under his Command, to be obedient to his Orders as Lieutenant General & Commander in Chief. And he is to observe and follow such Orders and Directions from time to time, as he shall receive from me, or the future President of the United States of America,_____ This Commission to continue in Force during the Pleasure of the President of the United States for the Time being.

By Command of the President of the United States of America.

James M'Henry
Secry. of War

Given under my Hand, at Philadelphia this Fourth day of July in the Year of our Lord One Thousand seven Hundred and ninety eight and in the twenty third Year of the Independence of the United States.

John Adams

Registered
John Caldwell Ch. Clk.
Department of War.

Drawn & Engrav'd by Thackara & Vallance. Philada.

270

ONE FINAL CALL
TO DUTY

By 1798 not much time remained to the old gentleman. Increasingly aware that he might soon be "looking into Domesday Book," Washington nevertheless could not bring himself to refuse command of the United States Army when relations with France deteriorated and the threat of war became imminent. On the facing page is his commission as commander in chief, signed by President John Adams on July 4, 1798. That same year the French artist Charles St. Memin drew the last portrait ever made of George Washington — the profile reproduced here. When he wrote his will, Washington was careful to provide for the disposition of his swords. One went to each of his nephews, along with an injunction that they were not to be unsheathed except in self-defense "or in defence of their Country and its rights." The so-called "Prussian" sword below was bequeathed to George Steptoe Washington, son of his brother Samuel. It had been made for the General by Theophilus Alte, a Prussian armorer, who engraved on it the legend: DESTROYER OF DESPOTISM, PROTECTOR OF FREEDOM, STEADFAST MAN, TAKE FROM MY SON'S HANDS THIS SWORD, I PRAY THEE, THEOPHILUS ALTE AT SOLINGEN. The son Alte entrusted to present it to Washington pawned it instead at a tavern in America, and only through the intercession of friends did the sword finally reach the intended recipient.

——— To each of my Nephews, William Augustine Washington, George Lewis, George Steptoe Washington Bushrod Washington and Samuel Washington, I give one of the Swords or Cutteaux of which I may die possessed; and they are to chuse in the order they are named. ——— These Swords are accompanied with an injunction not to unsheath them for the purpose of shedding blood, except it be for self defence, or in defence of their Country and its rights; and in the latter case, to keep them unsheathed, and prefer falling with them in their hands, to the relinquishment thereof

G Washington

THE LOST DANCE

One of the last notes in George Washington's hand is the poignant message on the facing page, declining an invitation to participate in the Alexandria assemblies he loved so well. The "crayon" or pastel likenesses above of the elderly couple whose dancing days were over were made in 1796 by James Sharples, and only barely did they survive the vicissitudes of time. Until Martha's death they hung at Mount Vernon; then they reverted to her grandson, George Washington Parke Custis, who declared at the end of his life that the miniature of Washington was "The finest and purest likeness of the Chief. . . ." Custis left the portraits to his daughter, the wife of General Robert E. Lee, and during the Civil War, when the Lee home was occupied by Federal troops, they were spirited away for safekeeping. In 1865 they reappeared, to be sent by boat to Lexington, Virginia, along with Lee's other personal effects. En route the ship sank in a canal and although the pictures were recovered they were badly damaged and had to be restored. In 1917 the last surviving child of General and Mrs. Lee wrote from Lexington, "I have . . . somewhere two small crayon portraits of Gen. and Mrs. Washington by Sharpless [sic] which were still hanging on the walls here on one of my visits years ago, and which . . . were already injured by the damp and cold of an unused house. . . ." What Custis termed "The finest and purest likeness of the Chief" has deteriorated almost beyond recall.

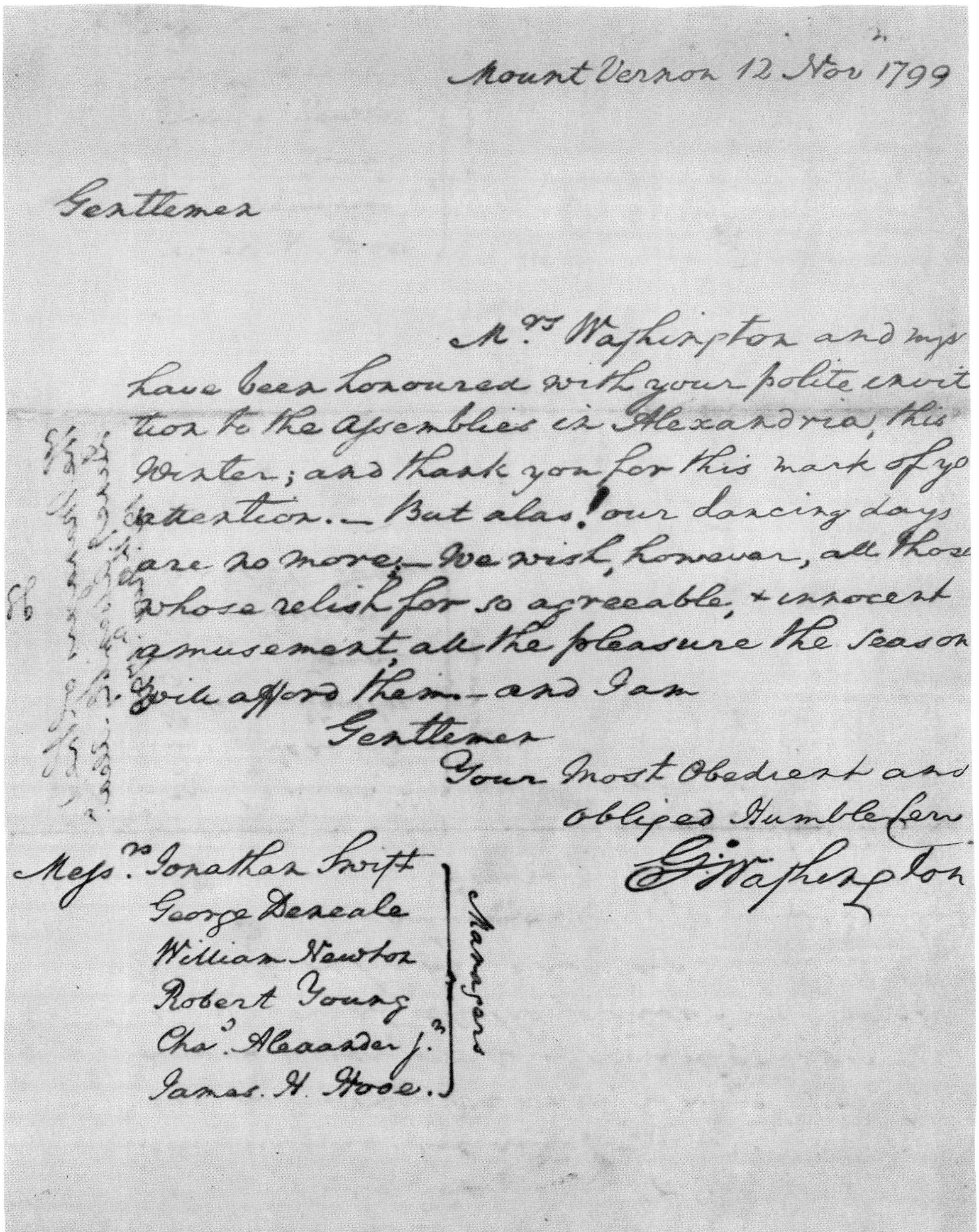

Mount Vernon 12 Nov. 1799

Gentlemen

    Mrs. Washington and myself
have been honoured with your polite invitation to the assemblies in Alexandria, this
Winter; and thank you for this mark of yo
attention.— But alas! our dancing days
are no more;— We wish, however, all those
whose relish for so agreeable, & innocent
amusement all the pleasure the season
will afford them— and I am
      Gentlemen
       Your most Obedient and
       obliged Humble Serv
        Go. Washington

Messrs. Jonathan Swift
George Deneale
William Newton
Robert Young
Chas. Alexander jr.
James H. Hooe.

CHRONOLOGY

George Washington born at Pope's Creek, Virginia, on February 22 (February 11, O.S.)	1732	
Family moves to Little Hunting Creek tract (later named Mount Vernon) on the Potomac River	1735	
Family moves to Ferry Farm, on the Rappahannock River	1738	
	1739	*War of Jenkins' Ear (1739–1742)*
	1740	*War of the Austrian Succession (1740–1748)*
Father, Augustine Washington, dies	1743	
Meets Lord Fairfax and his son, George William	1744	*France and England declare war*
Goes to live with half-brother Lawrence Washington at Mount Vernon; is assistant surveyor for Lord Fairfax on surveying expedition to the Shenandoah Valley	1748	
Appointed official surveyor for Culpeper County, Virginia; helps lay out the town of Alexandria	1749	
Sails to Barbados with ailing Lawrence; contracts small pox	1751	
Commissioned major in the Virginia militia; joins Masonic order; Lawrence Washington dies	1752	*Land south of the Ohio River is ceded to Virginia by the Iroquois Indians; Ohio Valley is defended by the French*
Sent to the Ohio Valley by Governor Robert Dinwiddie to deliver an ultimatum to the French at Fort Le Boeuf	1753	*Albany Congress*
Commissioned lieutenant colonel of the Virginia militia; fights in battle of Fort Necessity; resigns commission in October; leases Mount Vernon from Lawrence Washington's widow	1754	*French and Indian War (1754–1763)*
Becomes aide-de-camp to General Braddock; after battle at the Forks of the Ohio becomes colonel of Virginia troops responsible for frontier defenses	1755	*General Edward Braddock becomes British commander in chief in America; dies after battle with French and Indians at the Forks of the Ohio; French build Fort Duquesne*
Goes to Boston to visit Governor William Shirley, new British commander in chief; visits New York	1756	*Seven Years' War (1756–1763)*
Attends conference of colonial governors at Philadelphia; retires from the field because of illness; returns to Mount Vernon	1757	
Becomes engaged to Mrs. Martha Dandridge Custis; in command of Virginia Regiment, joins General John Forbes' expedition against Fort Duquesne; elected to the House of Burgesses from Frederick County, Virginia (re-elected in 1761); resigns commission; enlarges Mount Vernon	1758	*Fort Duquesne evacuated by the French; is rebuilt by the British and renamed Fort Pitt*
Marries Martha Custis	1759	
	1760	*George III of England begins reign (1760–1820)*
Inherits Mount Vernon	1761	*James Otis speaks out against the Writs of Assistance in Boston*
Chosen vestryman of Truro Parish in Fairfax County, Virginia	1762	
Visits the Dismal Swamp to investigate drainage and canal project	1763	*Proclamation of 1763*
Elected to the House of Burgesses from Fairfax County, Virginia (re-elected in 1768, 1769, 1771, and 1774)	1765	*Stamp Act passed*
Repeatedly visits the Dismal Swamp to inspect operations	1766	*Stamp Act repealed*
	1767	*Townshend Acts passed*
Journeys to western Pennsylvania and Ohio with James Craik to select land to be given in grants to Virginia veterans of the French and Indian War	1770	*Lord North begins ministry (1770–1782); Boston Massacre*
Poses for first portrait by Charles Willson Peale	1772	*Revival of the Committees of Correspondence*
Enrolls step-son "Jack" in King's College in New York; step-daughter "Patsy" dies; George William and Sally Fairfax move to England	1773	*Boston Tea Party*
Presides over meeting that adopts Fairfax County Resolves; attends the first Virginia Provincial Convention at Williamsburg; attends First Continental Congress at Philadelphia; enlarges Mount Vernon	1774	*Intolerable Acts passed; Louis XVI of France begins reign (1774–1792)*

Attends Second Continental Congress; named commander in chief of the Continental Army; commands Continental troops around Boston	1775 Battles at Lexington and Concord, Fort Ticonderoga, Bunker Hill; Sir William Howe succeeds General Gage as British commander; Montgomery and Arnold lead unsuccessful campaign to capture Quebec
Occupies Boston; wages unsuccessful battles at Long Island, Kips Bay, Harlem Heights, White Plains; retreats through New Jersey; defeats Hessians at Trenton; enlarges Mount Vernon	1776 Declaration of Independence; Congress moves from Philadelphia to Baltimore
Defeats British at Princeton; in winter quarters at Morristown, New Jersey, till May; repulsed by British at Brandywine and Germantown, Pennsylvania; welcomes the Marquis de Lafayette as member of personal staff; moves army to winter quarters at Valley Forge in December	1777 Americans lose Fort Ticonderoga to John Burgoyne; Burgoyne surrenders to Horatio Gates at Saratoga; Conway Cabal against Washington
Leads battle of Monmouth Court House in New Jersey; takes up winter quarters at Middlebrook, New Jersey	1778 Sir Henry Clinton succeeds Howe as British commander; France recognizes U.S. and enters war; Savannah, Georgia, falls to British
Discovers Benedict Arnold's treason	1780 General Gates defeated by British at the battle of Camden, South Carolina
Meets with French general Rochambeau in Connecticut; accepts surrender of Cornwallis after battle of Yorktown, Virginia; step-son "Jack" Custis dies	1781 Mutinies of Pennsylvania and New Jersey troops are quelled; Articles of Confederation are ratified
	1782 Sir Guy Carleton succeeds Clinton as British commander; British evacuate Savannah; preliminary articles of peace are signed in Paris
Elected first president of the Society of the Cincinnati; says farewell to officers at Fraunces Tavern in New York City; resigns commission; returns to Mount Vernon on Christmas Eve	1783 Cessation of hostilities; British evacuate New York City; Congress orders army disbanded
Becomes president of the new Potomac Navigation Company	1785
Completes enlargement of Mount Vernon	1786 Annapolis Convention; Shays' Rebellion in Massachusetts
Presides over Philadelphia Constitutional Convention; brother John Augustine Washington dies	1787 The Federalist papers are published
Elected chancellor of William and Mary College	1788 U.S. Constitution is ratified
Unanimously elected President of the United States; inaugurated at Federal Hall, New York City; mother, Mary Ball Washington, dies; tours New England	1789 John Adams becomes Vice-President; first Congress is organized; French Revolution begins; John Jay is appointed first Chief Justice of the U.S. Supreme Court
Visits Rhode Island; moves to Philadelphia, new temporary U.S. Capital	1790 Alexander Hamilton, first Secretary of the U.S. Treasury, gives Report on Public Credit and Report on the Bank
Tours southern states	1791 Congress passes excise tax on whiskey; Congress divides on constitutionality of the Bank; boundaries of Washington, D.C. are laid out
Unanimously re-elected President	1792 Lafayette is imprisoned
Inaugurated for second term as President at Independence Hall, Philadelphia; issues Proclamation of Neutrality in war between Britain and France; lays cornerstone of Capitol Building in Washington, D.C.	1793 Louis XVI is executed; France declares war on Britain; Thomas Jefferson resigns as Secretary of State and is succeeded by Edmund Randolph
	1794 Whiskey Rebellion is put down without armed clash; John Jay is sent to England as special envoy to settle outstanding disputes, resulting in Jay's Treaty
	1795 Alexander Hamilton resigns as Secretary of the Treasury; Edmund Randolph resigns as Secretary of State over Jay's Treaty controversy
Publishes farewell address	1796 John Adams is elected President; Thomas Jefferson, Vice-President
Retires from office, returns to Mount Vernon	1797 Adams and Jefferson are inaugurated; XYZ Affair
Appointed lieutenant general and commander in chief of the U.S. military forces	1798
Dies at Mount Vernon on December 14	1799 Napoleon overthrows the Directory

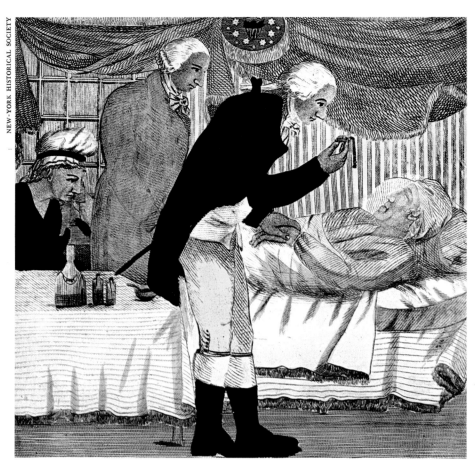

This early nineteenth-century print shows Washington on his deathbed, attended by two of his doctors, with Martha, seated at left, looking on.

ACKNOWLEDGMENTS

The Editors appreciate the generous assistance provided by many individuals and institutions during the preparation of this book. They especially wish to thank the following:

Alexandria-Washington Lodge No. 22, A.F. & A.M., Alexandria, Virginia
    Oliver Lloyd Onion
Boston Atheneum
    Jack Jackson
Geoffrey Clements, New York
George Cushing, Boston
George Washington Masonic National Memorial, Alexandria, Virginia
    Edward Buckmaster
Clark Kinnaird, *George Washington, The Pictorial Biography*
Library of Congress
    Dr. Paul Sifton

The Mount Vernon Ladies' Association of the Union, Mount Vernon, Virginia
    Charles Wall
    Christine Meadows
    John Castellani
New York Public Library
    Maude D. Cole, Rare Book Room
    Elizabeth Roth, Prints Division
    Roberta W. Wong, Prints Division
Newsweek Books
    Susan Storer
Woodlawn Plantation
    George M. Smith

INDEX

Page numbers in italic type refer to illustrations.